# The Death of Trotsky

## Also by Josh Ireland

*Churchill & Son*
*The Traitors*

# The Death of Trotsky

## The True Story of the Plot to Kill Stalin's Greatest Enemy

Josh Ireland

DUTTON

DUTTON

An imprint of Penguin Random House LLC
1745 Broadway, New York, NY 10019
penguinrandomhouse.com

Photograph on page 13 courtesy of Fine Art Images/Süddeutsche Zeitung Photo; page 47 courtesy of Album/Alamy Stock Photo; page 79 courtesy of the Picture Art Collection/Alamy Stock Photo; page 165 courtesy of SuperStock/Alamy Stock Photo; page 215 courtesy of Associated Press/Alamy Stock Photo; page 259 courtesy of Associated Press/Alamy Stock Photo

LIBRARY OF CONGRESS CATALOGING-IN-PUBLICATION DATA
Names: Ireland, Josh, 1981- author
Title: The death of Trotsky : the true story of the plot to kill Stalin's greatest enemy / Josh Ireland.
Other titles: True story of the plot to kill Stalin's greatest enemy
Description: [New York, New York] : Dutton, [2025] |
Includes bibliographical references and index.
Identifiers: LCCN 2024055779 | ISBN 9780593187104 hardcover | ISBN 9780593187111 ebook
Subjects: LCSH: Trotsky, Leon, 1879-1940—Assassination |
Trotsky, Leon, 1879-1940—Exile | Revolutionaries—Soviet Union—Biography |
Exiles—Soviet Union—Biography | Exiles—Mexico—Biography |
Mercader, Ramón, 1914-1978 | Mexico—Politics and government—1910-1946
Classification: LCC DK254.T6 I74 2025
LC record available at https://lccn.loc.gov/2024055779

Printed in the United States of America
1st Printing

The authorized representative in the EU for product safety and compliance is Penguin Random House Ireland, Morrison Chambers, 32 Nassau Street, Dublin D02 YH68, Ireland, https://eu-contact.penguin.ie.

To Victoria and Ivy

Stalin: "Death solves all problems. No man, no problem."
Trotsky: "I do not know personal tragedy."

# Contents

# The Death of Trotsky

# Prologue

## I

At some point in the afternoon of 17 July 1937, a tall, round-faced Ukrainian in his late thirties, whose bright eyes contrasted vividly with his smooth black hair, sat down in a hotel room in Paris to write a letter to the Central Committee of the Communist Party of the Soviet Union. Nobody, he believed, knew where he was or what he was planning. He was, effectively, in hiding.

The letter did not come easily to him; its composition had stretched out over several nights. It was probably the most important document he would ever write. He also knew that it might prove to be his death sentence.

He had been born Nathan Markovic Poreckij, in 1899, in Podwołoczyska, which was then in Galicia, part of the Austro-Hungarian Empire. Over the last two decades, he had acquired new names, each signaling a different identity: Ignace Poretsky, Ignatz Reiss, Ludwig, Ludwik, Ludwig Wauer, Hans Eberhardt, Steff Brandt, Raymond, and Walter Scott. Some knew him only as "the Fat One." Even his son did not know his real name. For twenty years he had been a dedicated revolutionary, serving as a Soviet spy in Vienna, Prague, Paris, and Amsterdam. All of this helped make him into something of a paradox: a man with a reputation as one of the Soviet Union's greatest spies who barely seemed to exist. Years later, two British intelligence officers exchanged exasperated memorandums, trying to establish even basic facts about the man they knew as Ignatz Reiss: "You say that the sum of your knowledge on this man is not impressive," one of them sighed, "but by comparison our own information on him is even less so."

His agents knew almost nothing about him. They understood that it was wise not to ask. His discretion was so absolute that they knew neither whom they were working for nor what the end results of the tasks they were assigned would be. He did not rely on extortion or intimidation to force people to work for him; he only asked, gently, if they might want to involve themselves in something "bigger."

This is why the men and women in the networks liked him. They thought him intelligent, patient, and considerate. One called him "the finest man I have ever met in my life."

But over the last few months, a few of these agents had received strange letters from him in which he had expressed, guardedly, a "critical" attitude about the Soviet Union—about that "bigger" cause. They struggled to make sense of them. Then they each received another that was more categorical: he was going to make a break with the regime. His disgust—both at what had become of the revolution that was so precious to him and at his own moral compromises—had reached such a pitch that he could carry on no longer. He had dedicated his life to building socialism. That had justified a great deal. And yet now Joseph Stalin had begun murdering "his own people," men and women who Reiss knew were innocent of the grotesque crimes they had been accused of.

Not long after he had made his resolution, he received a letter from Abram Slutsky, head of the Foreign Department at the Commissariat of Internal Affairs (NKVD), who urged him to return to Moscow. "Your nerves seem to be on edge, come without delay, it is time we talked things over and straightened things out." Reiss knew that comrades of his had received similar, superficially friendly communications inviting them to come home. They had either disappeared or been shot. He did not want to suffer the same fate.

Slutsky's letter was followed by another, which was little more than a confused note from Gertrude Schildbach, one of Reiss's agents who was in Rome. Having lost contact with the Reiss family, she wanted to get back in touch; she said that she urgently needed his advice.

Schildbach, who worshipped Reiss and had a clammy, almost obsessive attachment to his family, had a short, squat body, an oversized head, glasses with very thick lenses, and blackened, protruding teeth. She was lonely, emotionally volatile, and probably delusional. Less than a year before, she had taken up a new posting in Italy, but now she wrote to him to say that she was in difficulties. Reiss glanced at the note without realizing that its significance lay not in what it said, but that it had been sent at all.

Reiss continued preparing for his defection. That summer he arranged for the sum of $7,660 to be placed to his credit in New York—in a savings account bearing the name of Stephen Brandt (one of his aliases; the last name was also his mother's maiden name). He talked to his wife about his plans and started taking tentative steps to warn his networks that something significant was about to happen. On June 11, the day that Marshal Mikhail Tukhachevsky and eight other Red Army generals were executed, he traveled to Amsterdam to meet with Richard Sneevliet, the head of the Dutch Trotskyists.

By that afternoon in July 1937, as he sat in his Paris hotel room, having done everything he could to ensure that he had slipped surveillance, all that was left for him to do was to finally cut the cord.

> I should have written the letter I am writing you today a long time ago, on that day when the Sixteen [Old Bolsheviks tried in Moscow in August 1936] were massacred in the cellars of the Lubianka [*sic*] on the orders of the "Father of the People."

> I kept quiet then and I did not raise my voice at the murders that followed, and as a result I bear a heavy responsibility. My guilt is grave, but I will try to repair it, to repair it promptly and thus ease my conscience.
>
> Up to this moment I marched alongside you. Now I will not take another step. Our paths diverge! He who now keeps quiet becomes Stalin's accomplice, betrays the working class, betrays socialism.

The letter continued in a similar vein for several pages; its ending somehow even more incendiary than its beginning:

> What is needed today is a fight without mercy against Stalinism! The class struggle and not the popular front, workers' intervention in the Spanish revolution as opposed to the action of committees.
>
> Down with the lie of socialism in one country! Return to Lenin's international! . . . I am joining Trotsky and the Fourth International.

In a postscript, he noted that he was returning his Order of the Red Banner: "It would be beneath my dignity to wear an order also worn by the executioners of the best men of the working class in Russia."

He made several copies of the letter by hand and wrote a separate letter to Slutsky to inform him of his intentions and assure him that he wouldn't spill any Soviet secrets.

Once finished, he handed copies to his secretary, Lydia Grozovskya, to be sent through the embassy post. If, as Reiss intended, the letter was forwarded through the usual channels to Nikolai Yezhov, the head of the NKVD in Moscow, he would have ample time to make the arrangements that ensured his safety.

This done, at seven p.m., he headed to Café Weber to meet his friend and fellow agent Walter Krivitsky. The two men were together for only a few minutes, but Krivitsky could tell that there was something pressing on Reiss's mind, "a matter of supreme importance to him." They agreed that Reiss would call Krivitsky at eleven the following morning at the Hotel Napoleon, where he was staying. Reiss also told Krivitsky that as a precaution he would change hotels; he gave Krivitsky his new address.

Two hours later, Krivitsky received an urgent summons from the deputy head of foreign services at the NKVD, Mikhail Shpiegelglass. They met at a café on the Paris Exposition grounds. Here, with the Eiffel Tower looming above them, the small, stout, Shpiegelglass explained that he had been sent to Paris to identify a traitor who, that spring, had established clandestine contact with Richard Sneevliet. A happy coincidence had revealed his identity.

Shpiegelglass had had Reiss's letter in his hands just an hour after it had been dispatched. He immediately passed the news up the chain of command. The instant that Stalin learned of Reiss's treason, he ordered Yezhov to kill not just Reiss but his wife and child. He wanted it to be a warning to anybody else considering doing the same: Stalin did not permit Soviet agents to leave his service.

Shpiegelglass began to hint that Krivitsky should arrange the liquidation. Krivitsky pretended not to understand and tried to divert the conversation into other channels. But Shpiegelglass became more insistent.

Krivitsky wavered. He knew that his own fate rested on his conduct that night. Shpiegelglass continued to push him. Then clarity. "At that moment I realized that my lifelong service to the Soviet government was ended."

Another agent, Theodore Maly, a cadaverous-looking former Hungarian priest who had been close to Reiss, arrived shortly afterward, summoned by Shpiegelglass. Shpiegelglass became distracted. When he occasionally disappeared to go to another pavilion, Krivitsky assumed he was speaking to another agent. A little later on, Shpiegelglass ordered Maly to take an iron bar and beat Reiss to death in his hotel room. Maly refused. The night continued. All around them, darkness fell.

At around midnight, as Reiss, unaware that the Paris NKVD had already been charged with arranging his death, devoted himself to the preparations for his final departure, his telephone rang. When he answered, the caller hung up without speaking. They did not need to; he understood instantly that somebody was trying to warn him that he was in danger. He needed to leave Paris urgently. He wrote some farewell letters, including to Schildbach. Between one and three in the morning, his preparations were interrupted by three more calls. Each time, he answered and was met with only the click made by someone on the other line putting down their handset.

At ten o'clock the following morning, as Krivitsky waited to see if his friend would call, his telephone rang. It was Maly.

"You can come over. He won't show up."

Nausea clambered up Krivitsky's throat as he contemplated the possibility that Reiss had already been caught. The night before, during the moments when Shpiegelglass had absented himself, Krivitsky and Maly had rung Reiss's room four times, but they weren't sure if their message had been understood. Krivitsky leaped into a cab and dashed to Maly's quarters. The Hungarian was waiting for him.

"He's got away! He left his hotel at seven this morning."

Krivitsky knew that his own immediate future had become extremely uncertain, but Reiss had escaped. For the first time that morning, he found he could breathe freely.

After Reiss had checked out that morning, he traveled by train to the Valais, Switzerland, to meet with his wife, Elsa and young son,

Roman, in a house she had taken in a mountain village called Finhaut. His arrival shocked Elsa, who stared uncomprehendingly at her husband. It had been ten days since she had last seen him; in that time his hair had turned completely white.

## II

Reiss had contacted the representatives of Leon Trotsky—Stalin's "enemy number one"—because he knew that if he tried to hide from the NKVD, if he tried to go it alone, he would only be deferring the inevitable. He believed that by meeting with Sneevliet and coming out into the open, "Stalin's arm [would] be too short to reach me."

That August, Reiss revealed to Elsa that he had been in touch with Sneevliet and Victor Serge, another Russian exile who had thrown his lot in with the Trotskyists. They were going to meet in Reims on 5 September to discuss the political consequences of Reiss's defection and the publication of his declaration. Since Elsa and he were planning to leave the mountains for a pension in Territet, he proposed that they should travel together and then on to Lausanne, where he would catch the night train to Reims. He had also made a plan, reluctantly, to see Schildbach during the couple of hours he waited for his connection.

Reiss invited Elsa to join them. Later she realized that she should have asked him when, exactly, he had got in touch with Schildbach. And yet at the time it had seemed unimportant. The days at Finhaut went by without incident. The only unusual event came just before their departure. A group of people passed the family on the road. A young blond woman, whom neither Reiss nor Elsa recognized, smiled and waved.

It was a short trip. The couple set off after lunch, leaving their landlady to look after their son. They traveled from Territet to Lausanne along the shore of the lake in a tiny suburban train. It was one of those radiant early autumn days; the water sparkled, the air still felt warm.

Reiss sat opposite his wife, looking at her strong gray-blue eyes and sober clothes. Recently, the lower part of her face often appeared to be clenched with tension. Neither gave any thought to Schildbach; they were much more focused on the forthcoming encounter with Sneevliet.

They spoke little, their silence broken only when Reiss glanced at the conductor, who reminded him irresistibly of a Ukrainian friend who had been shot in Kiev: "Doesn't he look like Maximovich?" Elsa didn't see the resemblance but nodded all the same.

Reiss fell asleep for a few minutes. His wife examined his face; his suntan only superficially obscured the traces of his ordeal. "When he opened his eyes, suddenly there was a lonely, forlorn look in them; he must have seen, in his short dream, his friends."

At the station in Lausanne, he bought some stamps for their son, who was a keen collector; then they went to a big café nearby to meet Schildbach. Their friend rose to greet them. Elsa was struck by how pale and anxious she seemed, but also reflected that "perhaps we gave the same impression—the circumstances hardly warranted a relaxed get-together."

On her lap, Schildbach cradled the handbag that Reiss, who was punctilious about gifts, had sent her for her last birthday. Both husband and wife noted that this woman who had always been so inelegant had suddenly become well-dressed. While Elsa complimented Schildbach before talking more generally about their plans and their son, Reiss stared at Schildbach as if wondering about her changed appearance. Seeming to respond to this scrutiny, she explained that she was returning to Rome to marry a rich Italian industrialist.

At one point, Elsa noticed a pretty box of chocolates sitting on the windowsill beside them. She reached out mechanically to touch the box but Schildbach tore it roughly from her hands and put it in her handbag, saying: "It's not for you." Their friend's voice wavered and she appeared on the verge of tears; she turned her face to the window so that Reiss could not see her. An unnecessary precaution: he still seemed distant, barely following the conversation. After arranging to meet Reiss again the following evening to continue their conversation, Schildbach hurriedly left the café, claiming that she was late for a date.

A little later, Reiss and Elsa went their separate ways. As he took his leave, he told her, "Take good care of our boy and don't worry. I will be back on Monday night."

SHPIEGELGLASS'S PLANS TO liquidate his former comrade continued. Reiss's letter had been his first piece of luck. The second was his correspondence with the unhappy Schildbach, which had also been intercepted; this was the thread the NKVD could use to trace his movements. As long as he continued to write to her, it did not matter how far he traveled, they would always be able to find him.

There were a couple of false starts: in early August, a handful of agents followed a lead to a house near Versailles. They stayed there for a number of days, waiting for Reiss to turn up. Searches in Châtenay-Malabry and Grenoble also ended in failure. But then at the end of August, there was another breakthrough.

Renata Steiner, an attractive young Swiss woman whose desire to live in the Soviet Union had been parlayed into an agreement for her to work for its secret service, was driven to a café in the Place d'Italie in Paris to rendezvous with a Russian she had never met before.

The Russian took her across the street to the Dupont Café, where a man she was introduced to as "Leo" was waiting for her. Leo asked her if she could drive. She assured him that she could. He then ordered her to meet him at the Gare de Lyon on the departures platform at eleven p.m. on 28 August. Then he told her that she had to leave the same evening for Bern, where new instructions would be waiting for her. Leo handed her a sealed letter, a tube of pills, and an expensive-looking box of chocolates.

On her arrival in Bern, she was greeted by another member of the network, Roland Abbiate, aka François Rossi—a Russian expatriate, former hotelier in Prague, and citizen of Monaco. Rossi relieved Steiner of the various items she'd brought with her, and installed her in the Hotel City. Her next task was to rent a gray Chevrolet from the casino garage, and on Rossi's orders, she made a round trip to Paris, bringing with her a letter from Leo.

On the morning of Friday, 3 September, Rossi summoned Steiner to the station at Bern, where he introduced her to Schildbach. It is not clear when the NKVD managed to dissolve the loyalty Schildbach felt toward Reiss and his family or what inducements it employed, but here she was, about to betray a man she had once adored. The trio set off in the car for Martigny but they were then forced to halt in Salvan, because the roadway was no longer passable. Renata Steiner was left to make the last leg of the journey, climbing up to Finhaut on foot, by herself.

The following day she spotted Reiss with his family. She waved at the little boy, then rushed to call Rossi's room. Schildbach answered. "The Uncle has left," said Steiner.

LATER THAT AFTERNOON, Gertrude Schildbach and François Rossi had a quick meal before leaving the Hotel de la Paix in Lausanne, where they had been staying in separate but interconnected rooms, registered under their own names. Nobody at the hotel saw them again. Their luggage—which included articles of clothing, personal papers, and an expensive box of poisoned chocolates—remained in their rooms. Their bill of eighty francs had not been paid. Their gray Chevrolet crossed to Lausanne. At some point they picked up a passenger, the short-legged and bullnecked Etienne-Charles Martignat.

Whatever fragments of affection Schildbach retained for Reiss and his family had stopped her from handing them the poisoned chocolates, but she could not escape her task entirely. As agreed, she met her old friend for dinner in a café. After some time, they came out and began walking on an unlit, deserted road, intending to find a taxi. The Chevrolet pulled up alongside them. Inside were Roland Abbiate and Etienne-Charles Martignat, who carried with them a blackjack and a Soviet PPD-34 submachine gun. Reiss only understood what was happening when it was already too late. He threw himself at Schildbach, snatching a lock of her hair. It did him little good. Reiss was hit by a salvo of bullets from Abbiate's submachine gun and killed instantly. The group pulled Reiss's body into the car, drove off, then dumped the corpse by the side of a road three miles away.

In the early hours of the following morning, a resident of the Chamblandes quarter in the town of Pully near Lausanne was out walking his dog when he stumbled upon a corpse riddled with machine-gun bullets. Five bullets had been fired into the head; seven had pierced the body. A clenched fist contained a tuft of gray hair. The man had not been robbed. His jacket contained a Czech passport in the name of Hans Eberhardt (the Swiss police had received an anonymous tip a few days earlier identifying a man named Eberhardt as a dangerous trafficker in coins and drugs) and a rail ticket for Reims that had been punctured by a bullet.

As the Swiss police rifled through the corpse's pockets, Richard Sneevliet and Victor Serge were still waiting anxiously at a small, deserted, poorly lit snack bar in Reims where they had arranged to meet Reiss. "This is strange," said Sneevliet. "Ludwig is always punctual." They moved on to the post office, still puzzled by his absence, and then wandered aimlessly through the town, before stopping to drink "amazingly good and cheap champagne" in a cabaret. They registered the entry of a young woman with "platinum hair and the look of a tourist" and her date, and discussed Trotsky's political missteps. Sneevliet talked about his friends who had lost their lives in the Spanish Civil War and about the suicides of both of his sons. At no point did they realize that they were being watched.

A telephone call informed Elsa Reiss that her husband had been killed. She was stunned, and yet her son, who watched her then and in the days that followed, would always remember how calm she was. She did not panic, nor did she lose her composure when speaking to the Swiss and French police. She simply told them that this was not an ordinary crime and that if the police wanted to find the killers, they should pay a visit to the Soviet embassy in Paris.

But nothing was done, nobody was arrested. France's socialist government did not want to damage its relationship with the Soviet Union.

Perhaps the most telling item among Rossi's and Schildbach's abandoned possessions was a detailed map of Mexico City. Further investigation revealed that the Russian consulate in Lausanne had made three passport applications for a man called "Rossi," who was proposing to travel to Mexico.

This information was telling because it showed that while the elimination of Reiss was important to Stalin, his true target—the object of a rabid obsession that had already destroyed thousands of lives and derailed the foreign policy of one of the greatest nations on the planet—was ten thousand kilometers away in Coyoacán, a suburb of the Mexican capital. Leon Trotsky, once a comrade of the Soviet dictator, now his greatest enemy, had been exiled from the USSR almost a decade before. Stalin regretted this decision almost as soon as it had been made. This regret soon metastasized into paranoia. It was this paranoia that had created the conditions that led to the defection of a man like Reiss, who had devoted so much of his life to the revolution. And it was this paranoia that for years had kept Trotsky and his wife "waiting, with sure inner knowledge, for the assassins."

Trotsky knew he would be murdered. For him, the only question was when.

# Part One

Joseph Stalin

# 1

# Death Solves All Problems

When did Joseph Stalin decide to crush, or destroy, or kill Leon Trotsky?

Perhaps it was the first time these two men met—in 1907, at the Russian Social Democratic Labor Party's Fifth Party Congress in a damp, shabby church in London. Trotsky claimed later not to remember even seeing Stalin, who apparently remained mute for the whole three weeks of debates and arguments.*

Trotsky was tall, with broad, muscular shoulders, a "great head," abundant hair, and curiously small hands. He looked, at times, like a bird of prey: most of all because of his "mouth—big, crooked, biting. A frightful mouth."

He was vain. There was something instinctively theatrical about him. He was always "calculating the effects of his gestures, his pauses and intonation." He loved dressing up in gloves and shapely clothing—the things that the revolution he identified with so closely was supposed to be sweeping away.

He was clever, with an insatiable desire to exceed others. Even

* Trotsky: "The fact remains that I first learned about Koba's presence at the London Congress from [Boris] Souvarine's book and subsequently found confirmation of it in the official records."

when he became one of the most infamous figures on the planet, he never quite stopped being a clever schoolboy desperate to show others how much he had learned. Many thought he was the most dazzling speaker of his era. The kind of man who could make old, familiar ideas appear new and fresh. Even when he was wrong—and Trotsky was often wrong—he was still intoxicating. His arguments were original, surprising, and often brilliant. When he talked, his face lit up and his eyes flashed. Witnesses spoke wonderingly about his voice's "electric crackle."

And yet none of this would have mattered had he not married his fine words and fine gestures to immense courage and a queer instinct for those moments when history's tectonic plates were shifting.

This precocious son of an illiterate Jewish farmer from an obscure part of what is now Ukraine, he emerged as a national figure during the revolution in 1905 that briefly shook the Russian Empire's foundations. Somehow this shortsighted dandy who had never worked in a factory, nor spent a day in uniform, nor even studied at a university, found he could fire the imaginations and mirror the emotions of workers, soldiers, and students. He was just twenty-five, and yet, standing at the head of the St. Petersburg Soviet of Workers' Deputies, he spoke with an authority that exceeded even that of the tsar. (When a gendarme tried to arrest Trotsky while he was in full flow, the young revolutionary rounded on the startled police officer: "Please don't interfere with the work of the Soviet. If you wish to speak, kindly give your name and I will ask the assembly if they wish to hear you.") His glory was, of course, short-lived. Prison, then exile, followed.

This was the second time he had been banished to Siberia. His earliest revolutionary activities, when he was still known as Lev Davidovich Bronstein, had been brought to a sharp halt by his arrest in 1898. He spent two years behind bars awaiting trial—during which he married his first wife, Aleksandra Sokolovskaya—before he was sentenced to four years in the farthest-flung corner of the Russian Empire. He studied philosophy, had two daughters with Aleksandra, and then, in 1902, urged by his wife ("Go, a great future awaits you"), he escaped in a hay wagon.

> In my hands, I had a copy of the *Iliad* in the Russian hexameter of Gnyeditch; in my pocket, a passport made out in the name of Trotsky, which I wrote in it at random, without even imagining that it would become my name for the rest of my life. . . . Throughout the journey, the entire car full of passengers drank tea and ate cheap Siberian buns. I read the hexameters and dreamed of the life abroad. The escape proved to be quite without romantic glamour; it dissolved into nothing but an endless drinking of tea.

One thing led to another and he found himself in London, where he met Vladimir Ilyich Lenin, a man whose respectable clothes, neat beard, and "strange, faun's face" were scant disguise for the ruthless, uncompromising will to power that lay beneath. How, asked one of his political opponents, can you deal with a man who "for twenty-four hours of the day is taken up with the revolution, who has no other thoughts but thoughts of the revolution, and who, even in his sleep, dreams of nothing but revolution?" The party he led, the Russian Social Democratic Labor Party, was perhaps the most extreme of the many socialist groups formed in Russia during this period. They were "millenarian sectarians preparing for the apocalypse," willing to sacrifice everything, willing to countenance any amount of bloodshed, if it meant they could depose the hated tsarist regime and completely transform society. Their ambitions were not limited to Russia. Revolution there would simply be the first act in the eventual, inevitable worldwide triumph of the working classes.

But although Trotsky would one day call Lenin the "greatest leader of the proletariat in the history of mankind," for more than a decade, they both found themselves embroiled in the factional struggles that saw the party split into two warring sides: the Bolsheviks, who argued for a smaller, more tightly organized party; and the Mensheviks, who favored a looser organization. Lenin led the Bolsheviks. Trotsky initially supported the Mensheviks, though later he adopted a more independent position, calling himself a "non-factional social democrat." This was not enough to save him from the rancor that surrounded these disputes. Lenin, whose gift for vituperation was unmatched, called Trotsky a "Little Judas," a "scoundrel," and a "swine." Trotsky was just as vicious in return—abuse was a common currency in the incestuous world of exiled Russian revolutionaries; it was only years later that he came to regret his invective.

His second exile began with another daring escape that allowed him to rejoin the family he had started with Natalia Sedova, whom he had met in Paris in 1902. Over the next decade and a half, they moved through London, Vienna, Paris, Spain, and finally New York, where in February 1917 he learned of the uprising in Russia against the tsar. As fast as he could, he scrambled to return home.

JOSEPH STALIN WAS compact and ungainly, with a withered left arm and a pockmarked, sallow face whose expression told nothing of what he felt. Most of the time his sunken watchful eyes were the color of the Georgian wine he loved to drink; except for when they were angry, when they turned a "lupine" yellow. When he walked, it was with a limp; the second and third toes of his left foot had grown together.*

In meetings he spoke rarely and in a low, monotonous voice. Occasionally, his tone softened still further, and his Georgian accent emerged. At other times he simply smoked a Dunhill pipe packed with cigarette tobacco and doodled (phrases such as "Lenin-teacher-friend" or, as one foreign visitor noted, a drawing of wolves).

Melodramatic and boastful, moody and capricious, a twitchy, ner-

---

* When still a young boy, he was hit by a runaway phaeton, which permanently affected his gait.

vous wreck obsessed with illness, Stalin was a bundle of appalling contradictions. He was a frustrated poet and a fine singer who destroyed every intimate relationship he entered. He possessed both an uncontrollable temper and extraordinary willpower. He was capable of bewildering recklessness and cold-blooded displays of control. Much of his behavior was possible because he despised pity, sympathy, mercy. Some people dated this rejection of ordinary human values to the death of his first wife. He had pointed at the coffin and said to a friend, "Soso, this creature softened my heart of stone; she died, and with her died—my last warm feelings for all human beings." At this he moved his right hand to his heart: "It is all so desolate here inside, so inexpressibly desolate." It's also possible his moral deformation occurred during his harsh childhood. On one of the very few visits he made to his mother in Georgia, Stalin asked her why she had beaten him so often.

"That's why you turned out so well" came the reply.

Nobody was better than Stalin, a man who read Machiavelli constantly, at spotting weakness in another person or institution. (He possessed an uncommon talent for snatching more from situations than they appeared to offer.) And nobody could sink their teeth so viciously into that soft spot, tearing and ripping until he had got exactly what he came for.

Stalin was an exceptional student who might have become a priest, but instead ended up as a gangster-revolutionary. Like Trotsky, he had come from one of the far corners of the Russian Empire—in his case, Georgia. But he had traveled little and felt uncomfortable among the cosmopolitan exiles who made up much of the party. He loathed the way they talked, the jokes they told; he loathed émigré life, foreign countries, the intelligentsia—all the things that Trotsky embodied.

The two men felt an immediate and almost physical revulsion for each other. Stalin hated Trotsky's delicately balanced pince-nez and sweep of dark, glossy hair, his self-confidence, eloquence, and authority. Trotsky was repulsed by the Georgian's pockmarked face, his coarse manners, his provincialism.

Their paths crossed again—once they both returned to St. Petersburg in 1917 after the tsar had abdicated following the revolution in February of that year. Trotsky arrived in Russia on 17 May 1917. It was clear that his sympathies now lay with the Bolsheviks, who realized that the ferment into which Russia had been thrown offered them an unprecedented, perhaps unique, opportunity to establish, for the first time in history, a true workers' state.

While the party's leader, Lenin, was in exile in Finland and other Bolsheviks wavered just as it looked as if power were in their grasp, Trotsky was a force of nature: agitating, organizing, leading, doing everything he could to help prepare the coup that would allow the Bolsheviks to supplant the floundering liberal Provisional Government that had succeeded the monarchy. Then, on the night of 25 October 1917, with Lenin now back in St. Petersburg, the insurrection began. In the course of a little under twenty-four hours, a handful of violent idealists seized control over an empire of millions of souls.

During these months, Trotsky and Stalin saw each other everywhere: at meetings, conferences. Stalin had obviously become an important figure—he was Lenin's "wonderful Georgian"—and yet Trotsky appeared unable to see him as a personality in his own right. He might have registered the way Stalin's cold eyes fixed on him each time they passed each other in a corridor, or he might have noticed Stalin sitting on the other side of the room, but Trotsky never seemed to recall if Stalin had even spoken. (Trotsky on Stalin's revolutionary record: "The sum total of Koba's revolutionary activities during the years of the First Revolution seems to be so inconsiderable that willy-nilly it gives rise to the question: *is it possible that this was all?*")

Stalin was not just incensed by the way that this strutting peacock dismissed and disregarded him; he was jealous of how he himself had been supplanted in the Bolshevik firmament. By most measures, Stalin's life was already a success. He had made an astounding journey from being the child of illiterate parents to thriving at the heart of a revolutionary government. But it was Trotsky, not he, who emerged as a preeminent figure once the Bolsheviks were in power. It was Trotsky, who had been a Bolshevik for only a matter of months, who was seen as Lenin's right-hand man and likely successor. And with the onset of civil war—which pitched the Bolshevik Red Army against the White Army, a loose coalition of factions from across the political spectrum united only by their desire to thwart Lenin's increasingly repressive regime—it was Trotsky who was made war commissar.

TROTSKY WELCOMED THE civil war that followed the Bolshevik coup in October 1917.

He was intoxicated by the Bolshevik triumph, which he called "the festival of the oppressed." His entire life had been devoted to an almost abstract idea of change. And now it had *come*. Despite the Soviet state's parlous position, he was suffused with hope. A better future seemed to be just within reach. And his vision for this future was ecstatic: a universal order that would set the human spirit free.

In one celebrated passage, he talked lyrically of how human beings would change under socialism.

> Man will become incomparably stronger, more intelligent, more subtle. His body will be more harmonious, his movements more rhythmical, his voice more musical; the forms of daily existence will acquire a dynamic theatricality. The average human type will rise to the level of Aristotle, Goethe, Marx. It is above this ridge that new summits will rise.

Every atom in his body was obsessed with revolution. There was nothing more important to him, nothing he believed that was not worth sacrificing to make it work.* He once told a biographer that he

---

* He always struggled with the idea that the working classes in whose name he claimed to act might not actually support the revolution.

and the party were perfectly happy to "burn several thousand Russians to a cinder in order to create a true Revolutionary American movement." He meant it. Nothing, he said, was more humane in a revolution than the utmost ruthlessness.

And now a chance to show this ruthlessness had arrived. With victory, the Bolsheviks would be able to eliminate the nation's exploiting classes once and for all. The jet-black hair and lively bright blue eyes of the new war commissar appeared everywhere. He was carried in a train stuffed with weapons, uniforms, and felt boots. It had a printing press (occupying two carriages); a telegraph; radio and electric power stations; a library; a garage complete with trucks, cars, and a petrol tank; and a bath as well its own secretariat, team of agitators, and twelve-man bodyguard (who, when not protecting Trotsky, looked out for food such as game, asparagus, and butter.) Over the course of the war, one of his companions estimated that they traveled the same distance as they would have if they had circled the world five times.

Just Trotsky's presence at the front was sufficient to raise morale. Troops lined the route and greeted him with great cheers or renditions of "The Marseillaise." Clad head to toe in black leather, he would then proceed to act with extreme, flamboyant decision: setting up revolutionary tribunals to try turncoats; giving instant orders to repair supply problems; creating new divisions on the spot.

He was fond of rewarding those soldiers who distinguished themselves in battle with gifts such as watches, binoculars, telescopes, Finnish knives, pens, waterproof cloaks, and silver cigarette cases. Once, when in Bogorodskoe, he was presented with twenty men but found he had only eighteen gifts. With a flourish he gave one man his watch and another his Browning pistol.

There was another side to this largesse. One of the carriages on Trotsky's train was set aside as a revolutionary tribunal to deal with deserters and cowards. It was suspected that some of those shot for treachery on Trotsky's orders weren't guilty. But that was not the point. The word "ruthlessly" appears with *extreme* regularity in his Red Army orders.

It was Trotsky—the man with the phenomenal cultural range* and princelike bearing†—who had argued, "We must rid ourselves once and for all of the Quaker-Papist babble about the sanctity of life."

It was Trotsky who ordered the slaughter of sailors from the Kronstadt naval base who had risen up against the Bolsheviks. These rebels, who Trotsky himself had once called the "adornment and pride of the revolution," were disappointed by the way the Bolshevik government had diminished the civil rights of the working classes and become increasingly consumed by a mania for centralization and bureaucratization. This challenge could not be tolerated, so Trotsky sent sixty thousand troops from the Red Army to crush them. Revolutionary justice was applied without mercy.

It was Trotsky who, when faced with a peasant rebellion, approved of the measures introduced by the local commissars, which included the burning of insurgent villages, "the merciless execution of every single person who has taken direct or indirect part in the uprising," and the execution of every fifth or tenth adult male inhabitant. "The nests of these dishonest traitors and betrayers must be destroyed," he said. "These Cains must be exterminated."

And it was Trotsky who, as much as any other leader, was intimately involved in the construction of the apparatus of terror—including helping to create the Soviet secret police, the Cheka (an abbreviation of the All-Russian Extraordinary Commission, the forerunner of the NKVD)—that allowed the Communist Party to subjugate a population of millions. In a very profound sense, he combined what was most attractive and most repellent about Bolshevism.

* He would later become (arguably) Russia's leading literary critic. "The range of his interest was immense—he wrote articles on Freud, Futurist poetry, Constructivist architecture and Shakespearean tragedy; he studied chemistry and physics and foretold the releasing of energy from the atom."

† Even at the age of five, he had been famous for his "beautiful manners."

---

THE CIVIL WAR was an opportunity for Stalin too: it gave his desire for recrimination and revenge a physical form. He used his own authority to persecute Trotsky's proxies. (At one time, he imprisoned four hundred of them in a barge moored on the Volga River—many starved or were shot or died when the barge sank. "Death solves all problems. No man, no problem," Stalin said when he learned of the tragedy.) He placed articles filled with insinuations and crude exaggerations in *Pravda*,* sent telegrams full of administrative slander, interfered with Trotsky's orders, and tried to undermine his authority.

In response, Trotsky attempted several times to remove Stalin from any position with military responsibility, complaining to Lenin by effectively accusing Stalin of sabotage: "I consider Stalin's [conduct] a most dangerous ulcer, worse than any treason or betrayal."

STALIN WAS CONVINCED that if Trotsky were to ever become the Bolsheviks' leader, the revolution would be in mortal danger. But while Stalin identified Trotsky—the man he derided as an "operetta commander, a chatterbox, ha-ha-ha!"—as his main obstacle to securing power once the ailing Lenin died, Trotsky remained insouciant. It was as if he could not believe his comrade could also be a threat. Trotsky was the man who had done more than almost anyone else both to help the Bolsheviks seize power and to protect their prize during the Russian Civil War. For this he was celebrated and vilified in equal measure; his notoriety stretched across continents. Trotsky did not see, until it was far too late, that his opponent was both stranger and more gifted than he thought possible.

* The Communist Party's official newspaper. "*Pravda*" means "truth."

## 2

# Liar, Traitor, Scum

By the early 1920s, Trotsky appeared to be better placed than anyone to succeed Lenin, who had been weakened by illness and the consequences of an attempt to kill him by the half-blind Socialist Revolutionary Fanny Kaplan, who shot him three times without landing a mortal blow.

And yet almost everyone, not least Trotsky himself, was surprised by the ease and speed with which Trotsky was defeated by Stalin. Trotsky's downfall was not a struggle or a duel, although it has often been described in those terms. It was an assassination.

This was partly due to Trotsky's own flaws. He had cultivated no constituency within the party. He might make a coruscating, exciting speech to party members, but then disappear from the hall as soon as he had finished. He took no time to meet the Bolshevik faithful.

Trotsky despised a great number of people and thought they were unworthy of his respect. He made no attempt to hide this. Sometimes he appeared to go out of his way to broadcast it. He consistently failed to offer support or sympathy to those who took his side, and often attacked their views. Max Eastman, who admired him deeply, was pained by the realization that Trotsky was completely indifferent "to my opinions, my interests, my existence." He ascribed this disregard to the fact that

> in youth he stood prodigiously high above his companions in brain, speech, and capacity for action, so that he never formed the habit of inquiring—he was always telling. *His* knowledge and true knowledge, *his* view and the right view, were identical. There is no bragging or vanity in this, no preoccupation with himself. Trotsky is preoccupied with ideas and the world, but they are his own ideas and his own view of the world. People, therefore, who do not adulate, go away from Trotsky feeling belittled.

Wonderingly Eastman noted, "He has never asked me a question." Trotsky's gift for friendship, Eastman said, "is actually about on the level of a barnyard fowl."

Trotsky understood that he had an unfortunate capacity for wounding others. The problem was, he did not realize how damaging this was to him or how it might be exploited by others. A passage in his biography of Stalin exemplifies this blindness: he remembered how "whenever I had occasion to tread on the corns of personal predilections, friendships or vanities, Stalin carefully gathered up all the people whose corns had been stepped on. He had a lot of time for that, since it furthered his personal ends."

Where Trotsky mocked young Bolsheviks for perverting the revolution, Stalin could recall, seemingly without effort, the names and biographies of mid- and lower-level functionaries, even those of service staff. He listened to their concerns and appeared to identify with them. This man who called gratitude "a dog's disease" also put obscure party functionaries' children to bed, insisted on lighting the fires in the apartments of the other Politburo members, and gave his allies thoughtfully personalized gifts.

Alongside this, Stalin employed the colossal patronage at his disposal as the party's general secretary to promote his allies. He ran rings around the other members of the Politburo, such as Grigory Zinoviev and Lev Kamenev,* playing on their fears of Trotsky to advance his own interests and, depending on whom he was talking to, portraying himself as either the most moderate man in the room or the hottest fire-breather in the country.

Stalin—who, with his rival under close surveillance, could read his mail and listen to his phone calls—stopped Trotsky's name from being adopted by towns and factories and strangled sympathetic mentions of his name in the press. Trotsky's followers were expelled from the editorial boards of party organs, they lost what had been their automatic freedom to write in the party press, and many were removed from the prestigious positions they held and sent to obscure postings in distant countries.

Then, as soon as Lenin died in 1924, the ground really began to move beneath Trotsky's feet. He failed to return from a holiday in the Caucasus to attend the funeral. Stalin, however, acted with incredible speed and deftness, choreographing Lenin's deification (against the wishes of both the dead leader and his family) and using this to enhance his own power.

He presented himself as Lenin's chief follower and interpreter, a position that rendered him almost invulnerable. Simultaneously he maneuvered Trotsky into looking as if, rather than defending the revolution and its ideals, he were prosecuting a personal vendetta against it. Stalin—who, having long kept a record of the paradoxical and clever things that Trotsky carelessly tossed out in conversations, was ready to use them against him—created the idea that his rival was the proponent of an anti-Leninist political tendency: Trotskyism.

Stalin quoted from unpublished letters Trotsky had written before the Great War ("the whole edifice of Leninism at the present time is built on lying and falsification and bears within it the poisoned element

---

* Who was married to Trotsky's sister Olga.

of its own disintegration"), distorting what he found and omitting essential context. Trotsky called Stalin's activity "one of the greatest frauds in the world's history," but he was helpless against a man who had a genius for inflicting moral damage on others.

Slowly, relentlessly, Trotsky could feel his power slipping away: he noticed how people went quiet and looked either embarrassed or slightly bitter when he entered a room.

But at a time when he was supposed to be locked in an existential struggle, he appeared to lack application or drive. At critical moments, he left to take holidays in the Caucasus or to seek medical treatment in Berlin. On one occasion when the Politburo planned to review Trotsky's factional activity, he was out hunting with a friend. At other times he sat in the Politburo reading French novels as if nothing else in the world were more important.

Throughout this period he was plagued by inexplicable illness.* He suffered from colitis, insomnia, and a "persistent and unaccountable fever." He often said, "My head is empty."

Most worrying of all for someone who prized action, there were whole days when he felt as if his energy had been extinguished. Trotsky, who had displayed supreme bravery on the battlefield, was reduced to maundering "almost neurotically about most of his ailments," whose outbreaks seemed to coincide, with uncanny accuracy, with the times when things were going against him.

Belatedly, he tried to organize opposition to Stalin, striking up new alliances with old foes like Kamenev and Zinoviev. But they appeared to be playing different games with different rules. As an exasperated-sounding Kamenev once said to Trotsky, "Do you think that Stalin is now considering how to reply to your arguments? You are mistaken. He is thinking of how to destroy you. Morally, and if possible, phys-

* This ailment puzzled doctors in Russia, France, Germany, and Mexico.

ically as well. To slander you, to trump up a military conspiracy, and then, when the ground has been prepared, to perpetrate a terroristic act. Stalin is conducting the war on a different plane from you. Your weapons are ineffective against him."

There were still moments when Trotsky could knock his opponent off-balance. At the Fifteenth Party Congress, in 1927, Stalin, halfway through delivering his report, started mocking Trotsky's prose style.

> Leninism as a "muscular feeling in physical labor." New, original, profound, no? Did you understand any of it? [Laughter] All that is very beautiful, musical and, if you want, even grand. It is only missing a small thing: the simple and human touch of Leninism.

Enraged, Trotsky rose, pointed his finger, and declared that Stalin's malevolence threatened the very existence of the party: "The first secretary poses his candidacy to the post of grave digger of the revolution."

There was a sudden freedom about the way Trotsky spoke, as if something had been unleashed within him. Stalin was so shaken and humiliated by this assault that he turned deathly pale and lost all composure. Instead of defending himself, he rushed out of the hall, carried by his curious, pigeon-toed gait, and slammed the door behind himself. Afterward, Trotsky's friends gathered at his Kremlin apartment. They were all frightened by what they had seen because they knew that there would be grave consequences. Yuri Pyatakov gulped down a glass of water as if it might wash away his agitation. "You know I have smelled gunpowder," he said, "but I have never seen anything like this. This was worse than anything! And why, why did Lev Davidovich [Trotsky] say this? Stalin will not forgive him unto the third and fourth generation!" A little later, when Trotsky entered, he found himself confronted by Pyatakov. Trotsky looked tired, almost broken by the strains of the last months, and yet he calmly waved his hand, dismissing his friend's anxiety. As far as he was concerned, the breach with Stalin was irreparable now, so why waste time worrying about a few angry words? The following day he was expelled from the Politburo.

Events took their course, and it was soon clear that Trotsky's defiance had come too late. He was allowed to address the Central Committee one final time, in October 1927, to defend himself against a resolution proposing to expel him and Zinoviev from the Central Committee as punishment for their oppositional activity.

Trotsky walked into a wild atmosphere, adjusted his pince-nez, stretched one arm out, and read a confused, passionate speech hurriedly without looking at the crowd before him. His voice had an unfamiliar timbre and could barely be heard above the shouts and insults.

He used his extended arm to try to protect himself from a hail of books, inkwells, and tumblers. When he started quoting again from the damning testament Lenin had dictated before his death, "Remove Stalin, who may carry the party to a split and to ruin," he was greeted with calls of "Liar," "Traitor," "Scum," "Gravedigger of the revolution."*

Trotsky simply stretched out his arm again and continued, occasionally pausing to wait for a break in the wall of abuse. Then he started to discuss recent provocations by NKVD agents, and the furor reached another level. The chairman of the session rang the bell again and again. One member of the audience threw an enormous volume of economic statistics at Trotsky. Another tossed a glass of water.

Stalin remained calm throughout the excitement. Occasionally, he'd look around the hall, before returning to corrections of his own speech. He added a new title, "The Trotskyist Opposition Before and

* Stalin was initially horrified when the contents of the testament were revealed: "He shit on himself and he shit on us!" But damning as they were, Trotsky was never able to deploy them effectively, and Stalin had his own sly way of neutralizing them. In response to Lenin's statements about his rudeness, he admitted, "This is completely true. Yes, I'm rude, comrades, in connection with those who rudely and treacherously destroy and split the party. I did not and do not hide this."

Now," and then drew a pack of wolves in the margin of his text, using a red pencil to fill in a crimson background.

Trotsky's expulsion was confirmed. Without showing any outward signs of emotion, he glanced at the platform, collected his papers, stuffed them into his ancient briefcase, and left, pursued by catcalls and abuse hurled at him by men who had once been proud to call him a comrade. Most of them would be dead within a decade—disappeared, imprisoned, or driven to such desperation that they blew their own brains out.

Gray-faced, Trotsky scrambled into the car that was one of last few emblems of his old status, and he was driven away. It was an unpleasant way for him to celebrate the tenth anniversary of the revolution. It was also the last time that he and Stalin ever saw each other.

In the months that followed, a defeated, horrified Trotsky was white with overwork, feverish, and subject to an insomnia even sleeping pills could not relieve. In the mornings, he would open newspapers, glance at them, then throw them down in disgust.

After he refused to recant and confess to ludicrously confected "crimes against the Party," he was condemned to internal exile in Alma-Ata, a town in the far corner of Kazakhstan on the Chinese border. On the morning of 17 January 1928, the NKVD sent a detachment to his Moscow flat.

They found their target still dressed in his frayed pajamas. Trotsky was handed an arrest order but refused to accept its terms. He; his wife, Natalia Sedova; and two guests locked themselves in one of the apartment's rooms. For a while futile negotiations were conducted through the glazed glass door until the agent in charge telephoned for instructions. Within seconds there was the sound of shattering glass, and an arm reached inside the door to open it. There was still time for a moment of farce: one of the NKVD agents, who had already been behaving strangely, began to repeat, "Shoot me, Comrade Trotsky, shoot me." Trotsky recognized him as an officer called Kishkin who had often been by his side on his armored train during the Civil War.

"Don't talk nonsense, Kishkin," he replied coolly. "No one is going to shoot you. Go ahead with your job."

Minutes later, with a look of "stunned hauteur" on a face that had been turned yellow by liver problems and malaria, Trotsky was driven by car to catch the Trans-Siberian Express.

# 3

# ATTRITION

Trotsky was optimistic when, a year later, Stalin threw him out of the Soviet Union. This was the third time he had been expelled by a Russian government. Each time, he had returned to a new coup—first 1905, then 1917. And now he was forty-nine and at the peak of his powers!

He was skeptical about the stability of the political situation in Russia and dismissive of Stalin's political abilities. In his view Stalin's rule would be a mere "interlude" that would be succeeded by a revival of revolutionary spirit or by the triumph of counterrevolution, which would mean the return of capitalism.

Trotsky also struggled to believe that his own opposition movement—those communists who had chosen to support him against what they saw as the bureaucratic degeneration presided over by Stalin—could be annihilated. After all, the Bolsheviks had survived tsarist oppression and exile. Over time, this conviction gave way to a more careful perspective: it was possible he would never return to Russia, and equally possible that he would die before his cause prevailed, but it *would* prevail. He issued confident announcements that belied the increasingly dire state of his movement. "Let there remain in exile not three hundred and fifty people faithful to their banner, but only thirty-five. Let there remain even three—the banner will remain, the strategic line will remain, the future will remain."

Even this confidence, however, eroded as Trotsky passed first through Turkey—where he was lodged near Istanbul on the island of Prinkipo—then France, and finally, Norway. During his previous exiles, he had been largely unknown, something that had protected him. Now he was infamous. He was one of the best-known figures from the Russian Revolution and its bloody aftermath, events that still had the power to send shivers of terror down the spines of European politicians who feared that Trotsky might inspire proletarian revolts in their own countries. Newspapers were unable to determine whether Trotsky was a true outcast or a Trojan horse sent to stir up revolution by Stalin. And few governments, even left-leaning ones, felt comfortable offering Trotsky a home. He was living, he said, on a "planet without a visa."

In France, where he had been offered asylum in 1933 (with the caveat that he could not live in Paris nor even close to it), he felt equally persecuted by the government, the press, and his political enemies. He had to remain strictly incognito, which he achieved by shaving off his thick, gray goatee so that he resembled a bourgeois French intellectual. But each time his identity was discovered, he was forced to move. He had become a homeless refugee permanently in danger.

There were times when he was changing hotel rooms five or six times a month. And yet whatever he did—he once spent several days hiding in the attic of one of his son's friends—he always seemed to be followed by silent, enigmatic, and yet relentless figures. Each time this man—who hated breaking his habits and who could not write when traveling and knew that every moment he was out in the open he was exposed to danger—moved home, he was assailed by the same set of symptoms: "a profound uneasiness, fever, sickness, psychological disturbance." These precautions could only ever achieve so much. He could not move without Moscow knowing about it. He could not write, or receive, a letter without Moscow reading it. His correspondence was either confiscated or simply intercepted by the NKVD, which sent monthly digests of its findings to Stalin.

And then in 1935 after the French government agreed to a treaty of mutual assistance with the Soviet Union, he was told that he was no longer welcome in the country. Norway, with its left-leaning government, seemed to offer refuge. Soon he discovered that this too was just an illusion: as pressure from Stalin's government on their Norwegian counterparts grew, attempts were made to make his residence conditional on his remaining silent on all political matters and consenting to having his incoming and outgoing post inspected by the police; he then spent 108 days under a cruel form of house arrest, forbidden from even taking walks outdoors.

The discomfort Trotsky experienced during the first part of his exile was exacerbated by the knowledge of his impotence.

The man who had led two revolutions and inspired the Red Army to victory in the Russian Civil War could now count on only an ever-dwindling number of weakened supporters, who were scattered across the world. These supporters all had to accustom themselves to living in a political wilderness—they were socialism's lepers. The ostracism and isolation they all experienced inevitably intensified internal dissension. Many gave themselves up to arguments in which it was difficult to see where the personal started and the political ended. Trotsky allowed himself to sink into these squabbles between puny figures, with his attempts at mediation devouring his time and fraying his nerves.

And even if he could sometimes persuade himself that he was "sharpening the mind and the will of a new Marxist generation," he could not resist making bitter comparisons between his Western followers and their Bolshevik forebears.

The only two groupings that Jean van Heijenoort—a talented

French mathematician who was one of Trotsky's most loyal and able secretaries—heard Trotsky express unqualified admiration for were coal miners from Charleroi and Teamsters from Minneapolis. Mostly, he thought of his friends stranded in Russia, lying condemned in prisons and gulags, but since 1933 almost completely beyond his reach.

This was the part of his impotence that hurt him most: exile had forced him to become a distant spectator to the liquidation of his family and supporters.

ONE OF STALIN'S great talents was torturing other human beings. He knew he could employ the apparatus of terror he had inherited from Lenin and then expanded and refined himself. But he also knew that he could achieve effective results without resorting to dungeons or knuckle-dusters. It was not necessary to arrest someone to make their existence unbearable.

Pressure was ramped up on the country's remaining Trotskyists. They were fired from their jobs; expelled from the party for being a "demoralized petit-bourgeois element," a "corrupt person," or a "profiteer"; arrested; and beaten. Or they simply found that their lives had been made complicated in unexpected ways.

Occasionally, some of Trotsky's followers might be summoned from their workplaces to the NKVD offices. Here they would be left standing in the corridors for hours before they were released without any explanation. When they returned to their offices or factories, they could offer no credible explanation as to what had happened. When the process was repeated, their comrades would become suspicious and eventually start to believe the rumors planted by the NKVD officers, who claimed that they had employed the Trotskyists as informers. Once discredited, the Trotskyists could be arrested for their real "crimes."

It had become increasingly clear too that, just as Pyatakov had warned, to be related to Trotsky was another kind of crime. As Olga Grebner, his son Sergei's first wife, said bitterly, "He brought misery to everyone he came in contact with."

IT HAD NEVER been easy to be one of Trotsky's children. He had abandoned his first wife and their two daughters in 1902, and while he might sometimes remember to send one of his girls a birthday card, he was barely a presence in their upbringing.

Despite this neglect, Nina and Zina supported him fanatically. Both tried to defend him when the attacks on him started in the Soviet press and even after he had been exiled. Nina soon learned that there was a price to pay for this loyalty. Stalin, frustrated that for the moment his old enemy was out of reach, inflicted cruelty on those within striking distance. Nina's husband, Man Nevelson, was arrested and later shot, and she lost her own job due to her "Trotskyist convictions." Every aspect of her life became harsh and uncomfortable. When she fell ill with tuberculosis, only Zina would, or could, care for her. No doctor dared—they knew what the consequences would be.

Her father, hundreds of miles away in Alma-Ata, remained almost completely unaware of the decline in her health or her persecution because his communications with the rest of the USSR had withered. Few letters made it through to him. Many others, including ones carrying important information, vanished. He could infer what *might* have been happening to his children only from the indirect, confused reports of Stalin's reprisals that did reach him.

A telegram Zina sent in June 1928 when it was clear her sister's condition was deteriorating—*Nina is calling for you all the time, hoping that if she sees you she will get better*—took seventy-three days to arrive. By then it was too late; she had died in Zina's arms aged just twenty-six.

Trotsky's only consolation was that the sickness that had killed her saved her from the misery of the gulag.

---

ZINA, TROTSKY'S FIRSTBORN, had been fixated with her father ever since their first real encounter, when she was five. She was enraptured by his physical poise and sartorial elegance, perhaps because she was the child who most closely resembled him. And yet she was also almost a stranger to him. In the fifteen years between the moment he had left a dummy in his bed to deceive the police as he abandoned the family home and his return to revolutionary Russia in 1917, he had not seen her more than three times.

Zina wanted, more than anything, to be able to help him, and yet he resisted her efforts, keeping her at arm's length. After a long and at times humiliating struggle, in 1931 she joined her father in Prinkipo, his refuge near Istanbul. But the psychological instability that had affected her for some time became evident. As memories, desires, and grievances that she'd previously kept hidden or suppressed surged toward the surface of her mind, her behavior grew more unpredictable, her thoughts lost coherence.*

She pined for the daughter she had left in Moscow and fretted about the disappearance of her husband, Platon Volkov. More than anything, she believed that she was unwanted by the father she adored. She often repeated, "To Papa, I am a good-for-nothing."

Trotsky was troubled by the lack of affection he could provide his daughter but seemed incapable of improving the situation. Zina eventually, albeit reluctantly, took his advice and sought psychiatric treatment in Berlin, leaving her six-year-old son, Seva, in Turkey. Little improved. She was lonely, embarrassed by the anxiety she believed she was causing her family, and torn to pieces by the thought of others caring for her children. Her ability to look after herself diminished. She struggled to manage her monthly allowance and moved into a

---

* Her presence in Prinkipo coincided with a number of inexplicable fires in the house as well as the devastating conflagration that burned many of the family's most cherished possessions, including Trotsky's library.

"low-grade boarding house" where she lived alongside outcasts, madmen, and criminals.

A further blow came on 20 February 1932, when the USSR stripped Trotsky and every member of his family who was abroad at the time of their Soviet citizenship. Zina had been desperate to return home to see her daughter, Alexandra, and perhaps even her exiled husband.

Trotsky arranged for Seva to join her in Berlin, but this was not sufficient to arrest her depression.

In her last letter to her father, she wrote: "Instinct has terribly keen eyes which see in the dark . . . What is more frightful is that it hits infallibly and mercilessly those who are in its way. . . . do you know what has sustained me? *Faith in you* . . . And this is not instinct."

Then, a week after Seva's arrival, the German authorities—at the insistence of the Soviet embassy—ordered them to leave Berlin. Zina had no money, no passport, and little hope. On 5 January, she left Seva with neighbors, barricaded herself in her room, and opened the gas taps.

When they learned of her death, Trotsky and Natalia shut themselves away in their room, occasionally opening the door a fraction to ask for tea. Trotsky wrote to Alexandra: "Zinushka is no longer alive. I turned to wood." When he emerged from his seclusion a few days later, "his features appeared ravaged. Two deep wrinkles had formed on either side of his nose and ran down both sides of his mouth."

At little later, he addressed an open letter to party leaders in Moscow, talking of how the decree that took away his daughter's citizenship had broken her. She "did not choose death of her own will," he wrote. "She was driven to it by Stalin." He knew, as well as anyone, the role he had played in Zina's decline, but it was easier to push the wrenching guilt he felt outward.

"There was not even a shadow of any political sense in the persecution of my daughter—there was nothing in it but purposeless, naked vengeance."

More pain would follow before long.

# 4

# Kremlin Complexion

As Trotsky scuttled from one country to the next, desperately trying to find sanctuary, his rival barely moved at all.

Stalin had last traveled abroad before the Great War. He would not do so again until 1943. He had almost no personal contact with the millions of people over whom he ruled. Instead, they wrote to him. During his flawed, brutal attempt to collectivize the nation's agriculture that began in 1928, he received tens of thousands of letters filled with bewilderment, misery, and terror. This made no difference. His regime's machinery carried on grinding his population's lives into dust. Occasionally, he might reply to a party member in such a way to help burnish his legend as a simple, humble comrade: "You speak about your 'devotion' to me. Maybe the phrase just slipped out. Maybe . . . But if it didn't just slip out, I would advise you to discard the 'principle' of devotion to individuals. It is not the Bolshevik way. Be devoted to the working class, to its party, its state. That is what is needed and what is good."*

* Nikita Khrushchev, the future Soviet leader, claimed that Stalin inserted the following paragraph in a draft of his own *Short Biography*: "Although he performed his task as the leader of the Party and the people with consummate skill and enjoyed the un-

Stalin did not tour factories or construction sites. He sequestered himself with documents and reports, watched film commentaries, or simply stood, seemingly lost in thought, in front of vast maps. It was the maps he loved most of all. He would trace the route of the Trans-Siberian Express with his finger, or find Magnitogorsk, the Dnieper hydroelectric dam, the White Sea–Baltic Canal. And, of course, there were also the towns and cities that had been renamed in his honor: Stalingrad, Stalino, Stalinsk, Stalinabad. His map was so big that to reach a region like Kolyma in the distant east, he would have to take several paces.

Stalin led the nocturnal existence of a poet or a gangster. When he was in Moscow, he rarely emerged before eleven in the morning and would not sleep until it was almost dawn. And yet he was not indolent. Stalin existed in a single dimension: his work. It was perhaps the only force in the Soviet Union that had more power than he did.

He was always reading a stream of files: requests to exempt tractor and combine drivers from military service; a proposal for the construction of new houses for the army; a report on a speech by the Polish leader Józef Piłsudski; extracts from the Czech press; a request to intervene on behalf of a schoolteacher in the Sasov district who was subject to unwanted advances from a local functionary.

This devotion meant that Stalin's life was lived behind the Kremlin's thirteen-foot walls, or in airless rooms full of the fug of smoke and cheap cologne. He very rarely walked or took exercise of any kind.* Occasionally, when he was staying at Kuntsevo, he ventured outside into his dacha's grounds. His staff would see a stooping figure take one or two turns around the paved path before coming to a halt by a flower bed or lilac bush.

But Stalin would still be working late into the evening even as he

---

reserved support of the entire Soviet people. Stalin never allowed his work to be marred by the slightest hint of vanity, conceit or self-adulation."

* He thought activities such as hunting and fishing were aristocratic pastimes.

sat at the dinner table in his apartment with his cronies, sipping Georgian wines, talking, taunting, and plotting. He stopped only after midnight to watch films. Then he would be driven out of Moscow, through thick pine forests and a ring of checkpoints and fences to his austere camouflage-green dacha, where he usually slept, alone. No guards or servants stayed in the compound with him.

The men in Stalin's inner circle who shared this unreal, upside-down existence with him developed what became known as "Kremlin Complexion"; their skin took on a sickly, chalky color except where it was marked by livid blotches: a sign of the way Stalin could effect a physical as well as a moral transformation in those closest to him.

STALIN WAS THE most powerful man in one of the most powerful nations on the planet. Every single one of his old rivals had been forced to abase themselves. At the party's Seventeenth Congress in 1934, known as the Congress of Victors, Nikolai Bukharin, who had once mocked Stalin's lack of foreign languages, announced, "By his brilliant application of Marx-Lenin [*sic*] dialectics, Stalin was entirely correct when he smashed a whole series of theoretical premises of the right deviation which had been formulated above all by myself."

Kamenev—the man who had once, while talking with Trotsky, called Stalin a "ferocious savage"—argued, "This era in which we are living . . . is a new era . . . it will go down in history, without doubt, as the Stalin era, just as the preceding era went down in history as the Lenin era, and each of us, especially us, has the obligation to resist with all means and all our energy the slightest wavering of this authority."

There was one exception: Trotsky. In exile he produced a torrent of articles and books that insulted, mocked, and denigrated Stalin, who read them in the course of a single night before emerging the following day "seething with bile."

Trotsky was an alternative leader—the conscience of the revolution ready to sweep back in once its promise had been betrayed. Worse still for Stalin, he had traveled abroad with his capacious archive.* What if everything he had built could be destroyed by a single piece of paper plucked from one of Trotsky's files?

The Central Committee could order the "correcting" of history, which meant, "Memoirs were censored and expurgated; documents were concealed or destroyed, and encyclopedias re-written." Maxim Gorky was forced to alter the page in his *Recollections of Lenin* that discussed Trotsky. He cut out any praise of Trotsky and instead hinted that Lenin had always distrusted Trotsky. All of Trotsky's achievements in the Civil War were attributed to Stalin.

But even this assault on objective reality was never enough. Stalin had emerged from the battle for the leadership of the party victorious and yet somehow even more riddled with self-loathing and suspicion.

Trotsky knew that his rival's inferiority complex was allied to an infinite hunger, and capacity, for vengeance, noting that *"personal revenge"* had always been a significant element in his repressive policies. "Joseph knew how to persecute and how to avenge himself. He knew how to strike at weak spots."

Kamenev had once told Trotsky how in the summer of 1923, he had spent a day drinking and talking with Stalin, Karl Radek, Alexei Rykov, and Felix Dzerzhinsky† in Stalin's first dacha, Zubalovo. After

---

* During the 1930s, while talking with cronies, Stalin was told about Trotsky's most recent speech. In response, Stalin snapped: "We made two mistakes on that occasion. We should have left him for a time in Alma-Ata, but on no account should we have let him out of the country. And the other one was, how could we have let him take so many documents with him?"

† Felix Dzerzhinsky, the first leader of the Cheka. Dzerzhinsky was a fanatic even by the standards of his fellow Bolsheviks, although this communism was shot through with a vein of equally passionate religiosity. He once mused to his brother Kazimierz: "If I ever concluded that God did not exist, I'd put a bullet through my head."

In Warsaw before the Great War, while serving a sentence in one of Poland's most feared prisons, he shocked both his fellow inmates and the guards by his willingness to volunteer for all of the most unpleasant tasks, such as cleaning the filthy buckets used as latrines. When he was asked why he did so, he replied: "Someday there will be a really dirty job to be done and someone will have to do it; and that will be I."

they'd finished the wine, they sat on their balcony and conversation talked to "personal tastes and predilections." What was the finest thing in the world?

"Books," said Kamenev.

Radek, slyly, said, "A woman, your woman."

Rykov said, "Cognac."

Stalin: "The greatest delight is to mark one's enemy, prepare everything, avenge oneself thoroughly, and then go to sleep."

His comrades called this his "theory of sweet revenge."

Stalin never forgot anything. He stored past grievances and indiscretions in his "icy, computer-like memory." This man—who wore shoes with built-up heels and would always try to be a step higher than anyone else when photos were taken, who could not bear it when anybody else was praised, or even awarded a medal—was preternaturally touchy and possessed a very un-Georgian inability to take a joke. Stalin's daughter, Svetlana, said that if he was told that somebody had criticized him, or opposed him in some way, he underwent a "psychological metamorphosis."

> At this point—and this was where his cruel, implacable nature showed itself—the past ceased to exist for him. Years of friendship and fighting side by side in a common cause might as well never have been. . . . "So you've betrayed me," some inner demon would whisper. "I don't even know you any more."

Trotsky had belittled and abused Stalin publicly while he was still in Russia, and the flood of insults continued unabated while he was in exile. This could not go unrequited.

All of this—the inferiority complex, the seething desire for vengeance—was magnified by the paranoia that was one of the defining traits of a man who lived in an unreal atmosphere of terror he had largely created himself. The number of people that Stalin, who

Khrushchev described as "sickly suspicious," trusted could be counted on the fingers of one hand.

His paranoia was so intense that the gardenias outside his dacha's windows had to be cut at a height of less than two feet—to ensure that nobody could hide behind them. If Stalin ever detected a glance from one of his bodyguards he didn't like, that man would never work for him again. He would often look at someone and ask: "Why are your eyes so shifty today?" or "Why are you turning so much today and avoiding looking directly in my eyes?"

In the days when Trotsky had sat across from him at the Politburo table, Stalin had been able to make a precise calculation of his weaknesses and flaws and expose them mercilessly. And yet now that he was in exile, the Georgian struggled to maintain any sense of proportion.

His assessment of the threat that Trotsky posed was a paranoid fantasy. When Trotsky—whom Stalin addressed in his mind as "Leib Davidovich," using the Yiddish form of Lev*—spoke, Stalin feared that he did so "for all of the silent supporters and the oppositionists inside the USSR." Stalin was convinced that Trotsky's accomplices were fomenting, plotting, spying. And he was also convinced that these enemies were multiplying.

This man who remembered everything seemed to have forgotten that there had never been a time when Trotsky enjoyed widespread support within the party. He had perhaps only a few hundred followers at the time of his expulsion. Many of them had since recanted—and were forced to abase themselves.

Stalin did not, or could not, appreciate the extent to which his rival had neither a "serious social base, nor a serious program." Or that anti-Stalinism could have only an incredibly narrow appeal for a movement with worldwide ambitions.

The picture of Trotsky painted by Stalinist mythology was of a di-

* Trotsky's Jewishness undoubtedly informed Stalin's hatred for him.

abolical figure who was in alliance with Nazi Germany, Japan, and the capitalist powers that surrounded the Soviet Union, and who had tentacles that reached into every corner of Soviet society.

Nevertheless, the liquidation of Trotsky became the chief objective of Stalin's foreign policy. In the fevered corners of Stalin's imagination, his credibility and authority depended on the extermination of his former comrade. Trotsky was, in his own words, Stalin's "enemy number one." Stalin could not bear the idea that most people who called themselves communists saw Trotsky as synonymous with the October Revolution and the creation of the Red Army. He could not forgive Trotsky for the way he had ridiculed Stalin in front of other Bolsheviks or denounced him to the Central Committee as the "gravedigger of the revolution."

The hatred—his frustration at not being able to solve the Trotsky "problem"—churned within Stalin constantly. He could not stop thinking about this man whose power he had destroyed years before. Sometimes the frustration spilled out without warning. Stalin had invented his name, his biography, even his nationality to serve his remorseless ambition. He had done this so he could play his part in history—he was not going to let Trotsky stop that.

# Part Two

Ramón and Caridad Mercader

# 5

# A Perfect Communist Family

Ramón Mercader del Río (or Jacques Mornard, or Frank Jacson, or Ramón Ivanovich López, or Carrasco—he went by many names during his life) was tall and slender and had abundant curly dark hair; he was handsome enough, some said, to have passed as a movie star. Almost everybody who met him said how pleasant and easy to get along with he was. His conversation was entertaining, partly because, though his knowledge was shallow, he knew a little about a lot and had a great memory. "This meant he could talk easily about everything: electronics, radio engineering, cybernetics, the Big Bang, astronomy, quantum mechanics." All of this was enlivened by a sense of humor and a strikingly vivid imagination. Almost a mythomaniac, said two psychologists who spent thousands of hours in his company. (They liked him despite, or perhaps because of, this.)

Ramón was perceptive, meticulous, and scrupulous. His reactions were unusually swift. His hands possessed the sensitivity of a highly skilled watchmaker, and he was so manually dextrous that he could disassemble and then reassemble a rifle in just half a minute or perform tricks with cards that astonished experts. A keen gymnast and "serious sportsman," he was also so strong that he could fold a ten-centime coin in two with his fingers. His memory was photographic, and he could learn highly complicated instructions quickly and then recall them accurately. Ramón spoke Spanish, Catalan, French, and English perfectly.

Although his large green eyes struggled to make out objects in the distance, which meant he generally wore glasses, the rest of his senses were acute. He could follow a chosen path in the dark and detect the slightest sound. All of this was allied to intelligence, decisiveness, steady nerves, and almost perfect self-control. Perhaps most significantly of all, he was a gifted actor who appeared to actively enjoy deceit.

Ramón was, in short, the perfect spy. He was also a fanatic communist, desperate to remake into a utopia the imperfect world into which he had been born. It was precisely these qualities that sent him on a journey that ended with him killing Leon Trotsky in cold blood in his study in Mexico City.

His mother, Caridad, who had set him on that brutal path and was by his side right up to that final, vicious moment, was also extraordinary in her own way. Once Luis, Ramón's younger brother, asked her why people on the street were looking at her. "All my life they have looked at me and admired me," she said. "Always. I'm used to it."

Caridad was "a beautiful creature with green eyes," white hair, and light olive skin. Her bewitching looks were married to an unsettled, anxious temperament. Tall, imposing, and elegant, she dressed well and with great taste. Luis remembered her in nylon stockings, "which had just been invented," brown snakeskin shoes, and stiletto heels. But more notable even than these was her penetrating, domineering gaze. Photos show her eyes burning with an almost impossible intensity.

This force of personality was matched by great physical strength, vigor, and "iron health." She did whatever she wanted, leading an existence that appeared ungoverned by conventional morals or beliefs.

Ramón idolized his nervous, unstable, charismatic mother, and she adored him. Their identification was so close that when he was asked to provide a description of her, he gave one that was almost identical to the one he'd given of himself. Photos of mother and son taken during the Spanish Civil War show them looking almost like twins.*

Eustacia María Caridad del Río Hernández was born into an aristocratic family in Santiago de Cuba on 29 March 1892, at a time when Spain was still clinging on to its last scraps of empire.

Her upbringing was conventional (although she liked to boast that her family mixed with both the Castros and the Bacardís). She was educated in Barcelona, Paris, and Brighton. By the time she returned to Cuba, she had mastered Catalan, Spanish, English, and French.

After a brief spell back in Cuba, her parents moved permanently to Barcelona on 23 October 1910. Her predisposition to mysticism saw her serve as a novitiate in the Order of the Carmelite Descalzas.

This did not last. Before she had turned nineteen, she was married to Don Pablo Mercader Marina, a man from a noble if financially precarious Catalan family who was six years older than her and possessed a "retiring and conservative disposition"; he was also a fervent Catholic and a Catalan separatist, later a militant in the Estat Català grouping. (Ramón seems to have had conflicting memories of his father. At times he talked of him "with undisguised dislike" as "a fat, sluggish and physically dull man, who was harried by petty phobias." Don Pablo had a preoccupation with cleanliness and a fear of disease—it was said that he used to have his vegetables washed in potassium permanganate before they were cooked.)

Early on there were signs that something was different about

* Ramón became critical—"very harsh," Luis said—when discussing their mother, and not just of how she lived her own life, but of how she had treated their father, who was, Ramón said, "too good and meek."

For his own part, Ramón argued that the idea that Caridad had exerted an overdue influence over him was overstated—and that she had impacted on her children more by her absence than by her presence. "We have almost always lived alone," he argued, "or rather, without her."

Caridad. She was educated, but at the same time restless and daring. In 1912 she was threatened with excommunication for having flown over El Prat de Llobregat with her godfather.* And there had always been something reckless about the way she rode, swam, and hunted. There were too many car accidents, too many occasions when she was hurled off her horse.

Still, five children followed in quick succession: four boys and one girl: Jorge, Ramón (born in 1913), Pablo, Luis, and Montserrat. Growing up in a mansion with a large garden and stables, the children learned to speak French and English perfectly, just as their mother had. ("At home, we speak French until one o'clock in the afternoon," Jorge told a girlfriend. "After one, we speak English." The children were forced to learn under threat of no dinner.) They were also given a strict, conservative religious education in line with their father's beliefs.

Ramón was quiet and well-behaved. He had an instinctive sense of right and wrong and a belief in the value of punishment. "When I was small," he recalled, "I never refused a punishment if it was just, but rebelled if it was unjust. For example, once when my mother scolded me for having eaten some apples, she told me that next time I would be punished and that she would stand me facing the wall. One day when she was not at home I ate some apples and then put myself facing the wall. When my mother arrived, she found me standing there."

Along with his siblings, he went to school, played sports, learned languages, but saw little of either parent. Don Pablo worked at the family business; his wife swanked around with the aristocracy and the upper reaches of the bourgeoisie at the Lyceum.

It was only once Caridad had turned thirty-three that her life swerved in an unexpected direction.

* At that time a woman who took to the air was considered to be challenging God in heaven: a mortal sin.

This was due in part due to a collapse in the family's fortunes. The family's textile business had been run so badly by their father's elder brother that he'd had to emigrate to Buenos Aires to escape his family's wrath. Don Pablo was "left with nothing" and was reduced to doing odd jobs, such as working as an accountant for small publishing companies, to try to help his family cling on to their position. What he could earn was not sufficient to cover even the essentials, and Caridad was forced to give private math classes.

She also felt suffocated by the fact that her life had become a well-ordered procession of childbearing. After a point, Caridad refused "even the most normal sexual relations" with her husband. Don Pablo's response was to take his wife to brothels to watch through hidden peepholes as men made love to prostitutes. This attempt to "normalize" her did not increase her desire to go to bed with him; it simply deepened her resentment.

And now she began to pursue disturbing interests.

The math lessons she was giving led her into the company of new sorts of people.

She started to paint and to associate with intellectuals and bohemians. She read Voltaire and stopped seeing those friends and family members she thought were stuffy. Ramón later said that when his mother compared his father to her new friends, he seemed impossibly provincial, small, and reactionary. In turn her husband's friends and relatives thought she was eccentric.

There were late nights, drugs, intoxicating ideas. At some point Caridad began injecting heroin. Worse still, she became involved with a group of anarchists, helping them plant bombs in factories owned by her husband's family. When the anarchists were arrested, they sent personal letters to the judges threatening them with death if they continued the trials until sentencing. José del Río, the municipal judge of Barcelona who was responsible for assigning cases to individual judges, was Caridad's brother; somehow, she had discovered the judges' identities and shared them with her friends.

Caridad's involvement could not remain hidden for long. One night, her brothers, accompanied by psychiatric nurses, put her in a straitjacket and took her away in great secrecy. For three months she was confined to the Nueva Belén hospital in Sarrià-Sant Gervasi. She was subjected to cold showers and shock treatments, treated as if she were genuinely insane, and prevented from contact with the world outside. "I was," she said, "really afraid I'd go crazy."

This was the moment that she began to truly hate the Mercaders and the social class they represented. The Mercaders, she told Luis, were "sons of bitches."

In 1925, when Ramón was twelve, Caridad left her husband and took her children to Dax, France. Here they lived on a farm near some woods in which they went with a pig to look for truffles. There were hens and geese that were being fattened for foie gras. Caridad had a mare, Conchita, with whom Pablo, Ramón, Jorge, Montserrat, and Luis played.

After Dax, they moved to Toulouse, where Caridad ran a small restaurant and Ramón and Jorge attended a school for hotel management. But at some point the accumulated turbulence and trauma of the previous years began to press too powerfully on her. She tried to commit suicide and was rushed to the hospital, where she was confined for a significant period of time. Don Pablo returned to his children's lives, coming to France to pick them up and bring them back to Barcelona.

Don Pablo Mercader's attempts at reconciliation with Caridad failed. By 1928, the break was complete and Caridad moved to Paris. She was joined there by her daughter, from whom she was "inseparable." Montserrat, aged thirteen, had escaped from a convent. In Paris, Caridad joined the fifteenth section of the French Section of the Workers' International (Section Française de l'Internationale Ouvrière [SFIO]), which, while not avowedly communist, was aligned with Moscow.*

* Her involvement might have gone deeper. It is suggested that her relationship with the NKVD dates to this period.

Luis was sent to a boarding school run by nuns. While his father visited every Sunday and took him away for two weeks each summer, he remembered seeing his mother, accompanied by Ramón, who was living in the family home, only once during this period.

Jorge, who had graduated as a chef de cuisine, found a job on the *Atlantique* ocean liner on the Bordeaux–Buenos Aires route. Ramón, though qualified as a maître d'hôtel, worked as a messenger at the Barcelona International Exposition, in a hotel at the Plaza de España, and then as assistant to the chef at the Ritz in Barcelona. He found that his education, manners, and ability to speak several languages allowed him to settle easily in such a prestigious environment.

RAMÓN HAD RETURNED to a city gripped by revolutionary turmoil. In the aftermath of the triumph by a coalition of Republican parties in the elections of spring 1931, which led to the declaration of the Second Spanish Republic, King Alfonso XIII fled into exile. What followed were several years of turbulence as factions from across the political spectrum jockeyed for power. The new government's nationalization of public services, banks, and railways, as well as its redistributive land reforms and attacks on the Catholic Church, enraged those on the Right. Then, after a conservative party, the CEDA (Spanish Confederation of the Autonomous Right), won a majority in the 1933 election and was reluctantly invited into the government, Spanish socialists unleashed an insurrection on 1 October 1934. This revolt was crushed within two weeks but it was clear that violence had become an established part of Spain's politics, both means and end. Moreover, the two sides seemed increasingly irreconcilable. One religious figure observed that children in his parish no longer played cops and robbers; instead they divided themselves into leftists and rightists.

Ramón was at this struggle's epicenter. By the early thirties, he had already, like his mother, become a proud communist. Leftists like Ramón and Caridad were entranced by the Soviet Union, a nation that had been transformed by a “real” revolution. It allowed them to believe in the possibility of “a new society, a new man, a new relationship between the rich and poor, more social justice.” A country where the power of the Church and the big landowners, who, they argued, had kept a large part of Spain stuck in the Middle Ages, would be diminished.

These new beliefs led him to reject the rest of his family. He seldom visited them. When he did, he gave away little about his activities, limiting himself to sour comments about current events.

He moved out of the family home—where Luis and his father still lived—and began spending his time with other young fanatics. To the rest of the Mercaders, it was as if he had become wrapped up in a strange religious sect. Some of them suspected that he was involved in the wave of terrorist activities in the city—though how far, they dared not speculate.

Before he could be conscripted, Ramón volunteered to do his military service in the Jaen Infantry Regiment. Life in the army appealed to him; he began to consider a career. He liked wearing the uniform, and the discipline and order matched the personality of the boy who had “always been very rigid in his way of being. Always very precise, impeccable. He knew what he wanted and what he had to do.” But although he was swiftly made a corporal, and it was recommended that he be promoted to sergeant, his political beliefs became an issue. According to Luis, this was a crushing disappointment to Ramón, a “failure” that would be “his lifelong gripe.”

Ramón could at least channel his frustration into politics. He fought alongside other communists in the bloody scuffles that followed the 1934 uprising and helped organize the Cervantes Artistic Recreational Circle, which was a front for an underground cell of communist youths.

During this time, Ramón lived in a boardinghouse above a shoe-repair shop. At nights he met his comrades in a bar, the Joaquín Costa on Calle Guifré, where their secretary worked. This turbulent but exciting routine was abruptly terminated when on 12 June 1935 he, along with seventeen others, was arrested for communist activities in a police raid at the bar. The police recorded him as being a writer and bachelor, then sentenced him to prison. He spent three months in Barcelona, before being transferred to the prison of San Miguel de los Reyes in Valencia. He was freed when the Popular Front came to power in February 1936 and declared a general amnesty. With this, he returned to Barcelona.

It was around this time that Caridad reappeared in her son's life. In 1935, she had been expelled from Paris by the police—presumably as a result of her own political pursuits. Unable to come within seventy kilometers of the capital, she moved to Bordeaux. Sometime later she was expelled from the country entirely. At one point she was held by police for several days during which she was severely beaten, suffering numerous blows to her head so severe that she lost her sight for over two weeks.

In the summer of 1936, as political tensions continued to rise in Spain, both Ramón and Caridad were involved with the People's Olympiad, an event organized by the Catalan Left as a rejection of the "Wagnerian spectacle" in Berlin. It was attended by workers and peasants from across Europe, including Italy and Germany. There were socialists, anarchists, and communists. The sporting level was low, but that was probably beside the point.

Ramón combined a role on the organizing committee with being captain of the horse-riding team. One witness from the time remembered him as "good-looking, with distinguished manners, although at times authoritarian, especially if the subordinates did not fully comply with orders."

The young Catalan leftist Teresa Pàmies, one of the leaders of the Unified Socialist Youth of Catalonia (JSUC), also recalled his good looks, as well as a rigid, almost priggish strain in his character. Ramón was haughty and sectarian and let it be known that he didn't think that dancing, even the sardana (a traditional Catalan dance), was an appropriate activity for young communists.

This, however, did not seem to have stopped him from attending dances or attracting attention from women when he did so. Ramón had a reputation among the young leftists he mixed with as a playboy, "a kind of Communist Don Juan" notorious for his many conquests. Marina Ginestà was one of them. There was even talk of marriage, though this was discouraged by Caridad. His priggishness was accompanied by an elegance in his dress that sometimes edged into flamboyance. Pàmies noted that he was a "show-off" who seemed a bit too proud of his uniform: "fabulous" leggings worn over café au lait trousers.

This trait persisted throughout Ramón's life. Even when deeply depressed at the beginning of a long stretch in prison (he passed his days either lying in bed or standing with one shoulder against a wall of the cell and arms folded, smoking a cigarette, deep in thought), he would be up to bathe in ice-cold water before reveille was called, he would shave perfectly, and he would be the first to appear in the courtyard.

His ostentatious hygiene, his distinguished manners, and his preference for speaking in French or English rather than in Spanish made his fellow inmates think him a snob—"*un apretado.*"

But for the moment, there were more pressing issues for his comrades to consider. On 17 July, before the Olympiad opened, the Spanish press reported that right-wing officers in the Spanish army stationed in Africa had mutinied. The revolt spread rapidly across the country over the next two days. A civil war had begun.

# 6

# BLACK WORK

Two thousand miles away, in Moscow, another kind of civil war was beginning.

The Terror, when it came, was the product of both Stalin's ambition and his paranoia.

In December 1935 a case that had originally concerned Stalin's old comrade Zinoviev—in which he had been convicted of being complicit in the assassination of Sergei Kirov, the head of the Communist Party in Leningrad—metastasized with terrifying speed into a huge conspiracy that appeared to implicate hundreds of party members.

The accused who were brought into court looked gray, thin, sleep-deprived. Some shook with fear. "Babbling deliriously," they confessed to bizarre and horrifying crimes in a process that was almost completely choreographed by Stalin. This specialist in the pitiless application of pressure was the author of the whole grisly farce, dictating to the presiding judge* the words he wanted him to speak and personally

* Andrey Vyshinsky presented as sober and respectable; with his "trim gray mustache and hair, neatly dressed in stiff white collar and well-cut dark suit," he looked like a prosperous stockbroker, but this disguised his moral decay. Robert Conquest, author of *The Great Terror*, met this indefatigable survivor toward the end of his life. Conquest came away disgusted by the presence of a man who he felt was "both physically and spiritually a creature who gave life to the worn image of a 'rat in human form.'"

proofreading the transcripts to make sure everybody said their lines correctly. The two central witnesses, Zinoviev and Kamenev, had been broken by sleeplessness and an endless parade of carefully weighted threats. In return for a promise from the Politburo that their lives and those of their families would be spared, they had agreed to testify. It did them little good.

Zinoviev spent the last moments of his life begging for a reprieve. Staring feverishly around him, he claimed that he was the victim of a fascist coup. Somehow, despite Stalin's macabre history of betrayals and traps, Zinoviev appeared unable to understand that he had been deceived. "Please, comrade, for God's sake, call Joseph Vissarionovich. Joseph Vissarionovich promised to save our lives!"

In some accounts he began to hug and lick the boots of the NKVD agents who had come to escort him to his death. Disturbed by the spectacle Zinoviev was creating, a lieutenant took him to a nearby cell and without ceremony fired a single round into the back of his head.

Kamenev summoned a last, hopeless burst of dignity, and yet he met the same fate. The bullets that had killed the two old Bolsheviks were pried, still warm, out of their skulls, wiped clean of foamy brain matter, and conveyed to Genrikh Yagoda, the head of the NKVD who named them "Zinoviev" and "Kamenev" and placed them reverently among his collection of pornography (including 165 lewdly carved pipes) and ladies' stockings.

That same day, 25 August 1936, as fourteen more party members were shot in the cellars of Moscow's Lubyanka Prison on charges related to the "Anti-Soviet Trotskyite-Zinovievite Center" and thousands more arrested (which led to confessions, which led to more arrests), Trotsky and his son were sentenced to death in absentia.

THE PURGE THAT Stalin unleashed in the months that followed allowed him to consolidate his power by destroying every potential rival to his position, but also by making fear a basic fact of existence in the Soviet Union.

The man charged with overseeing this vicious new phase was the slight, limping Nikolai Yezhov, who replaced Yagoda as head of the NKVD on 27 September 1936. Stalin did not believe Yagoda had been sufficiently aggressive in his pursuit of Trotskyists and other threats to the Soviet Union. He would have no such qualms about Yezhov.

Before the revolution, Yezhov had written poetry and had a reputation as "Nicky the booklover." Now, with his dark hair cut into "an irregular, shining crew cut," bad yellow teeth, and gray-green eyes that were as greedy as a hyena's, he was one of the most feared men in the entire country.

Standing at barely four feet, ten inches, even in his coarse, reddish high-heeled boots, and with one leg shorter than the other, he was known as "the dwarf" or "the lame." His extraordinary appetite for violence was masked by a permanent smile that hovered somewhere between sarcastic and cynical and that made him repulsive even to his closest collaborators. One man who met him in the 1920s remembered him as almost insignificant: "Yezhov did not at all resemble a vampire. He was a small, slender man, always dressed in a crumpled cheap suit and a blue satin shirt. He sat at the table quietly, not talking much, somewhat shy, drank little, did not interrupt, only listened attentively, slightly bending his head."

Another witness was more perceptive: "I don't know of any more ideal functionary than Yezhov. Rather, he is not a functionary, but an executor. After charging him with a task, you don't have to check up on him: he will accomplish the mission. Yezhov has only one, indeed essential, shortcoming—he does not know where to stop."

The man Stalin called "Blackberry" devoted himself so utterly to persecution that his own health disintegrated. At various points he was treated for colitis, anemia, lung catarrh, exhaustion, tuberculosis of the lungs, angina, sciatica, malnutrition, neurasthenia. Parallel to this was an addiction to alcohol that saw titanic drinking bouts in his working day.

But Trotsky was essential to this project too. For years a distorted caricature of him as a monstrous figure had existed within Stalin's psyche—the incarnation of a particular kind of nightmare. Now Stalin ensured that his old rival played the same role in the whole country's imagination: "the cause and incarnation of all that was evil."

As always with Stalin, it was difficult to establish exactly where his mental sickness ended and his pragmatism began. The idea of Trotsky tortured him, and yet Stalin was able to make use of his existence. As one historian noted: "Had there been not Trotsky, Stalin would have had to invent him. Or more precisely, Stalin invented the Trotsky he needed, a task that looks simple only in hindsight."

Stalin had worked hard over the last decade arranging a moral assassination of Trotsky. The show trials gave him the chance to tie these threads together. Trotsky and his plots were the explanation for everything that had gone wrong in the Soviet Union—the "badly bungled policy of industrialization, the parlous state of the transport system and the terrifying number of industrial accidents" could all be blamed on him.

A handful of those caught up in the conspiracies were reformed Trotskyists. Most had no connection. Few had met him. Even fewer had ever shown any sign of supporting him, either in public or private. Some were guilty of no more than having unintentionally used the same phrase that Trotsky had once employed in a letter to the Soviet authorities. What was increasingly clear was that this latest purge was directed not just at ex-oppositionists but also at Stalin's own followers.

Because this was the problem with Trotskyists: like the witches who had plagued early modern Europe, they were, somehow, everywhere and nowhere. Though on the inside they were distorted by a secret evil, they bore no external marks that revealed their true nature.

They walked among their fellow citizens, plotting, following the malign orders of their leader, and there was no sure way of identifying them. How could you be confident that your boss, or your neighbor, or your oldest comrade was not harboring the sinister desire to sabotage the utopia that was being built here in the Soviet Union?

The bigger error, Stalin believed, was not arresting those who were innocent; it was failing to stop the guilty. After all, and he knew this as well as anyone else, only a tiny group was needed to foment a revolution. In 1937 he observed that if just 5 percent of those arrested were guilty, it would be a "good result." Yezhov shared this indifference as well as his leader's paranoia. "Better too much than not enough," he said. If "an extra thousand people are shot, that is not such a big deal."

The victims were accused of terrorism and of wanting to restore capitalism with the support of the German and Japanese governments. In return, they would offer Germany land and welcome German capital into the country. If the two nations went to war, they'd sabotage the Soviet fighting machine. All of this had been agreed when Trotsky and the Nazi Rudolf Hess met clandestinely. After this, in another secret meeting, with Pyatakov in Oslo in December 1935, Trotsky had set out the entire program of sabotage.

The accusations were barely believable. In the surreal miasma created by Stalin, an explosion on 23 September 1936 in the Tsentralnaya mine in Kemerovo could be blamed not on the revolting conditions in which the workers who had built it existed, or on the fact that safety standards had been abandoned in order to satisfy the relentless demand for results, but on a "Trotskyite nest" in West Siberia.

Rykov could confess with a straight face "that in 1932 we took measures to spread plague among pigs, which resulted in a high pig mortality; this was done by inoculating pigs against the plague in a wrecking fashion."

And Isaak Zelensky, who had been running the state consumer distribution network, could dredge from his memory the following: "I cannot recall the month just now, but I can mention the following fact. In 1936 fifty carloads of eggs were allowed to spoil, from wrecking motives."

As THE TERROR wore on, "ordinary" people began to disappear. Denunciations proliferated. One betrayal begat another. Fear contorted consciences. Some knew their arrest was coming: racked by nerves, they would eat little and try desperately to call people who they thought might help them. Lots of people kept a small suitcase with two changes of underwear in readiness. They might take steps like transferring their savings and valuables to their partners or destroying private papers. In case either of her parents was arrested, Zoya Zarubina, the stepdaughter of NKVD operative Leonid Eitingon, was shown by her mother how to collect warm clothes and take her eight-year-old sister to a distant relative who lived in the country.

The victims, clasping small suitcases with their toothbrushes and dressing gowns, would leave surrounded by NKVD agents. Many wives fainted as they watched their husbands being dragged away. Once the victim had been removed, their apartments would be searched, and cash, radios, bicycles, coats, linen, even little teacups would be taken away.

Arrest was almost invariably followed by interrogation and torture. Huge importance was placed on obtaining a confession, no matter how outlandish. Stalin did not just want to liquidate his opponents but to destroy them morally and politically. Husbands were tortured in front of their wives; daughters raped while their fathers were forced to watch. Fingers were slammed in doors; prisoners were beaten with broken-off chair legs. One favored technique was the "conveyor" in which the victim was interrogated for hours, or days, by unceasing relays of Chekists. Some went seven days without sleep or food. Degradation worked where pain, or exhaustion, could not. One man broke once his head had been rammed into a spittoon "brimful of spittle." Another's capitulation came after an interrogator pissed on his head.

People broke, became unrecognizable as human beings. Some were so damaged by their interrogation that they lost the ability to speak or use their hands; their interrogators would have to take the pens and sign their confessions for them. It was not unusual to find one of these documents marked by blood sprayed by a body in motion.

More than half of those arrested during this period were executed. Execution was officially called the "Highest Measure of Punishment" (known in the USSR by its acronym, VMN). Stalin called it "black work." At the beginning the liquidations took place in the basement of the infamous Lubyanka. The victims would be forced to change into white underclothes, then led to death cells where they would be shot in the back of the head with Tokarev pistols, either as they were standing against the wall or as they walked in.

A doctor would be brought in to certify death. This document would be the last thing placed in the victim's file. Later, Yezhov created a special abattoir in the courtyard of an NKVD building close to the Lubyanka. It had a wall of logs to absorb bullets and facilities in which to wash away blood and brain matter.

Unsurprisingly, many of those involved in committing these crimes drank heavily. Some were even known to have ended their own lives. This was the result of guilt, certainly, but perhaps also the looming understanding that at some point, they too would become victims.

# 7

# SUPER-BANDIT

Trotsky was still in Norway when news of the first wave of show trials reached him. Natalia talked of how the "nightmare descended on the quiet house in Wexhall, and the nauseating stench of the bloodshed in Moscow began to envelop us even here."

The Western press reported the increased tempo of arrests and the relentless search for plotters. Trotsky was dazed by the strange, almost incomprehensible turns of fate, by the moral degradation of the revolution he had given so much to, and by his own centrality to the fantasies being woven in the Soviet Union's capital.

In the pages of *Pravda* and *Izvestia*, men like Karl Radek or Christian Rakovsky (in his diary, Trotsky wrote: "Rakovsky was virtually my last contact with the old revolutionary generation. After his capitulation there is nobody left"), people Trotsky and Natalia remembered as friends and fearless, upright comrades, were now demanding the blood of "that super-bandit Trotsky" or writing, "No pity for the Trotskyist Gestapo agents! Let them be shot!"

It did them little good. They were merely "dead men on furlough." Often, before the ink on their denunciations had dried, they were consigned to the gulag, but this was no consolation to Trotsky.

"[F]rowning and feverish," he immersed himself in research, annotating accounts of the trials with red, blue, and black pencils. His study filled up with pieces of paper, galley proofs, and manuscripts as he produced closely argued but futile refutations of Stalin's paranoid fantasies.

Trotsky's anxiety at the situation made it hard for him to get on with his other work. Instead of writing, he would wait for his secretary to bring him newspapers. Sometimes, his indignation was so great that he could not sleep. In the evenings he listened to Radio Moscow. On the nights he could make out the city's distant chimes, it allowed him to reminisce about his time in the Kremlin. But it also forced him to listen to constant talk about the criminality of Zinoviev and Kamenev—the "unfinished enemies" following the promptings of "the Fascist hireling Trotsky." He was shattered by their executions, even more so by the fact that those responsible had been awarded the Order of Lenin.

"The thinking of mankind is bogged down in its own excrement," he concluded. "I do not think that in all of human history anything could be found even remotely resembling the gigantic factory of lies which was organized by the Kremlin under the leadership of Stalin."

Stalin also followed the progress of the trials from a distance. Sitting in one of his holiday dachas in the far south of the Soviet Union, he received from the NKVD packages containing transcripts of their interrogations and confrontations as well as newspapers, memos, and telegrams. He read them at the wicker table on his veranda like a theater producer eagerly tracking the reception of his latest show.

Steadily Trotsky became more isolated. The number of letters he received in Norway from Russia dwindled, then stopped altogether. He was surrounded by policemen playing cards, Natalia and Trotsky were now under house arrest—and yet he felt more alone than ever before. It was as if he were trapped in a room with "the ravings in the newspapers from Moscow."

---

As the persecution of Stalin's enemies within the Soviet Union accelerated, it was increasingly obvious that nobody who shared blood or family ties of any kind with Trotsky was safe.

Two months after the murder of Kirov, Trotsky learned that Aleksandra Sokolovskaya Bronstein, his first wife, had been arrested and exiled, first to Tobolsk, then to a remote part of Omsk province. His two granddaughters, whom she had been caring for, were sent to an elderly aunt in Ukraine. His brother, Alexander, had spent the twenties and thirties working as an agronomist in a provincial sugar mill. When Trotsky was deported in 1929, Alex was expelled from the party, exiled, and forced to make a public repudiation. This was not enough to save him. One night in the summer of 1936, he was arrested. On 25 April 1938, he was shot as "an active, un-disarmed Trotskyist."

Their sister Olga, who had married Kamenev, was arrested in 1935, then sent to a concentration camp. She was shot in 1941. Her son was executed in 1938, her older son in 1939.

Platon Volkov, Zina's former husband, was arrested although already in exile and sent even farther away. And then came the hardest blow of all: the disappearance of Sergei, the Trotskys' younger son.

The gentle Sergei had grown up in the Kremlin. Stalin's son was often a guest in his room. Unlike many others, he took the ideas of socialist equality with which he'd been raised at face value. He was disgusted by the comfort in which the *nomenklatura*, the regime's privileged bureaucrats, lived. He refused to jump the queue at the doctor's office, and when sent a new jacket by the Moscow Soviet, he continued wearing his old patched one. He believed that even his parents lived a "bourgeois" lifestyle and hated their cultural tastes. On one occasion he berated them for listening to a radio broadcast of *Eugene Onegin*, the Tchaikovsky opera. For him, this was unacceptably decadent.

At the age of twelve, he turned his back on politics. At sixteen he left home. Not long after, driven by his passion for gymnastics, he joined a circus but was eventually persuaded by his new wife, librarian Olga Grebner, to resume his studies and became an engineer.*

Trotsky stopped writing to Sergei after 1929 because he didn't want to give the authorities reason to harass his son. Instead, Sergei and his mother corresponded, though they were careful to write only of his health and his work in academia. Sometimes the letters dried up; then a postcard would come out of the blue and the conversation could resume.

A few days after Kirov's assassination, Sergei posted to his mother a letter about the subjects he lectured on at the Higher Technical School in Moscow and the demands this made on him. It was only as the letter drew to a close that he added: "something unpleasant is brewing, so far it has taken the form of rumors, but how all this is going to end I do not know."

A week later, 12 December 1934, he sent another update about his work, but this was accompanied by an alarming conclusion: "My general situation is very grave, graver than one could imagine."

His parents waited in vain for news. In May 1935 they learned that their twenty-seven-year-old son had been arrested two months earlier, on 4 March. Five agents had searched his home for several hours, taking away his books and a portrait of Trotsky. He spent two to three months in the Lubyanka, where he was charged with "espionage, aiding and abetting his father, wrecking." Then he was banished to Siberia.

His second wife, Genrieta, disappeared soon afterward. Trotsky and his wife found out only when an international money order they had sent her came back with the sinister message: "no forwarding address." Trotsky was shattered by the idea his son was suffering a "hangover after someone else's feast." He desperately tried to convince

* His only book, written with two colleagues, was called *Light Generators of the Autotractor Type*; it was published by the Scientific Autotractor Institute.

himself that Sergei was still alive, perhaps sequestered in a far-flung camp. At times, he considered suicide. "Perhaps if I were to die, they would set him free?" he wondered before returning to waiting desperately for news. There was nothing they could do beyond releasing plaintive public appeals, which were invariably met by terse, unhelpful nothings from the Soviet Union. In the diary Trotsky kept during this time, his entries about Sergei alternated with reflections about the Bolsheviks' killing of the Romanov children in 1918—Tsar Nicholas II's offspring had also been been punished for nothing more than the name they bore.*

The following year, more news came in the form of a brief communiqué announcing the execution of eighty-three Trotskyists in the Far East. There had been an accident in the factory in Krasnoyarsk where Sergei had been allowed to work as an engineer. He was accused of having "organized the mass gassing of workers." *Pravda* published an article in which a foreman at the Krasnoyarsk Engineering Works accused, "This worthy offspring of a father who has sold himself to Fascism attempted to poison a large number of workers at this factory with gas."

That same summer, Sergei's first wife, Olga, received a postcard: "They're taking me to the North. For a long time. Goodbye. I embrace you."

Then silence.

AT ONE POINT in the bloody civil war that followed the Bolshevik Revolution of 1917, Lenin joked, "Do you know what [Trotsky] would reply when asked by the officer in charge of the firing-squad if he had any last wishes? 'Do you happen to have a comb, sir?'"

Now, though, something had shifted. The furrows that had ap-

* Trotsky concluded, somewhat unconvincingly, that the question of dynastic succession made the two situations different.

peared on Trotsky's face after Zina's death grew deeper still, just as his auburn hair grew grayer. Instead of wearing it "proudly" brushed back, he began to comb it to the side. Those around him noted that this fastidious man was taking less care of his clothes than before. It was now a rare sight to encounter him in one of his immaculate white suits.

Those around Trotsky and Natalia noted that they were preoccupied by their aging, with Trotsky apt to exaggerate his decline, just as he did his illnesses. "Old age," he said plaintively, "is the most unexpected of all things that happen to a man."

But he remained taller and more lithe than most people expected.* His movements were alert and his eyes, which retained their extraordinary lucidity, were capable of scrutinizing and dominating anybody upon whom they rested.

The slender Natalia was as reserved as she always had been. She continued to move with the exceptional grace that was one of her outstanding qualities. Her face, framed by fine ash-blond hair, retained its delicacy and sweetness, but it also showed the pain she had suffered over the last decade.

Natalia's life had been entwined with Trotsky's since the day, in the autumn of 1902, when they had met on the stairs of a Parisian apartment block on the Rue Lalande. Trotsky was a fugitive from a penal colony in Siberia, where he had left behind a wife and two daughters. Natalia Sedova was a clever young radical who had been expelled from her ladies' college in Kharkiv for "free thinking and reading seditious literature." She was now studying the history of art at the Sorbonne but was also already part of the group around *Iskra*† and had been charged with helping new arrivals find cheap places to eat and live.

She showed Trotsky the Louvre and told him about her life. One day the pair found themselves standing together looking at

---

* His height was a shock to anybody familiar with the "sickly and convulsed" figure shown in Stalinist and anti-Semitic cartoons

† *Iskra*, or *Spark* in English, was the underground newspaper managed by Lenin.

Baudelaire's tomb in the Montparnasse Cemetery. From that moment on, they were inseparable.

Natalia—whose comfortable life as the daughter of hereditary gentry had been broken apart at the age of seven when her father died of a heart attack and he was followed by her heartbroken mother a few months later—was as committed to revolutionary upheaval as her husband, and she was as viscerally disgusted as he was by the exploiting classes that they wished to remove.

During the long years of their first exile together, she spent her days looking after her children and devoted her nights to serious reading. Her sons grew up believing that she never slept. While other Bolsheviks—such as the Radeks, who had appropriated a set of grand-ducal rooms in the Kremlin—had been happy to exploit their status, Natalia set a much more modest example, continuing to make shirts for her boys out of old tablecloths.

Most of all, though, she self-consciously devoted herself to her husband. She believed that she was a modern woman, but also that she was the partner of an exceptional human being. As she told one of her husband's secretaries: "This is his work; this is his life. My life is to help him do it—to create the conditions for him that he should not have the slightest difficulties in his, and to live, live by this, and to *delight* in his work, his ideas."

Trotsky discussed his ideas with her, even if he rarely took on board her reservations—it was more important to her that he should be content and comfortable than that he should always be right. And she, in turn, was one of the tiny handful of people whose feelings Trotsky appeared aware of. Their comrades noticed how he was always trying to meet her desires and needs—at least insofar as he was able. This habit had strengthened during their exile. In France, then in Norway, they spent enormous amounts of time in each other's company—more than they had at any point in their lives so far.

The loneliness and pain were at times almost overwhelming, and yet the experience of it all drew them closer together.

# 8

# The Crucible

The Spanish Civil War changed everything for Ramón and Caridad. Perhaps their lives would have ended up on a similar trajectory had the conflict not broken out—they were already fanatically committed to their cause—but it certainly accelerated their journeys. It left them with physical and perhaps mental scars; more significantly, it also brought them into contact with the men who played a central role in shaping their future.

The revolt was the work of a conspiratorial network of military officers—including General Francisco Franco, who in the months to come emerged as its undisputed leader; they had begun plotting even before the left-wing Popular Front narrowly won the 1936 election.

Once the first shots had been fired in Spanish Morocco, the insurrection spread to Spain's major cities. On 18 July 1936, the Placa de Catalunya, one of Barcelona's main plazas, was occupied by rebel troops. They were confronted by crowds of armed workers at the edges of the plaza and its adjacent arcades. Caridad directed the attack against the rebels, leading the workers in a frontal assault on the machine-gun positions, which were overwhelmed by rifles and homemade grenades. The Placa de Catalunya surrendered, its commander was taken prisoner, and although many lost their lives, the action helped prevent a full-scale attack on Catalonia.

Around the same time, Luis, who was still living with his father, was summoned down to the street to see his brother. Ramón was

> seated, with the door open, in an enormous Hispano Suiza car, with a chauffeur, which he had requisitioned from the Belgian consul. He had a Winchester resting on his legs, and he began to explain its operation to me. It had a shoulder cartridge belt. He took out a cartridge and showed me how, with a knife, cross-shaped incisions could be made on the tip of the lead, with which to destroy a person. He told me that this type of rifle was mainly used for hunting lions and elephants. I was small, and that weapon thrilled me.

Ramón fought on the barricades—fierce, often hand-to-hand combat in a convent on Pau Claris Street as well as in the Drassanes metro station—where he met the teacher and textile worker and one of the founders of the Women's Anti-Fascist Movement (*Movimiento antifascista de mujeres* [MAM]), Elena Imbert, one of whose ancestors had joined the Paris Commune and been shot in 1871 in Père Lachaise Cemetery. Teresa Pàmies believed that while Ramón had many girlfriends, it was the exuberant, enterprising Elena—with her enormous black eyes, olive skin, and thick, dark hair—whom he had truly loved.

Though Seville and Cádiz, as well as large swathes of the more conservative north and west of the country, were captured by the rebels, who had started calling themselves *Nacionales*, or Nationalists, most of the country's major industrial regions, including the Basque Country and the east coast and center, were held by the Republicans, those still loyal to the government.

Both sides presented the struggle as an existential battle: on the one hand, the Republicans were fighting against the Nationalists' tyranny, and on the other, the Nationalists saw themselves as bravely holding back the forces of communism and anarchism to protect Christian civilization.

And yet there was a sort of gaiety to the opening weeks of the revolt. In Barcelona ties and jackets were abandoned for blue workers-style cotton overalls, often topped with the colors of whichever faction the wearer adhered to: red and black for anarchists, red for socialists and communists, gold and red for Catalan nationalists. Unless you wanted to look bourgeois, it was wise to avoid hats (except proletarian berets), dresses, jackets, or ties (except those with militia insignia). Those leaving for the front were handed skins of wine, hams, blankets, even ancient swords.

The cities were in a ferment of rumor and misinformation. There was shooting from every direction and it was difficult to know who was shooting at what; even so, cafés and restaurants were full to bursting. Banks had been taken over by workers' collectives; lipstick factories were converted to make munitions. Hotels were crammed with people who had previously believed them to be off-limits but who were now cheerfully eating in their dining rooms with elbows on tables covered in crumbs. Churches were closed or, sometimes, burned. Religious statues were decapitated or knocked off-balance as if they were about to faint.

On other occasions the horror was more straightforward. The bodies of the victims of the vigilantes who had operated in Madrid's old slaughterhouse, the Matadero, were laid out on display before burial long enough for vindictive members of the public to come to mock and stare.

COMBATIVE, DARING, ENERGETIC, Caridad thrived in the new world that the war had created. As always, she drew attention. Known as "La Mercader," she gained over the course of the war a reputation as a crack shot who could hit a target with gun or knife from thirty feet; she also later confessed in confidence that she had personally carried out twenty executions of Trotskyists and other "counter-revolutionaries." Her fellow combatants were also struck by her impressive physique: her height, her splendid teeth, and her short, prematurely white hair, which swept thickly around her head. She wore a leather jacket over a wide skirt and soldiers' boots, and she bubbled over with vitality and enthusiasm.

After her exploits in Barcelona, she led a communist brigade on the Aragon front. In August she was wounded under during an artillery bombardment; her intestines were perforated by Italian shrapnel as she sprinted through a field. After being operated on in Lérida and hovering for a while between life and death, she finally recovered and was released after three months, although she was afflicted by intestinal pain for the rest of her life.

A month later, Ramón was also wounded. He was part of a column of communist youth who had been charged with building trenches. When the detachment he led was ordered to cut a power line, he decided to do the job himself rather than endanger any of his men. The enemy opened fire as soon as he broke cover. Although he managed to cut the cable, he was hit before he could leap back to safety. A bullet tore through the tendons of his right forearm and he was taken to hospital in Lérida, where he met up with his mother.

He recovered in time to join in the bloody defense of Madrid, as well as the Guadalajara offensive, which ended in a Republican victory against Italian divisions advancing on the Spanish capital. Having shown promise as both an organizer and tactician, he was promoted to commander in the elite Fifth Regiment, which, while lavishly equipped, had come to be increasingly under the control of what were euphemistically known as "Russian technicians," as well as foreign specialists directed by the NKVD.

Teresa Pàmies saw Ramón for the last time in a Barcelona hospital, where he was being treated for dysentery. As she entered the room, a young nurse was reprimanding him for something with feigned severity; he managed to appease her with a mixture of flattery and banter. Pàmies could not have known that these skills at manipulation would one day be put to a different use.

It was clear that his new life suited him. Another friend found him "extremely cordial," if "somewhat exalted in his ways of expressing himself," and his excitement was reflected in the clothes he wore and the weapons he carried: a shirt open to the middle of his chest, a double-breasted jacket, a white scarf, a shiny-visored cap, a belt festooned with hand grenades, and a pistol with mother-of-pearl grips. He had learned to mimic the long strides of the commissars he'd seen in Soviet films. It was as if he were playing a role, except of course that the danger he faced, and the cause he fought for, was all too real.

# PART THREE

Leon Trotsky with the surrealist writer André Breton

# 9

# The Only Honest Government in the World

On a hot, tropical morning in January 1937, a ship carrying Trotsky, Natalia, and an escort of "fascist policemen" arrived in the Mexican port of Tampico.

Trotsky and Natalia had been offered asylum in Mexico by President Lázaro Cárdenas, who was himself responding to pressure from Spanish socialists and his country's most notable artist, Diego Rivera, who had emerged as an idiosyncratic supporter of the exiled Russian.*

Their party had finally left Norway on 19 December 1936. Policemen, pipes clenched in their mouths, waited outside in the gathering fog as an anxious Trotsky and Natalia, who had been given only a few hours' notice, packed their possessions. "Not one of our numerous migrations ever took place," wrote Trotsky, "in such an atmosphere of feverish haste, such feeling of utter isolation, uncertainty, and suppressed indignation." Occasionally, Natalia and he exchanged glances as they tried to parse the most recent turn in their fortunes. Each of

* The day before the November 1936 audience with Cárdenas at which Trotsky supporters Bartomeu Costa-Amic, Daniel Rebull, and Manuel Martínez planned to present their case for the Soviet exile, they met with Rivera to explain their idea. "Sons of shit, we hadn't thought about it," he exclaimed, and immediately pledged his support.

them worried that they might be walking into a trap, a fear that did not leave them for some days.

Over the course of the journey, though, Trotsky became excited about what lay ahead. The sea that carried them was rough, and the ship pitched and rolled, but he sat calmly working and reading "feverishly" about Mexico (in English), including books like Bernal Díaz del Castillo's *True History of the Conquest of New Spain* and Alfonso Reyes's *Vision of Anáhuac*. "Our planet is so tiny but we know so little about it!" he wrote in his journal.

And yet, as the tanker steamed into the harbor, Natalia was overcome with an unreasoning dread. She told the captain she would not leave the ship unless she saw the faces of friends. When, reassured by the sight of some of their supporters, Trotsky and she did eventually emerge to walk down the wooden pier, he strode confidently ahead, his chin high. Clad in tweed knickerbockers and a cap, he was carrying a briefcase and a cane. Behind him were a pale and fragile-looking Natalia, who anxiously watched her feet to make sure she didn't trip on the rough planks of the narrow dock, and the lissom, rebozo-draped Frida Kahlo. The wife of Diego Rivera, Kahlo had offered to let Trotsky and Natalia stay in her childhood home. Trotsky was suffused with excitement at stepping once more onto the soil of the New World. He reveled in the soil's warm breath and the fact that the oil derricks of Tampico reminded him of Baku.

Natalia's fear persisted. Every policeman startled her. She panicked each time she lost sight of Frida and the other friends who had come to welcome them, even if only for a second, and she panicked again when the train that collected them stopped at a small station on the outskirts of Mexico City, and Trotsky and Natalia were told to step into a waiting car filled with armed policemen.

They were not to be taken to prison, or an internment camp, or worse; it was simply a reflection of their circumstances. Natalia was married to a man with a target on his back.

---

MEXICO WAS A good home for Trotsky. "The contrast between northern Norway and tropical Mexico was felt not only in the climate," he wrote, almost ecstatically. "Torn free from the atmosphere of revolting self-will and enervating uncertainty, we encountered hospitality and attentiveness at every step." He told Victor Serge that the Cárdenas administration was "the only honest government in the world."

It was also very likely his only option. It was not just that he remained one of the most feared, vilified men on the planet. Stalin's revocation of his citizenship in 1932 had stripped him of even the most minimal diplomatic protection from the country of his birth. This also meant that any Soviet citizens who remained in contact with him became, overnight, guilty of associating "not just with a disgraced leader of a domestic opposition, but with a *foreign* conspirator."

Trotsky was isolated and alone, but he was also alive and at liberty, and this, perhaps, was enough. And yet, although Mexico offered a respite from many of the troubles that had plagued him for so long, it was not an escape.

Within days of his arrival, a cohort of experienced Soviet agents slipped into the country. They were there to watch him. Others, surely, would soon come; but they would have a very different purpose in mind.

THE HOUSE IN the residential suburb of Coyoacán in which the Trotskys spent the better part of three years was also the house in which Frida Kahlo (initially referred to by Trotsky as "Frieda Rivera") had been born and that in years gone by she had used for assignations with lovers.

Coyoacán was still separate from the rest of Mexico's capital. Getting there involved a long trip through cornfields. From here it was still possible to see the purple mountains that ringed the city, unobscured by the industrial fumes and traffic exhaust that blighted the lives of those living in the cacophonous, chaotic center, where even the still of the night was disturbed by the explosions of fireworks and dynamite stolen from mines. Evelyn Waugh called it the "most shrill and thunderous city in the world. Noise is the first, shattering greeting to the stranger, it is the constant companion of all his days."

Here, on Coyoacán's cobbled streets, the clip-clop of horseshoes and the squeak of peddlers' carts remained as familiar as the rumble of automobile tires. If Trotsky looked out of his window, he would see street sellers going from house to house, hawking their wares—"woolen rugs and serapes with brightly woven Indian designs; parrots, parakeets, and exotic songbirds; honeycakes, preserves and gelatins; charcoal-singed corn-on-the-cob sprinkled with cheese; slices of succulent jicama and radish smeared with lemon juice and chile."

And yet it was not quite an idyll. For one thing, Coyoacán was still subject dozens of times each year to the stomach-churning tremors that, while causing no serious damage, reminded every resident that the ground on which their existences were built was "unsettlingly alive."

It was to Coyoacán, a neighboring province to the south of Tenochtitlán, that Cortés had fled after the collapse of Aztec resistance to the conquistadores—somewhere that offered a respite from the stench of rotting corpses, the burned city with its shattered idols and wrecked and looted shrines; where he could plot a new era for the Valley of Mexico.

This ground had borne witness to the exploitation by the Spanish both of the environment—which had been completely transformed by their arrival (deforestation had left the "mountainsides corrugated and barren, as if their vegetation had been scraped away with a dull knife")—and of the natives, who had been cheated of their land.

And now Coyoacán abutted a city that for decades had been "a devourer of human beings," with a mortality rate that made it "the most unhealthy urban center on earth." Half of all infants died before they reached their first year.

But Mexico City's population was replenished by an unstoppable flow of rural migrants who crammed themselves onto soiled straw mats in cold, damp, typhus-ridden flophouses, or *mesónes*. The more permanent slums that sprang up were hardly any healthier or more comfortable. Seven or eight people slept in each room. There was no ventilation or sewage disposal; there were more sick wards than neighborhoods.

The poor themselves, clad in dirty white trousers and ragged white shawls and sandals, were reduced to eating biscuits leavened with lead chromate (used instead of eggs) and butter laced with linseed oil and drinking milk diluted with dirty water and thickened with animal brains discarded by slaughterhouses or coffee mixed with chickpeas and breadcrumbs.

Still, the Blue House, as Kahlo's home was known, was more congenial than anywhere Trotsky and Natalia had lived since the beginning of the twenties. Stepping into the low, blue-painted home—with its "sun-drenched patio . . . cactus, orange trees, bougainvilleas" and collection of pre-Columbian objets d'art—was like being transported to another world. Trotsky and Natalia were entranced by the parrots squawking in the foliage of the trees above, and the spacious, airy rooms.

When he allowed himself a break from his schedule of work, Trotsky walked in the garden, his upright posture, firm step, and authoritative gestures making him look like a Roman emperor, or as if it were 1918 and he were still war commissar.

Servants were on hand to meet any need, and given their experience of Rivera's and Kahlo's bohemian schedules, they were happy to accommodate Trotsky's desire to spend almost all his waking hours reading or writing. The food there was plentiful and good, and Trotsky in particular, because his health problems had left him picky about what he ate, enjoyed the Mexican cooking.

The Blue House was also close to the home in San Ángel that

Kahlo and Rivera had moved into after their marriage, and the families spent a great deal of time in one another's company: dining together, exploring Mexico City (although they had to be cautious as they did so and avoid the city's main attractions), and making excursions out into the country.

These trips, which Trotsky referred to as "walks," were less dangerous than venturing into the city but were still far from safe. As much as he enjoyed them, he denied himself the joy of escape for months at a time. The police had to be consulted in advance before the pleasure-seekers could set off in a convoy of armed vehicles, with Trotsky crouching down in his seat as they passed through the city; he could not risk being recognized.

Trotsky loved the Mexican countryside, especially when, with a skillful driver behind the wheel, they could veer off the paved highway onto obscure mud tracks littered with chuckholes, rocks, and bayonet-bladed cactus. For a moment he was able to pretend he was on a campaign with the Red Army.

A particular favorite destination was the edge of Hidalgo state, where they could hunt birds, deer, and bears and pick the famous *viejitos* (little old men) cacti with their long white hairs. While Natalia grabbed armfuls of orchids, Trotsky and his companions, picks and buckets on their shoulders, would launch themselves at the cacti. These trips ended with gigantic specimens being loaded, their roots trailing, into the backs of cars, ready to be brought back and planted at Coyoacán.

Even the strongest of Trotsky's guards sometimes struggled to keep up with him as he, in his blue French workers' jacket, exhilarated with freedom, scrambled up a steep slope with heavy cacti loaded onto his back. Bothered by neither the punishing Mexican sun nor the wind that whipped through his white hair, he'd work unrelentingly. Natalia affectionately called their expeditions "days of penal labor." "He was in a frenzy," she said, "always the first on the job and the last to leave . . . hypnotically driven by an urge to *complete* the job in hand." Here, more than anywhere else, he felt free of the worries that assailed him.

---

ONCE THEY WERE settled, Trotsky started working on books that he hoped would secure a wide audience (and thus big advances). But writing books was laborious, so he supplemented the income he received from these by selling his political correspondence for the years 1918 to 1922 to the International Institute of Social History in Amsterdam, giving seminars on current affairs for US students visiting Mexico, and charging for newspaper interviews. Still, he remained suspicious of talking to the press—he always felt as if editors would soften his words, no matter how careful a journalist was to reproduce them accurately.

In addition to writing as much as 80 percent of the articles in the *Bulletin of the Opposition*,* Trotsky spent a great deal of the first year in Mexico preparing for the Dewey Commission, an "independent" counter-trial presided over by the American philosopher John Dewey, a man Trotsky and his followers considered to be of unimpeachable impartiality and authority. This was probably true, but what was also true was that the commission was a Trotskyist front, albeit a well-meaning one. Trotsky believed that the commission's thirteen hearings, which took place in April 1937 at his house in Coyoacán, would expose the falsehoods of the previous year and turn world opinion against Stalin. But, given that the commission possessed no powers of subpoena or support from any government, it was unclear how it would achieve even half of what Trotsky hoped.

---

* Trotsky's main source of communication with the outside world, beyond his articles and books, was the *Bulletin*—a political journal. Though the *Bulletin* was printed in a small font to minimize cost, half of a run—never more than one thousand copies per issue—was on thin, expensive paper chosen because it helped when the copies were smuggled into the USSR. And yet only a tiny number of issues actually made their way into Russia after 1933. Those that made it were smuggled in under diplomatic cover or through merchant navy channels. For all the effort involved in getting them there, most probably ended up in the hands of the NKVD. Outside the intelligence organs, Stalin was probably one of the *Bulletin*'s very few readers in the USSR. Each issue (seized from arrested Trotskyists or obtained by Soviet agencies abroad) inflamed his hatred against Trotsky still further.

Nevertheless, Trotsky and his entourage prepared a refutation of every accusation that had been leveled against him, and backed each up with a blizzard of facts, documents, and logical arguments. Much was asked of Lev, who worked phenomenally hard. He had his helpers interview forty different people and send their depositions on to Mexico, where Trotsky's secretaries, as well as a new assistant, helped process the material. The new assistant, who was the daughter of a Russian, spoke the language fluently and could type excellently. She was also connected to the NKVD and immediately began passing information to them about life at Coyoacán. (It's possible she was also working for the FBI.)

In Mexico Trotsky learned much about the show trials that his Norwegian captors had kept from him: an unceasing stream of messages confirming the deaths of men Trotsky had fought with, men he had loved and who had loved him. But these men were outnumbered by those who had simply disappeared.

Just as distressing was learning that men he admired had had their spirits crushed—had allowed themselves to become implicated in Stalinist villainies. Trotsky found that he was haunted by the perversions of the Moscow trials. Obsessively, as if somehow it might make a difference, he carried on checking dates, counting the numbers of victims. An entire revolutionary generation was being annihilated, and the lonely, isolated Trotsky, trapped on another continent, could do nothing about it.

"We wandered about in our little tropical garden in Coyoacán," said Natalia, "surrounded by distant ghosts, each with a hole in his forehead."

THEY WERE WATCHED constantly.* There were the people who passed by, simply trying to get a sight of the house. More significantly, there

* The same curiosity could be found *within* the Blue House's walls. Frida's father had gone to live with his daughter Adriana, leaving his photo equipment stored in a room

were the Mexican police, who sent regular reports to the government*; Mexican communists, who were expected to supply Moscow with a constant flow of information; Stalinist agents; and Americans.

And yet Trotsky could, at times, still appear blithe about the danger he was in. This contrasted sharply with the attitude of the people around him. Visitors to the Blue House noticed that there were guns everywhere, in every room. The windows that faced the street were bricked up. As soon as there was suspicion that Trotsky and Natalia might be attacked from the house next door, Rivera simply bought it, evicted the neighbors, and brought in workmen to connect the two properties. Care was taken even when it came to buying food. An American volunteer during the Dewey Commission, John McDonald, was sent daily to buy yogurt for Trotsky, who was very fond of it. To avoid the possibility of poisoning by the NKVD, McDonald had to randomize the stores he bought it from.

Luckily, Trotsky and Natalia's hosts, whatever their own personal eccentricities, were avidly keen to ensure Trotsky's safety. In addition, both would offer him opportunities to divert his mind away from the hopelessness of his political position.

---

in the house. For him, Trotsky was like an arrival from another planet. "Who are these people? Who is Trotsky?" When Kahlo explained, he said, "Ah. How strange!"

Later, after noticing his daughter's growing interest in her guest, he warned her: "I want to advise you not to get involved in politics. Politics is always very bad."

* When Trotsky first saw the police guarding the Blue House, he was afraid—their presence reminded him of his incarceration in Norway.

# 10

## *PIOCHITAS*

Diego Rivera, one of the most extraordinary figures of his or any century, was born in 1886 in the silver-mining center of Guanajuato. The only surviving son of a middle-class couple, Diego claimed "a cosmic racial ancestry of white, Indian, and African blood." This boast, like many of the other claims that spilled out of his mouth, was only partly true. One of his first biographers, Bertram Wolfe, had to write a second biography twenty-four years after his first attempt in order to correct the torrent of exaggerations and lies he'd been fed. Rivera said that he could "suckle [the] young at his Buddhic breasts." He told Pablo Neruda that he was part Jewish and the real father of Erwin Rommel—something that had to be kept secret in case it caused an international incident (although he also told others that Pancho Villa was Rommel's real father).

Rivera claimed to have been a "wonder child" who walked and talked (in "ample paragraphs") before most other children, but began to draw before he was able to do either. He had a "preternaturally vivid" imagination and a hunger to find out how things worked—his mother once discovered him attempting to dissect the belly of a live mouse with a kitchen knife. This—following a number of other outrages—was enough to convince her that she had brought a demon into the world. Not long afterward, she had a nervous breakdown.

In the years since, Rivera had lived a bohemian existence in Paris, married three times, and become one of the most significant painters in the world. His work melded Renaissance traditions with the styles of Goya and El Greco, cubism, architecture, politics, and Mexican folk and indigenous art. For Diego, politics and art were inseparable. He and his colleagues had proclaimed the decadence of easel painting, the results of which were rarely seen outside the homes of the rich. Instead, they devoted their energies to public murals.

Painting gave him "sheer animal joy"; it acted on him like a narcotic and he hated anything that stopped him from doing it, whether it was sickness or revolution or a tax return. Sometimes he worked without rest for days on end, eating and sleeping on a scaffold.

He painted surrounded with friends and onlookers who listened as he talked of fighting in the Russian Revolution (he hadn't) or eating female flesh wrapped in a tortilla. "It's like the tenderest young pig," he claimed.

And he existed in a sort of benevolent chaos. As Frida explained:

> He sleeps in the bathtub, reads the newspapers while on the toilet, and spends hours playing with Don Fulang Chang [pet monkey]. . . . Diego is still losing all the letters that come into his hands; he leaves papers everywhere . . . ; he gets very angry when he is summoned to eat; he compliments all pretty girls; and sometimes . . . disappears with some female citizens who arrive unexpectedly, under the pretext that he is going "to show them" his frescoes. . . . His fountain pen runs out of ink; his watch stops working and he has to have it repaired every fifteen days; he is still wearing those big miners' shoes (he has been wearing the same ones for three years); he becomes furious when the car keys are lost, and generally these turn up in his

> own pocket; he never exercises and never sunbathes; he writes articles for the newspaper that generally cause a great uproar; he defends the IV International with cape and sword and is delighted because Trotsky is here.

His commitment to radical politics was sincere, if erratic. The Bolshevik Revolution had transformed Rivera's "mind and art completely." In 1922 he joined the Mexican Communist Party, at the time when it was changing from a party of revolutionary politicians to one of revolutionary painters, and he almost immediately became its leader.*

At around the same time, Rivera—along with two other artists, Xavier Guerrero and David Alfaro Siqueiros—set up *El Machete*, the most radical broadsheet in the city. Its pages were full of art manifestos and verses by radical poets, as well as attacks on poor labor conditions and lengthy disquisitions about communism. It was expensive, abstruse, and almost completely unappealing to the workers and peasants it was supposed to speak to and for.

For the ten years before Rivera welcomed Trotsky, his political commitment had wavered. This was partly because the government was no longer handing out generous commissions and partly because while Rivera's energy and charisma were never in doubt, his opinions were too unreliable, his friendships too heterodox, and his relationship with the government too ambiguous. Plus, he was liable to get so absorbed in painting that he forgot not only what time it was but what day of the week it was. He had also become disenchanted by the results of the revolution he had once greeted with such excitement, a process that was accelerated when he actually visited the Soviet Union in 1927. On his return he began to drift away from the party and ended up breaking with Siqueiros and presiding over his own expulsion.

---

* His membership number was 992, although it was extremely unlikely that the party was even close to having a thousand members.

> Diego arrived, sat down, and took out a large pistol and put it on a table. He then put a handkerchief over the pistol and said: "I, Diego Rivera, general secretary of the Mexican Communist party, accuse the painter Diego Rivera of collaborating with the petit-bourgeois government of Mexico and of having accepted a commission to paint the stairway of the National Palace of Mexico. This contradicts the politics of the Comintern and therefore the painter Diego Rivera should be expelled from the Communist party by the general secretary of the Communist party, Diego Rivera."

He then declared himself expelled, stood up, removed the handkerchief, and broke the pistol, which had been made from clay.

Supporting Trotsky was a way for Rivera to return to the political arena. Although he didn't join the Mexican section of the Fourth International—the political organization Trotsky had created to rival the Soviet-controlled Comintern (the international organization created to advocate for world communism)—until 1936, he had shown his support by painting a portrait of Trotsky in the Trotskyist's New York City headquarters. Back in Mexico City, he charged headlong into the lists, as if desperate to defend Trotsky. Until he did so, little importance had been given in Mexico's small intellectual circles to the struggle between Trotsky and Stalin—there were no more than thirty active Trotskyists in the entire country. And initially the friction did not extend beyond Rivera sparring with his old comrade Siqueiros. They attacked each other at public meetings and in magazine articles.

But everything was supercharged by the arrival of Trotsky.

Rivera watched, ecstatic, as journalists from across the world descended on his home in search of an interview with the old revolutionary. For his part, Trotsky basked in Rivera's energetic solicitude and was grateful for his financial support as well as his help in securing Trotsky a Mexican visa. He was proud to be able to count such a significant artistic figure, a man he called the October Revolution's "greatest interpreter," in the ranks of the Fourth International.

Trotsky, who had probably seen Rivera's work for the first time in Paris during the Great War, was captivated by the artist's defiance and power and by the way he mixed tradition and innovation in his work. Trotsky was also fascinated and at times puzzled by Rivera's personality.

The painter had a curious ability to divert Trotsky from the rigid structures of his days. Trotsky was invariably guarded and formal with almost everybody else he knew, no matter how long their shared history, and yet he felt as if he could relax in Rivera's company. Rivera was the only person who could visit Trotsky without making an appointment first and one of the few who could see him without a third person present.

The two men spent hours talking or riding horses in the nearby countryside. Trotsky's affection was such that he could overlook the vagueness of his new friend's politics.

Trotsky also liked the fact that Rivera increased his chances of meeting women. He was a man—according to Jean van Heijenoort—with "a vigorous interest in sex." Van Heijenoort noted that Trotsky became "especially animated and witty" around women. The strictures of his existence offered him few chances for this behavior, so when they arrived, he seemed determined to make the most of what came his way. "His was not a romantic or sentimental approach; it was direct and sometimes crude."

He was not above fondling a woman's knee under a table or making shockingly bold propositions.

At one point he became so carried away by the idea of sleeping with Cristina Kahlo, Frida's sister, that he began planning how he might scramble over the garden wall and make a dash for her house on Aguayo Street. He was eventually dissuaded from this course of action by the firmly expressed misgivings of his entourage and perhaps also a belated understanding that Cristina's fondness for him was not the same as sexual interest.

Frida, however, was a different matter.

FRIDA KAHLO WAS "nearly beautiful." Her tiny flaws—the heavy, beetling line of her eyebrows; the soft fuzz above her lips—only made her more alluring. When she was in New York, children, enchanted by her appearance, followed her in the street, asking "Where's the circus?"

She had an echoing, raucous laugh, a sensuous mouth and dark, almond-shaped eyes that looked at visitors so directly that they felt unmasked. She had an urchin's command of profanity, and and swore cheerfully and coarsely in both Spanish and English. "Her voice was *bronco*, a little hoarse. Words tumbled out intensely, swiftly, emphatically, punctuated by quick, graceful gestures, that full-bellied laughter, and the occasional screech of emotion."

A voracious reader with a photographic memory and a deep suspicion of established authority, she loved dancing and music and sex. She was one of the most talented artists of her generation, yet she spent much of her career overshadowed by her husband.

This color and thirst for life sat alongside pain. In 1925 the bus that took her home from school was rammed by a Mexico City streetcar. Her tiny frame was impaled on a metal bar in the wreckage, leaving her with a fractured spine, crushed pelvis, and a broken foot. The collision was so destructive, it stripped all the clothes from her body, which was discovered in the accident's aftermath covered with blood and the contents of a bag of powdered gold that had been carried by another passenger and had burst in the impact.

For the next twenty-nine years, she lived with constant agony, loneliness, and fatigue. There were miscarriages and therapeutic abortions, but never the baby she wished so desperately for.

"She lived dying," said a close friend. And yet this proximity to death produced something else in her. "I tease and laugh at death," she said, "so that it won't get the better of me." She called one of her dogs Pain.

Frida Kahlo said that she had suffered two accidents in her life: the streetcar and Diego Rivera. He, in his own way, understood this, confessing, "The more I loved her, the more I wanted to hurt her." Some betrayals, however, were harder to take than others. When Kahlo learned that Rivera had carried on with her younger sister, Cristina, she stopped wearing Tehuana costumes and cut off the long hair he loved so much.* An affair with the man she playfully called *Piochitas* (little goatee) and *el Viejo* was another way of gaining revenge.

Frida started to deploy "all her considerable seductive powers" on Trotsky. Kahlo and Rivera attended all the Dewey hearings. She sat, in her "brilliant Indian clothing and Tarascan jewelry," as close to Trotsky as possible; he was in a wide-brimmed hat adorned with a peacock feather.

She was also able to offer a great deal of practical support. Since neither Trotsky nor his wife spoke Spanish (Trotsky learned within months, but Natalia always had to wait for her husband to translate conversation into Russian or French), she became the couple's chief adviser and escort, with Cristina acting as occasional chauffeur. She gave them advice and helped them find servants they could trust.

And Trotsky was an easy door to kick down. There had always been attractive younger women in his entourage. And he had behaved correctly with these followers, who were probably too awed by him to consider flirting. But Kahlo was completely unlike anyone he'd ever met.

Jean van Heijenoort also, later, became Kahlo's lover. His biographer noted, "Whenever he described her appearance and personality, his mood changed. Physically his body seemed to grow lighter." She

---

* Rivera also had an affair with the younger sister of Lupe, his second wife. Lupe was so angry when she discovered them in flagrante that she destroyed a number of his best paintings and threatened to shoot his right arm off.

reminded him of what it meant to be free: "Frida . . . she would say *anything*, and so, you could tell *her* anything."

Trotsky started writing letters and slipping them into the books he recommended to Kahlo. He would then hand them to her, often in full view of their partners. He also began to slide under Frida's door every day a note saying "I love you" in different languages. They spoke in English to each other, which excluded Natalia, who did not understand it.

Within weeks of the end of the Dewey Commission, what had begun as a gentle flirtation escalated into a full-blown love affair conducted at Cristina's house. While Rivera remained ignorant (a good thing: Kahlo warned her male lovers that her husband was more than capable of murder), Natalia became jealous and profoundly depressed. She had been married—happily, she thought—to this man for thirty-five years. Her entire life was centered on Trotsky. When discussing the affair in letters, Natalia could bring herself to refer to Kahlo only as "F."

Others living in the house soon noticed the discord between the two women and a slight cooling between the two men. The affair shook the faith of Trotsky's loyal followers. He was the one who had lectured them on the need for revolutionaries to dedicate themselves absolutely to the cause, and who had sneered at Jean van Heijenoort over breakfast when he learned Jean had been to a local dance hall the night before.

The secretary Jan Frankel tried to talk to Trotsky about the political consequences if the affair became widely known. What would Moscow make of it? Would it affect his right to stay in Mexico? After all, Rivera had played a key role in persuading the president to allow Trotsky into the country.

In response, Trotsky exploded in anger and the relationship between the two men disintegrated, with Frankel retreating to his rooms elsewhere in the city. "At that point the general level of tension within the inner circle at the [B]lue [H]ouse in Coyoacán became nearly unbearable."

Perhaps on some level Trotsky understood that he was caught in something he could neither understand nor control. It was a relief, then, when in July, he made a trip with his bodyguard to a hacienda in the mountains. He had been exhausted by his efforts during the Dewey Commission. Even after sessions were over, he had continued to work to supplement evidence he had given. And as spring turned into summer, he was plagued by severe headaches, dizziness, and high blood pressure.

Always revived by exertion, he was looking forward to exercise: farmwork, riding, hunting. He also sent Kahlo an anguished nine-page letter begging her not to break off with him, telling her how much the weeks they had spent together meant to him.

But the moment had passed: "I am very tired of the old man," Kahlo told her friend Ella Wolfe.

It was as well for everyone that they pulled back. As van Heijenoort noted, "It was impossible to go on without committing themselves completely or without an incident with Natalia, Diego, or the GPU."

On 26 July Trotsky returned to the Blue House. On the face of it, everything was back to how it had been before. But there were no more secret notes; nobody ever used the word "love" when they were making farewells. Natalia swung between behaving coldly to her erstwhile rival and abrupt shows of affection. Trotsky asked Kahlo to return the letters he'd written her: "They could fall into the hands of the G.P.U." But she had already destroyed them.

Still, an affection remained, and Kahlo realized that Trotsky's arrival had changed something in her. In the following two years, she painted more than she had in her previous eight years of marriage. In a letter to her friend Lucienne Bloch, she declared that Trotsky coming to Mexico was the best thing that had ever happened in her life.

# 11

# Comrade Pablo

As always, what Ramón did was inextricably linked to his mother's own activities.

In October 1936, after she had finally recovered from her injuries, Caridad—accompanied by Elena, who acted as her secretary, and by her daughter, Montserrat—was sent by the committed communists of the Unified Socialist Party of Catalonia (PSUC) to Mexico. They traveled on the *Manuel Arnuz* on forged Mexican passports with the ostensible mission of finding homes for five hundred Spanish orphans, securing much-needed material support, and mobilizing Mexican public opinion behind the Republican cause.

They met with Lázaro Cárdenas and Vincente Lombardo Toledano, the leader of Mexico's trade unions, and secured an audience with Diego Rivera, who drew pencil portraits of Caridad and Montserrat.

Then, after a few weeks of intense activity, on 7 January—two days before Trotsky set foot in the country—they re-embarked for Barcelona, pursued by questions from the Mexican Ministry of the Interior but accompanied by ninety-six volunteers and having secured substantial quantities of guns and rifles for the Republic. More significantly, at least as far as the NKVD was concerned, Caridad had acquired knowledge of Mexico's terrain and environment that few of their agents possessed.*

On her return, she was greeted by tragic news. Her son Pablo had died on 3 January, killed by a tank that had crushed his machine-gun emplacement. When Luis told Caridad, her response shocked him. "I knew it," she said matter-of-factly. Then she explained that one day in Mexico she had suddenly felt very ill and told her companions: "They killed my son, they killed my son."

Not long afterward, Caridad took thirteen-year-old Luis in a chauffeur-driven Ford to see Ramón, who was stationed in the Alcarria region. It was a difficult journey conducted in icy cold conditions. They traveled all night and arrived at dawn, only to be stopped at a checkpoint by soldiers who said it was too dangerous to go any farther.

Word was sent to Ramón, but for an hour they shivered as they waited for him. Luis was dazzled by the appearance of his uniformed brother. There was a brief moment of fraternal affection. Ramón let Luis play with his pistol with mother-of-pearl grips, and then he brought out his trick of bending a coin with his fingers and giving it to Luis by placing it in the pocket of his trousers. But soon he and Caridad drew away to a secluded place to talk.

Their conversation was hushed; only occasionally did they raise their voices. Each time this happened, they would fall briefly silent, look around themselves suspiciously, and walk a few steps farther away from any potential eavesdropper.

After almost three hours, they stopped. They did not tell Luis what they had discussed or what had been agreed. "I don't know what they said, what happened," he recalled, and yet it was increasingly clear that an important decision had been taken. "I am convinced that from that moment on his bond with the NKVD had begun."

The family moved into the Bonanova tower, a smart building on

* They also carried a special gift for Luis from the Mexican communists: a 6.35-caliber pistol encased in a leather holster embossed with the Aztec calendar.

Paseo de la Bonanova in Sarrià that belonged to the Marquis de la Villota, a relative of theirs. Ramón used the property as headquarters for his men, who trained in the former nunnery next door. There were flashes of ordinary family life. Luis helped Caridad treat her angina with lemon juice; there was an attic at the top of the house containing expensive toys owned by their aunt's three children.

By April 1937 it was plain, even to Luis, a kid from whom information was routinely withheld, that Caridad and Ramón had some sort of relationship with *"los soviéticos."*

Elena Imbert, who had supplanted Marina Ginestà as Ramón's girlfriend, was also convinced that Caridad was responsible for Ramón's new affiliation: "[W]ithout his mother," she said, "Ramón wouldn't have done it."

THERE WAS ONLY ever a relatively small NKVD presence in Spain: fewer than ten operatives, of whom some were legal and two or three working undercover. The man in charge of the NKVD's operations in Spain was the forty-two-year-old Alexander Orlov. By turns cynical and explosive, he stood five foot eight inches tall, with a crumpled boxer's nose and an "unbecoming" dark mustache. As clever and devoted to the revolution as he was, the dapper Orlov was also venal—with a passion for rare watches and, while in Spain, valuable Moorish daggers.*

Orlov was an embodiment of Stalin's ambiguous relationship with the Republican cause. It was Orlov who helped spirit 70 percent of the country's gold reserves to the Soviet Union for "safekeeping." (Stalin: "[T]he Spaniards would no more see their gold again than see their own ears.")

* Orlov's NKVD colleague Pavel Sudoplatov said that he was posted to Spain after a tragic love affair with a young NKVD operator that ended with her shooting herself in front of the Lubyanka because he had refused to divorce his wife and ended the relationship.

Some time was, however, devoted to helping the Republicans prosecute their war. Orlov supervised training camps in Valencia, Barcelona, Bilbao, and Aragon that were attended by young Spaniards, German communists from the International Brigades, and even former tsarist officers hoping to earn the right to go home. They were taught how to derail trains and destroy communication centers, how to load Mausers quickly, and how to execute raids and ambushes while living off the land. They worked on their coordination and reflexes, attended classes to inculcate the correct ideology, and were taken on long marches carrying twenty-five-pound rucksacks.

Once trained, they were deployed deep into enemy territory, sometimes as far as three hundred kilometers behind Nationalist lines, to disrupt enemy communications, blow up bridges, attack arsenals, and ambush supply convoys and columns of troops.

Orlov might have boasted of causing havoc, but his true purpose, as Soviet intelligence later admitted, was "to build up a secret police force under NKVD control to effect a Stalinization of Spain." While at the beginning of the war the NKVD's first priority had been intelligence collection, all operations were gradually subordinated to what were referred to as "special tasks."

The Soviet intelligence services had been killing or kidnapping foreigners since 1926, the year that NKVD agents shot the Ukrainian leader Simon Petliura in Paris. At the heart of this operation was the Administration for Special Tasks (reorganized in July 1934 into Spetsialnaya Gruppa Osobogo Naznacheniya [SGON], Special Tasks Force).

Headed by Yakov "Yasha" Serebryansky, this elite NKVD service, working out of Paris and Brussels with just two hundred operatives, operated as a parallel foreign intelligence service, with a particular emphasis on sabotage, abduction, and assassination. Although it officially sat under the Foreign Department of NKVD security, its orders came from the Party Central Committee rather than Yezhov or, later, Lavrenti Beria.

The AST's essential purpose was to allow the NKVD to conduct terrorism abroad more efficiently and on a bigger scale. Its agents were seen as carrying out especially patriotic work—"the highest form of class vengeance against the enemies of socialism." As such, they were well rewarded and given rapid promotion.

The Estonian minister to the USSR, Ado Birk, was snatched off a Moscow street in broad daylight and never heard from again; the former communist courier Hans Wissengir was shot in Hamburg; the head of the NKVD in the US, Valentin Markin, was liquidated in New York; the GRU agent Jean Cremet was killed in Macao; Dmitri Navachine was assassinated in Paris; Juliet Stuart Poyntz disappeared in New York; Yevgeny Miller was kidnapped in Paris; and Ignatz Reiss was lured to his death on a quiet Swiss backstreet.

In the spring of 1937, at the same time as the Terror raged in the Soviet Union, Orlov and Serebryansky were ordered to move from the surveillance of Trotskyist groups in Spain to the extermination of their leaders. An order from Moscow read: "[O]rder issued by Comintern to PCE: 'Whatever happens, the final destruction of the Trotskyists must be achieved.'"

Orlov and his deputy, Leonid Eitingon, who was the AST's representative on the ground in Spain, had a list of foreign "literniks"—people to be liquidated. "Liter" referred to the letter-coded files opened on the targets. Files designated "A," for "active measure" (*aktivka*), were marked for assassination. Simultaneously, men began to disappear in hotel corridors. The bullet-ridden bodies of others were found in Barcelona's alleyways. In July 1937, Erwin Wolf, aka "Kiff" or "Nicole" or "N. Brown," left for Barcelona. A bourgeois with a burning desire to help the working class, he had been Trotsky's devoted secretary in Norway. Before Wolf departed, he met in Brussels with the writer and Trotskyist sympathizer Victor Serge, who tried to reason with him: "You must be mad! You are going to your certain death. You must realize that you are an essential witness of Trotsky's life and activities in Norway and that the G.P.U. will do everything they can to get rid of you."

Wolf nodded his high-domed head and assured Serge that he'd take every precaution. He was arrested almost immediately after his arrival in Spain, then released once it became clear that nobody could prove anything against him. Three days later he disappeared in the street.

Mark Rein, son of a Russian Menshevik, left Barcelona's Hotel Continental one day in April 1937 "without either his coat or hat" and never came back. Those who searched for him were wrong-footed by a letter addressed to Rein's friend Nicolas Sundelewicz (who would himself be arrested that July, accused of plotting to kill Stalin) in which Rein wrote that he'd had to leave for Madrid to deal with urgent business. A letter sent to Rein's father was recognized by him as having been written by his son. But he was puzzled by the fact that according to the stamp, it arrived in Barcelona on the same day it had been posted in Madrid; it was also missing the mandatory censors' stamp.

These fake letters, which were written and signed by people who were often dead well before they were posted, were one of Orlov's specialties. Further confusion was created by spreading rumors (often contradictory) about the missing people. One source suggested that Rein had been abducted by POUM* because he knew of its plans to launch an armed revolt. Another claimed that the anarchists were responsible.

Andres Nin, the leader of POUM, simply disappeared. And Nin was not so much the end as the beginning of Orlov's assault on Trotskyists. The scale of murder grew so excessive that to aid in the discreet disposal of its victims, the NKVD built its own crematorium, run by a Spanish communist from Salamanca.

---

* POUM was a revolutionary group of Catalan Marxists. They were not Trotskyists, and the tiny number of actual Spanish Trotskyists was not part of POUM, but the members of POUM had already declared war on Stalin, who they said had established "the bureaucratic regime of a poisoned traitor," and they had tried (briefly, ineffectually) to persuade the government to offer Trotsky sanctuary.

There was another benefit to the work Orlov invested in training idealistic young Spaniards in what was effectively the first Soviet spy school outside the Soviet Union. They joined members of the International Brigades in a clandestine program called CONSTRUCTION, in which they were trained in the art of *konspiratsia*. At some point they were extracted through France and into Western Europe before being given missions in their home countries. Secrecy was considered so important that to protect their identities, they were registered by number, not by name.

And so, once Trotsky moved to Mexico, Spain served as "a reservoir of agents" who could be employed to follow him there. It was not just that alongside their training in infiltration behind enemy lines, they were also being given the tools to operate beyond the peninsula. They possessed advantages that couldn't be taught; most notably they spoke Spanish and would be able to submerge themselves in the flood of Republican refugees who sought safety in Latin America. Cárdenas, the Mexican leader, had allowed thousands into Mexico. Orlov supplied Moscow with a number of agents who crossed the Atlantic to start providing the NKVD with reliable information. At some point, Caridad and Ramón also caught his eye.

Whether or not Caridad's connection with the Soviet intelligence services had started when she was in France in the late twenties or at some point later, her relationship with the main PSUC leaders in the Republican government had brought her into contact with members of the Soviet consular delegation in Barcelona. First, there was the Comintern's Ernö Gerö, alias Pedro or Edgar. And then, fatefully, Leonid Eitingon.

LEONID EITINGON WAS the kind of man who might one day be seen in southern France dressed as a common French street peddler without a necktie, wearing his beret whatever the weather; on another he might be spotted in the company of the British diplomat and Soviet double agent (and part of the infamous ring of spies recruited by the NKVD from Cambridge University) Guy Burgess. His presence in any given town or city generally tended to coincide with the assassination of one of the Soviet Union's enemies. He was as adept at arranging untraceable "accidents" as he was at pulling off bravura operations like the abduction of General Alexander Kutepov, head of a powerful White Russian émigré organization, in broad daylight on a Paris street.

Like many other revolutionaries, Eitingon had a bourgeois, Jewish background, with a father who worked at the local paper factory. At the beginning this merely rendered him typical; in the years to come, this unremarkable fact would come to feel more like a curse. His career was almost entirely devoted to inspiring terror in others. And yet he—just like almost all of his contemporaries—would be stalked by fear. It was not just that his less-than-impeccable, "cosmopolitan" background made him inherently suspect. As the thirties wore on and he saw hundreds of his contemporaries murdered by the system they had all worked so hard to protect, he came to understand how precarious his position was. There was a price to pay for having the wrong parents, and there was a price to pay for saying the wrong things. Most of all, there was a price to pay if he failed.

He was born Naum Alexandrovich Eitingon—he later changed his first name to Leonid because he did not want to draw attention to his Jewish origins—in Mogilev on the River Dneiper, an area of endless forests of pine and birch in what is now Belarus. His father died when Eitingon was just thirteen. In one of the several "autobiographies" the Soviet state required him to produce, he wrote that this loss ended his childhood. Desultory jobs followed. He cleaned toilets and compiled statistics in a local government office. Then the revolution came and he discovered the exhilaration that came with defending this incandescent political experiment that promised to transform the way he and everyone around him lived. In May 1920, when he was still only twenty, he joined the Cheka, the Soviet secret police.

Heavily built, with a narrow forehead, a scar on his chin (from a car accident), and "small, drilling eyes," Eitingon was determined to extract as much as he could from life. He was unusually talented—one person who knew him well described him as an "exceptional, complete personality"—and unusually ruthless, which explained his rapid series of promotions. (There was one exception to this. His favorite hobby, if one discounts seducing women, was hunting, except he never shot the animals: he was content to simply spot and track them.) But in numerous other respects, he was typical of a vast number of young men who joined the Soviet security forces. Like him they were idealistic and ambitious—they realized that the revolution offered them a route out of the provincial backwaters in which they'd been born.

EITINGON GAVE THE impression of enjoying the deception his craft demanded. Perhaps this is why descriptions of him are so slippery. One witness might insist on his having "soft brown eyes," another that they were "gray-green." To some he was handsome; others noted his ugliness.

What almost nobody seemed to dispute was the intelligence, or charm, of this stocky man. He could recite "Pushkin by heart to illustrate both the folly and heroism of everyday life"; was able to read a five-hundred-page book in a single night; was fluent in French, Castilian, and English (each spoken with a "Jewish" accent); and had eschewed the pretensions of other high-level bureaucrats in favor of a sly, generous sense of humor. (Like many charming people, he was perturbed when his charm didn't work. He sensed that the wife of one of his superiors disapproved of his personal lifestyle. Whenever he visited their apartment, he brought flowers as if trying to win her favor.) He was proud of his thick black hair, liked flashy clothes and women, but appeared uninterested in money: he lived without savings, all the furniture in his home was owned by the state, and his salary was spent on his adored wives and children.

This raffish cheer was not quite sufficient to hide the steel beneath.

As one contemporary noted, "He was a high-category spy, a nice and pleasant fellow but with an iron will: and when it was necessary he imposed it without hesitation." He always appeared to be in control. A glass of cognac would last him an entire evening. His eyes were watchful, piercing. To the wrong person, he could appear "unsympathetic, abrupt and authoritative in manner, hard in character." When Leonid was wounded in the leg in October 1921 during the Russian Civil War, his doctor, fearing gangrene, told him that it would have to be amputated. Leonid drew out his Mauser, pointed it at the doctor, and informed him he would shoot anybody who tried. For the rest of his life, he walked with a not-quite limp that meant one shoulder rose higher than the other.

Around the same time, he rounded up the most prosperous citizens of Gomel, his hometown, imprisoned them in the cellar of the local Cheka, then took them to an abandoned railway station, where he shot them. Many were Jews he knew well; some were relatives. His mother repudiated him in her synagogue, tearing at her clothes to show that he was no longer her son. She eventually forgave him; he carried on being promoted.

EITINGON'S SECRET WORK was varied and relied on his skill at quickly adapting to local conditions. He had been posted to Shanghai, where he spied alongside the infamous Richard Sorge; in Istanbul, as *rezident*, or station chief, he was charged with the surveillance of Trotsky; in France, he excelled at luring counterrevolutionaries back to their doom in the Soviet Union, and he ran a network that included an agent who had managed to place himself at the absolute center of the Trotskyist movement. It's possible that he first encountered Caridad during his time in Paris, though there are no records that can confirm this.

In Spain he was known, depending on who was speaking to him, as Leonid Alexandrovich Kotov, Alukov, Coto, Pierre, Tom, Leonov, or Comrade Pablo. He spent most of his time as *rezident* in the

NKVD's substation in the Soviet consulate in Barcelona, although officially he was simply a political attaché.

He arrived accompanied by an "attractive brunette," Alexandra Kochergina, an officer in the visa section who posed as his wife. Eitingon never troubled about the formalities of relationships. In Moscow he hadn't bothered to register his marriages and had in fact divided his time between two households. He saw no reason to change now that he had left the Soviet Union.

Another new arrival was a thirty-year-old interpreter, Eugenia Puzyriova. She eventually became his fourth wife. The trio took up residence in the spacious villa in the Ciudad Condal that the consul general Vladimir Antonov-Ovseenko had acquired, and they quickly started to send political reports home. Eitingon oversaw agent recruitment and the "illegals." But his main jobs were running Guy Burgess and directing partisan operations under the alias of Colonel Naum Kotov.

THERE IS NO record of how or where Eitingon and Caridad first met, at what point a transition was made from useful contact to something more significant, or when Caridad introduced Leonid to her son.

But we do know that Leonid liked Caridad's strength of character and was immediately aware of how useful it was that she spoke Spanish, knew Mexico, and had already established contact with the Mexican Communist Party.

A strong affection was established between Eitingon and the Mercaders.* Luis was adamant in describing Leonid as one of his closest

* There is much speculation about the exact nature of the relationship between Eitingon and Caridad. For a long time, it was taken as read that the Soviet lothario was sleeping with his Spanish contact. This would not have been out of character for a man who was almost entirely unencumbered by bourgeois anxieties about fidelity. Luis challenged this conception vigorously, calling it "nonsense and an easy and vulgar resort of male chauvinists and enemies to discredit a woman they hate." "Relations between them," he argued, "were genuinely friendly, fraternal, typical of communist

friends. (He liked Orlov too, calling him "very nice and very cheerful.") He would later live in Eitingon's house in Moscow, meet three of his wives, serve alongside his son Vladimir in the Red Army, and would become close to his daughter Svetlana and stepdaughter Zoya. During the uprising of 1937, a car, organized by Eitingon, was sent from the Soviet embassy to keep Luis safe.*

Ramón talked of the Russian with "deep admiration, as a very gifted and valiant person." He told his brother about an occasion when Eitingon had driven a tank, solo, toward Nationalist lines to distract the enemy long enough for his saboteurs to escape. And they had much in common. Like Ramón, Eitingon could have been seen as a show-off. They were confident, brave, and cosmopolitan. They enjoyed dressing well.† There was little, if anything, that either man did not think could be justified if it was in the service of the revolution.

As with so much else, it's difficult to be confident when exactly Ramón began to officially serve with the NKVD after he and his mother spoke that frigid dawn in the Alcarria. But we know, from the testimony of the fighter Kirill Khenkin, that he was operating with them by 1937. Khenkin remembered that Ramón was seen by others

---

comrades." He watched them for forty years and never heard anything even approaching an "amorous" phrase or allusion passing between them. His sensitivity about this topic was not surprising, since at least one writer has suggested, with perhaps undue confidence, that not only were Leonid and Caridad lovers but also that Leonid was in fact Luis's father. The dates do not support this.

* Luis was then sent to Paris to live with Montserrat and her husband, Jacques Dudouyt, so he could get the education no longer possible to obtain in Barcelona. He studied at the Lycée Michelet de Vanves until March 1939, when, with the Republic facing disaster, he asked to be sent to the front. After much to-ing and fro-ing, no fighting, and a spell in an internment camp for fleeing Spanish soldiers, he used his last few francs to scramble home to Paris. Not long afterward he departed for the relative safety of Moscow.

† Eitingon was scathing about the clothes of his fellow agents—anyone, he said, could spot an NKVD man walking the streets of a Western European city, "prancing along in his blue serge suit with its square shoulders—made to order by some Russian émigré tailor in the Latin Quarter. He struts down the Champs-Élysées for the special delight of French counterintelligence, and deludes himself that he's a second Colonel Lawrence."

as being part of Orlov's inner circle. He received (undefined) special privileges, because he was in the good books of senior officers. Ramón took part in raids deep inside Nationalist territory. He then graduated to helping train foreign volunteers to spy on one another. Ramón taught the young English communist David Crook to speak Spanish. More pertinently, he gave Crook the tools he needed to fulfill a particular mission: watching George Orwell.

It is hard not to think that Ramón had already been identified as somebody who might be able to carry out interesting work for the NKVD beyond the shores of Spain. It was Orlov who obtained Ramón's first false passport, a sign that he must have been aware of what his protégé was being groomed for. And then the moment would have come when Ramón's handlers began to explain exactly what they had in mind for him.

That he agreed is no surprise. To hate Trotsky and anybody who supported him would not have made Ramón in any way remarkable among the sorts of people with whom he mixed. It was another element of his personality shaped by the conflict.

He knew about the NKVD hunts for Trotskyists, and it is highly likely that he assisted them. There was, more generally, a feeling of intense gratitude toward the Soviet Union. With the Republic facing extinction, it was the only country to offer meaningful help. This engendered, one man remembered, a feeling of "unconditional" loyalty to the USSR. The writer Ilya Ehrenburg had witnessed militiamen in Andalusia going to their deaths shouting "Estalin!" The Unified Socialist Party of Catalonia, a communist organization of which Ramón was part, had long been critical of Trotskyist deviation. Spanish communists watching the show trials found them to be "a victory of socialism against fascism, imperialism and its agents, led by Leon Trotsky."

Luis Mercader recalled that "everyone had a visceral hatred for Trotskyism." For him, the most significant moment was the uprising in Barcelona in 1937, which was led by anarchists and alleged

Trotskyists: "It was barbaric that an uprising was organized in our rear. . . . An unforgivable rebellion."

It left seething, violent resentment. The communist Ricardo Muñoz Suay, who would go on to become a noted filmmaker, noted that "all of us . . . due to our deformed militancy, could potentially be Trotsky's murderers. In any case, I believe that none of those of us who in those years accepted without a doubt—or with a few—the need to exterminate the Trotskyists, as true allies of fascism, were disturbed by the news of the horrifying death of Trotsky, but quite the opposite."

All of this was allied to the encouragement Ramón received from his mother. And his family and its particular circumstances* had another impact on him. Like Leonid, he was all too aware that he had the wrong biography. His bourgeois zeal was an attempt to erase the "stigma of his class." Here, then, was his opportunity.

There was one last sighting of Ramón in Spain, in December 1937, when he visited one of the nurses who had looked after him in the hospital. When asked later about him, she recalled his fanaticism and a neurotic strain that caused him to talk often of his dream of performing great deeds. He told her that he would be going on an important mission, but said nothing about its location or its goal.

---

* Each of Caridad's five children was a communist, and three were NKVD agents. Jorge served in an unknown capacity. Montserrat was secretary to André Marty, also known as the "the Butcher of Albacete." For a while she was engaged to Daniel Béranger, another NKVD agent who operated with Eitingon's team in Spain, but then she married furniture maker Jacques Dudouyt and moved to France. During the war she worked for the Resistance, swimming across the Loire with messages for the French Communist Party.

But by this point, there was another fissure within the family. Caridad and Ramón took to dismissing Montserrat and her husband as "the pro-Trotskyites." They regarded her as "petty bourgeois" and laughed at her "communist feelings." These were not people who played with politics. For them it came above everything, even family ties.

# 12

# THE KID

There were no upper limits to Stalin's paranoia or vindictiveness. He was a greedy, indiscriminate hater. He understood Trotskyism as a particularly virulent virus: even fleeting contact could infect you, leaving marks that were impossible to wash off. Hundreds of thousands, perhaps millions of innocent people lost their lives, or were condemned to the various hells of Soviet incarceration, because somebody somewhere imagined that they were connected to Trotsky.

But those who were closest to his nemesis received the closest attention, and none was closer than Lev, Trotsky's elder son, the linchpin of Trotskyist operations in Europe.

Lev had always been the family favorite. He was kind, self-sacrificing, and idealistic. People were struck by his integrity, optimism, and energy. One friend recalled that he had the "vivacity of a young animal." His conversation was cheerful, liable to veer off in different directions before being interrupted when he stopped to look into his interlocutors' eyes or bite his nails. Signs of the nervous temperament that lay beneath his sanguine exterior, something that in time would be exacerbated by the incredible pressure that the Stalinist regime brought to bear on him, his "uneasy, cautious, isolated existence," and the deterioration of his relationship with his father.

---

Lev idolized his father and believed fanatically in his ideas. When the scale and aggression of Stalin's attack on his father mounted in the twenties, Lev dropped out of technical school to work as his father's assistant. When Trotsky was exiled, Lev, who had not been formally exiled himself, followed him: leaving his family without knowing when, or if, he would see them again. Lev stayed by his father's side until they reached Prinkipo, where the tensions in the relationship became so overpowering that both parties agreed it was best if they parted ways, even if Lev's loyalty to Trotsky, and his cause, never wavered. Lev carried on his work first in Berlin and then, after the Nazis took power in 1933, in Paris.

He knew that as he traveled around Europe effecting his father's business, he was being followed by the Soviet state. For almost a decade, every footstep he took was watched by hidden observers. Lev could never rid himself of the clammy certainty that he was being spied upon or that his mail was being intercepted. He feared being kidnapped, all too conscious of how lonely and vulnerable, and utterly dependent on a tiny yet fractious group of Trotskyists for protection, he was.

Renata Steiner, one of the central cogs in Reiss's murder, began her work in the service of the Soviets as part of a network drawn mostly from the NKVD's White Russian operatives in Paris, whose primary purpose was trailing Lev Sedov. The agents installed themselves in an apartment at 28 Rue Lacratelle, two doors away from where Sedov lived. They followed him wherever he went. A couple of them managed to make friends with Sedov and his partner Jeanne. Each day, they'd report back on the progress of this relationship. Occasionally, when Sedov and Jeanne were out, Sedov's nephew Seva, who was living with them after Zina's suicide, would hear the lock to their door rattle, as if somebody was trying to find a way in.

When, in the summer of 1936, Lev took a brief trip to Cap d'Antibes in the south of France, Steiner—an elegant dresser who wore her fashionable hat set at an angle over one eye—rented a room in the same pension and "urged him with strange insistence" to join her on sailing trips. In return, he invited her to his table to sit and watch the sea with him.

Sometimes, though, the surveillance was more intrusive. Victor Serge's experience of arriving in Paris would have been familiar to Lev. He was greeted by a hail of denunciations launched by the communist press. A welcoming telegram Trotsky sent Serge was lost—someone had intercepted it, but nobody knew how. This was a constant problem. Letters were sent but never arrived. Correspondence went missing.

Serge soon noted that the first floor of the house he lived in was rented by strangers who "kept watch over my comings and goings with no pretense of concealment."

Harassment was constant. At its most basic, it involved sending stooges to shout down Serge at public meetings. But it could also be more imaginative and disruptive. When the Spanish Civil War broke out, a police superintendent arrived with a search warrant. At one point as he searched the home, he looked in Serge's baby daughter's cradle for arms intended for the Republicans.

"I know, of course, that we can't take it seriously," he said, looking apologetic, "but you have been denounced."

Something similar happened in 1938, when King Leopold III of Belgium visited Paris. An accusation ricocheted around various departments in the French government suggesting that Serge was preparing his assassination. A senior Paris police official told Serge: "You can guess where that comes from, they're plaguing you and laughing at me."

This did not stop a card classifying him as being "suspected of terrorism" from being sent to every police force in Europe.

THE PERSECUTION LEFT the man the NKVD called "the Kid" with the "maturity and compassion of a much older man."

He suffered from persistent insomnia and led a pinched, penurious existence. Sometimes Sedov encountered old comrades in Paris or Berlin and was greeted with enthusiasm. Others, like Pyatakov, once a close friend, became "the Judas, the red-haired" who "turned away his head and pretended not to see me." Lev was constantly materially embarrassed. The very modest apartment he shared with his partner, Jeanne Martin des Paillères, and his nephew Seva, was barely furnished, dignified by just one "decent piece, an old Norman chest of which Sedov was very proud."

The couple barely managed on Jeanne's salary, and Lev spent nothing on himself. When his parents sent him back the royalty checks he collected from French publishers to be forwarded on to them, he took only a small portion of the money for himself, dividing the rest among friends who he thought needed it more or paying it into the Trotskyist movement's funds. A guest who smoked with him after dinner was surprised by how carefully he extinguished first his own and then her cigarettes. "That's that much less spent on smoke," he said before collecting the butts to put in his pipe the following day.

Lev never knew if he'd have money to pay the printer for the next issue of the *Bulletin*. And yet, as poverty-stricken as he was, he often suggested he would try to help his parents' finances by taking a job as a factory worker or by trying to secure an academic scholarship.

He also thought, endlessly, about the home he had left.

When Lev followed Trotsky to Alma-Ata, he had pushed aside his wife's objections to protect his father. Now he knew little of the family he had abandoned in Moscow other than that his wife was ill, poor, and suicidal: her life was broken, their child was unhappy, and Lev was not even in the same country as Trotsky anymore.

Despite his concern for his family, Lev had been so obsessed with the slender, dark-haired Jeanne when they first met in Prinkipo that he had threatened to kill himself if she did not leave her husband, Raymond Molinier. The tension this caused was part of the reason for his departure from Turkey. Molinier was a regular and useful visitor to Trotsky's home. In turn, Jeanne loved Lev, cared for him, but was imperious and possessive. Lev often confided in his friends how much she made him suffer. Worse, though ostensibly devoted to Lev and his father, she remained under the influence of her former husband* and sided with him in the group's virulent factional struggles, even after he broke away to form his own "mass organ," *La Commune.*

More generally, she often appeared to be working to isolate Lev from his friends. This meant that his comrades occasionally withheld important information from him. This lack of trust and the "absolutely solitary atmosphere" in which he existed cut him deeply and left him vulnerable to manipulation—something that would have fatal consequences.

TROTSKY PLACED STRENUOUS demands on his secretaries and assistants, but this was nothing compared to what he expected of himself and his son.

He was generally at great pains to appear courteous and calm at all times with strangers, but Lev saw another side of him. Lev was his most trusted critic and the person with whom he could share his most intimate thoughts and talk to about his ideas. He was also one of Trotsky's last links to the young Russian revolutionary generation. But in fits of pique, Trotsky blamed his son for the "disorder" in the secretariat, criticized his "sloth and sloppiness," or accused him of letting

---

* The corpulent, colorful Molinier, who always had a jovial smile or a curse on his lips and a toothpick clenched in his jaw, was dynamic, energetic, and—at least to begin with—always willing. He was a blackmailer as much as he was a revolutionary, and he liked to play the cynic—"We are Trotsky for the doctrine and Stalin for the method"—but his ambition was not enough to make up for his "almost total lack of political knowledge." He was a relentless, destabilizing prosecutor of factional struggle, introducing foreign militants into the organization before liquidating them once it became clear that they were not as pliant as he had hoped. Eventually, Trotsky tired of this former acolyte: "Peasants liken such characters to cows whose milking yields abundant milk—but whose kick always knocks over the bucket." Molinier disappeared after the outbreak of the Second World War and was rumored to have joined a traveling circus in Latin America.

his father down. When, eventually, they agreed to separate, there was regret on both sides, and also relief.

Lev was integral to the functioning of the Trotskyist movement, especially when his father was stranded on the other side of the Atlantic Ocean. It was Lev who translated, without complaining, the innumerable orders that streamed out of Mexico into direct action. He maintained contact with the Trotskyist groups scattered across Europe; kept lines of communication open with the Russian supporters who'd been sent to labor camps; ran networks of contacts that included sympathizers within Soviet commercial delegations and dockers in European ports who rubbed shoulders with Soviet sailors; supervised the printing of the *Bulletin*; argued with literary agents on his father's behalf.

He knew not only how to arrange secret correspondence in which an entire article could be transcribed onto an area the size of a postage stamp, but what it was like to wander hungrily through the streets of a foreign city for hours on end, trying to meet countrymen who'd been posted abroad or Western tourists on their way to Russia who could provide information or act as couriers for important messages.

At night, he tried to pursue the studies in math and physics that were his deepest passion and to correspond with his parents, writing to them about French political developments, the fortunes of the *Bulletin*, and their grandson Seva. But although he was always exhausted and frequently ill, he did not mention this to his father. Instead, he fretted about how cheaply a contract killer could be employed in the Mexican market.

All he received in return were further suggestions from his father that Lev had disappointed him. Nothing escaped Trotsky; nothing was too small to complain about. Lev was once upbraided for spelling "Turkey" incorrectly in a postcard.

Lev's personality was closer to his mother's. He was diffident and easily discomfited by strident personalities; only rarely did he feel able to confront his father. Instead, he confided in Natalia, who tried to mediate between the two.

In an April 1936 outburst to his mother, Lev wrote: "[I]t seems to me that all Papa's failings are getting worse with age: his intolerance, hot temper, teasing, even crudity and his desire to offend, do down and annihilate." Trotsky, Lev said, needed to accept that "an organization consists of living people." That was why people didn't write to him about sensitive topics. "Papa never recognizes when he's in the wrong. That's why he can't bear criticism. When something is said or written to him with which he disagrees he either ignores it entirely or gets back with a harsh reply."

LEV'S ANXIETIES ABOUT surveillance and abduction were not misplaced. Paris had more NKVD informers and agents than any other foreign city. The new Soviet embassy in Paris, a grand mansion called the Hôtel d'Estrées, was cover to set up across France a network of agents who posed as cultural and commercial officials, journalists, businessmen, and artists.

Central to the NKVD's operations was the Union for Repatriation of Russians Abroad. On the face of it, the Union was a sanctuary where well-dressed generals and venerable priests could mix with taxi drivers and other tsarist flotsam and jetsam. In practice it was a recruiting center for NKVD killers who could be used to prosecute the Soviet Union's war against the former White soldiers who had escaped to France after the Civil War.

The eminent Whites who could not be lured home were brought back more forcefully. In January 1930 a nurse working at a Catholic hospital near General Kutepov's house watched as a car pulled up alongside him, and a man dressed as a French policeman got out, arrested him, and drove away with him.

His successor, General Yevgeny Miller, met the same fate seven years later: again plucked off the street in broad daylight, then drugged. Next, he was transported in a wooden crate balanced on the back of a Ford truck to a merchant freighter at Le Havre. He was luckier than Kutepov, who—either because of a heart attack or an excess of chloroform—did not arrive in Russia alive.*

Given that both the White Guards and the Trotskyists had established their headquarters in Paris, it was hardly a surprise that the city should become the main center of operations for the NKVD Administration for Special Tasks.

The AST had a plan to liquidate Lev. By the time that Miller had "disappeared," matters were sufficiently advanced that a fishing boat had been hired in Boulogne. But the furor following Miller's abduction persuaded Serebryansky and his operatives to delay their strike.

There was another reason too. The AST's primary task was the surveillance and destabilization of Trotsky's followers, who were codenamed POLECATS by the NKVD. And Lev had inadvertently become such a valuable source of information that he was far more use to them alive than dead.

* Miller's luck did not last: he was shot in May 1939, having offered minimal useful evidence. The Soviet infiltration of his organization was so complete that there was almost nothing left for them to learn.

# 13

# POLECATS

At some point in 1935, a courteous, reserved young medical student called Mark Zborowski, who used the pen name of Etienne, made contact with the French Trotskyists. He told them that he was a sympathizer who had left Poland to avoid being kidnapped by the NKVD. Etienne—a family man who brought his son when he came to see other Trotskyists and who was always ready to talk about the "dreadful things that were happening" in the Soviet Union—had inside a few months established relations within the circle of European Trotskyists that included Jean van Heijenoort; Richard Sneevliet, a Dutch Trotskyist; and French Trotskyists Raymond Molinier, Pierre Naville, Gérard Rosenthal, and Jeanne Martin. Once he had cultivated the acquaintance of Martin, Etienne could effect a casual introduction to Lev as he walked past him in a corridor one day.

Before long the two new friends were seeing each other every day. Van Heijenoort found Etienne "sullen" and "colorless" and could not warm to him. But it was clear that Etienne was exactly what Lev had been searching for.

It did not matter that he "never asked Liova [Lev] a question that could provoke a political discussion of any sort or lead even to a serious conversation on a serious topic. He was obliging, always willing to fulfill the tasks with which Liova entrusted him. There was nothing you could grapple with in him, except his insignificance."

That he spoke Russian and possessed an "intimate feeling" for Soviet politics distinguished him from most of the other Francophone Trotskyists. Etienne was somebody that the lonely Lev could confide in. He seemed set apart from the quarrels and resentments that animated their comrades. Etienne worked closely with Lev's secretary, Lola Dallin, then known as Lola Estrina, a fellow Russian émigré who referred to Etienne as her "Siamese twin."* And they established a routine: Etienne would be with Lev in the mornings, and Lola in the afternoons.

Soon, this comrade, with his "helpless smile," became a member of the organization's Central Committee as well as of a small Russian committee that was designed to deal with the opposition in the USSR. This gave him access to all confidential meetings and information. Sedov made him his deputy so that Etienne could go to meetings he wasn't able to attend.

Lev also gave Etienne the key to his letter box, which meant that he knew every clandestine address and saw every letter that arrived, including Trotsky's instructions to the party.

Nobody worked harder, or gave more of themselves for the cause, than Etienne. Trotsky himself, whose sense of him came from the portrait painted in his son's letters, was so pleased with his contribution that he gave him an autographed photograph, a mark of his gratitude and the trust he invested in him. In return, a lavish note thanking Trotsky made its way to Mexico.

Writing to his father in August 1937 to apprise him of how the organization would run while he took a brief trip, Lev made his feelings about, and trust for, his comrade clear:

* Dallin, who died in 1980, has long been suspected of NKVD activities, but definitive proof of her role has not yet emerged. She was certainly sympathetic enough to Zborowski to invent paid jobs for him.

> In my absence my place will be taken by Étienne, who is on the closest terms with me here, so the address stays the same and your missions can be carried out as if I were in Paris myself. Étienne can be trusted absolutely in every respect.

He could not have been more wrong.

THE FIRST STAGE of an NKVD attempt at the liquidation of an enemy was usually the penetration of their entourage. And almost everything about Etienne's background made him an obvious target for recruitment by the Soviets. He was born in 1908 in Uman, in what is now Central Ukraine. Soviet intelligence's ranks had long been filled with natives of Russia's western provinces: Poles, Balts, Jews.

Although Etienne belonged to a wealthy Jewish family that had fled the revolution in 1921 to settle in Łódź, Poland, he was inspired by the Bolshevik attempt to remake society. Etienne claimed that his conservative family had been horrified by his communism and a combination of their pressure and police attention—he spent time in prison for organizing strikes—forced him and his wife, Regina Levi, to leave Poland for Germany, where he looked, unsuccessfully, for work. He then moved to France to continue his studies: medicine at the University of Rouen and philosophy at Grenoble. Life was hard. To pay for his education, he worked as a porter in a boardinghouse.

This experience changed his trajectory. In Grenoble he learned to hate the bourgeoisie. In particular, he felt bitter humiliation when he brought breakfast into their rooms and they made no effort to cover themselves when they opened the door to him. Instead, they looked through him as if he did not exist.

In 1932, he was approached by Boris Afanasyev, aka GAMMA, an NKVD "illegal" who suggested he should apply to the Soviet embassy in Paris and ask for repatriation to his motherland, where everything—including education and all medical costs—was free. Zborowski liked the idea and spent the whole day filling in the necessary forms, which his new friend promised to deliver personally.

But several months passed without anything happening; what was known as "cultivation" took its time. Just as Zborowski's patience was about to fray, GAMMA reappeared to tell him that if he was still keen, they should go to Paris to meet with someone who could help him get a visa.

Not long after Zborowski and GAMMA had taken their seats in a small café near the Porte d'Orléans, they were joined by another figure.

"This man will talk to you," GAMMA said. His name was Dmitry Mikhailovich Smirnov, the "legal" NKVD *rezident*.

They talked politely for a while about general topics, Mark's life thus far, and his intentions for the future. Three more meetings followed; at the fourth, the mood shifted. Smirnov told Zborowski that his visa was ready for him, but if he wanted to prove himself worthy of entering the Soviet paradise, he needed to demonstrate his loyalty. Zborowski indicated he was willing to do whatever it took. At the following encounter, his mission was laid out before him. "Our enemies are the Trotskyites, go and penetrate their gang for us."

THE KEEN STUDENT had much to learn, both about the rules of *konspiratsia* and the NKVD's own distinctive culture. Agents and subagents knew one another only by their respective code names. It was strictly forbidden to try to discover somebody's real name or to visit other agents at their homes. You could not make phone calls from your home except on entirely innocent matters. No letters could be sent directly to any of the other members of your group; they had to be sent to cover addresses, which were usually supplied by sympathizers who weren't active communists. Any written message was to be destroyed instantly; collecting documents and keeping a diary were considered criminal acts.

Correspondence about intelligence matters was conducted in code. Each section of service working abroad, whether legal or illegal, had its own code that was discarded at regular intervals and replaced by a new one.

Meetings between two Soviet agents had to take place in crowded locations, such as museums or post offices. Documents might be handed over in libraries or the gloomy interiors of cinemas. Other favored spots for rendezvous were the treatment rooms of "trusted dentists and physicians." If the chosen spot was a street corner, then it was important to choose a busy section at a time of day when the presence of two loitering figures would not seem remarkable.

Zborowski would have been taught how to throw off police surveillance by making convoluted journeys involving switching between buses and taxis, and how to develop the sixth sense needed to tell a provocateur from a genuine source.

He would also have begun to absorb the NKVD's distinctive lexicon, in which a radio transmitter was known as a "music box," cover for illegal activities was a "rocf," a passport was a "shoe" (and passport fabricators "cobblers"), the local communist party was known as a "corporation," and other Soviet intelligence agencies working in same country as "neighbors." Most sinister of all was *raschet*, literally "final account"—the physical liquidation of a hostile agent.

Moscow was delighted almost from the moment that the agent known in its files as TULIP, Max, Mack, and Kant began his work. He was supposed to be searching for evidence of Sedov's connection to Nazi Germany; but given that this did not exist, in practice he spent more time tracking Lev's and his father's movements. As long as Etienne could continue his work undetected, Trotsky would never be able to disappear from view.

Etienne, who had been supplied by his handlers with a camera and a special telephone number that allowed him to contact the embassy directly, also began sending material to his spymasters. Soon the NKVD files started overflowing with copies and originals of documents and letters that circulated among the Trotskyists. Anything of importance was passed immediately to Stalin. So, in March 1937, Yezhov forwarded to the Soviet leader "the continuation of Sedov's letter to Trotsky of 3 March. The information from the USSR that he cites in this letter allegedly came via Menshevik circles from a French newspaper representative or the agent Havas who left Moscow recently. The letter contains some omissions and lack of clarity, which is explained by the fact that it was taken down while being dictated."

The letters were combed through for clues about the Trotskyists' activities. Anyone unlucky enough to be mentioned, even in passing, in the intercepted correspondence was as good as condemned to death.

In August 1936, after Trotsky had been put under house arrest by the Norwegian authorities and fallen ill from the shock of the slanders in the show trials, Etienne passed on to Moscow the contents of a letter from Natalia to her son: "the 'Old Man' is very sick, has stopped going out altogether, he is sweating profusely which weakens him drastically. He should be in a sanatorium, but the Norwegian authorities are making his position more difficult." He was also able to inform Moscow of the forced boarding of Trotsky and Natalia onto the Norwegian freighter that transported them to Mexico.

In August 1937 Etienne reported that Lev had left Paris, entrusting the organization to himself. His haul included all current correspondence as well as a dispatch of documents to Trotsky. More significantly Lev had given him a small notebook that contained a treasure trove of addresses, including that of Trotsky in Mexico.

Etienne made a triumphant report: "As you know, we have dreamed about getting hold of it for a whole year, but we never managed it before, because 'Sonny' would never let it out of his hands. I enclose a photo of these addresses. We shall research them in detail shortly and send you [the results]. There are quite a few interesting addresses here."

His work was considered so valuable that Stalin regularly read his reports and used them as part of the choreography of his show trials.*

ETIENNE WAS NOT like other moles who went out of their way to exploit and intensify the factional disputes by contriving intrigues and organizing factions in the German Trotskyist group. He was instead, at least at the beginning, "rather like a mouse. He did not make himself conspicuous in any way. He always voted with the majority. One hardly noticed that he was there."

Nevertheless, some of the French comrades had their suspicions about him. The Trotskyists might have been leaky and easy to fool, but this did not mean that they weren't painfully aware of how embattled and vulnerable they were. Even innocuous details could, when looked at for too long, begin to seem dubious. Lev was not alone in being cautious about Victor Serge when he began to associate with them: he thought that there was something a bit suspicious about the circumstances of his release in 1936 from a Soviet prison. For a while Lev suspected Raymond Molinier of being an agent. Trotsky, who at the time was a keen advocate of the Frenchman, ignored his son's warnings and argued that given Lev had stolen Molinier's wife, he could hardly be expected to see the situation clearly. Later, Gérard Rosenthal—Trotsky's lawyer and a surrealist artist—began to wonder

---

* Although in his pose as a loyal Trotskyist Etienne worked hard to maintain contact with the followers scattered across Europe, he also remained committed to his studies. In 1933, the year he began meeting with his NKVD contact in earnest, he had joined the Department of History and Sociology of the University of Paris. Later he entered the same university's Institute of Ethnology. In parallel to this, he was completing studies at l'École des Hautes Études d'Histoire des Religions.

How much time did this leave for spying? His Soviet controllers were broadly delighted with his work, but they picked up on the pull that his academic life had for him. A report to Moscow described him as "a dedicated operative," but it also noted that "in terms of his personality he is not energetic enough and shows little initiative. He must be systematically guided in his future work."

whether Jeanne Martin was an agent, which led to a break in his relations with Lev.

The French Trotskyists, like their comrades across the globe, were incredibly prone to factional disputes. Power was hoarded jealously, and proximity to senior figures like Lev and his father was prized. It is not difficult to imagine the impact of so quick an elevation of a relative stranger—another *foreigner*—in such a group. Whether or not it was his intention to do so, Etienne's arrival had the result of heightening the atmosphere of tension and suspicion that already existed in the organization. It became ever harder to trust anybody else; and this, naturally, undermined their ability to function as an efficient unit. Suspicion pinballed around the group, touching first one, then another. All the while Etienne could continue his work, occasionally casting aspersions on others to keep his own reputation safe and further muddy the waters.

Raymond Molinier occasionally tried to follow Etienne, convinced that one day he would catch him with his NKVD controller. He never did. This did not allay his concerns, nor those of Pierre Naville, who had taken "an instant personal dislike" of Etienne. Although Naville was unable to exclude Etienne from confidential meetings, he could arrange matters so that, for example, the car sent to fetch Etienne to bring him to a given meeting would arrive only at the last minute so that he had no advance notice of the location.

Naville also asked searching questions about how Etienne, a student with no obvious source of income, could support himself. Although "obviously poor and always shabbily-dressed," he lived in a smart building. Etienne airily explained that because his wife worked as the caretaker, they didn't have to pay rent.

Even the more sympathetic Lola Estrina admitted that she was always a bit "amazed" that he could support his family. Initially, he claimed that he worked seasonally for a man who made radios. Six months of employment was enough to cover the next six months. But Lola pointed out that she could not remember him ever having worked for a spell of six months.

"What's the matter with you, did you lose your job?"

"Yes, I lost my job."

"How do you live now?"

Again, his story shifted. There was a legacy from his mother, he told her, enough for him to continue his studies and to live modestly. Unconvincing as it was, this explanation was enough for Lola.

Etienne made it known that he felt as if Naville were persecuting him. He made a show of putting up with the abuse, while also accusing the Frenchman of both chauvinism and anti-Semitism. He told others that Naville was simply trying to shake the confidence that Trotsky and his son had invested in him. When Naville attempted to raise his concerns with Trotsky, he was rebuked. "You want to deprive me of my collaborators."

So, unable to ever bring any compelling evidence, the frustrated Naville could only spread rumors.

If Lev had any criticism to make of the man who had become his closest ally, it was his "obsequious, flattering way." Others too found the "flowery praise he lavished on Trotsky . . . tasteless." He might say of somebody, "I have not had the honor to know him."

But Lev was also able to explain away Etienne's fawning when anybody asked him about it: "Etienne is still young in the movement. He does not have our tradition; after all, all he knows is Stalinism."

Ultimately, there was nothing that anybody else in the group could say that could shake Lev's faith. As he said to another comrade: "I have to stand up for Etienne. They don't like him and they don't trust him, but I know how devoted he is to me and to the old man. He would do anything for us and for the organization."

ONE INCIDENT THAT illustrates both how much trust Lev had in Etienne and how any incident could send accusations of treachery ricocheting around the group was the theft of Trotsky's archives.

In autumn 1936 Etienne warned Moscow that the perennially

broke Trotsky was selling part of his archive (much of which had previously been entrusted to Etienne for safekeeping) to the Paris branch of the International Institute of Social History.

Serebryansky rented a flat above the institute on the Rue Michelet so his comrades and he could maintain surveillance. He then instructed Etienne, who had by this point secured employment as a service engineer at a Paris telephone exchange, to cause a fault with the institute's telephone line. This gave Serebryansky the opportunity to establish the location of the papers and inspect the institute's locks.*

The theft of the fifteen numbered bundles of documents was neatly done, using a drill powered by an electric transformer concealed in a box filled with sawdust and cotton wool to deaden the sound. (This technique was absolutely unknown in France, and the special tools it required had never been used by French criminals.) It was also clearly not the work of common thieves, as the institute's money and valuables were untouched. Therefore, both the police and Sedov immediately suspected the NKVD.†

Sedov told the police that Etienne was above suspicion, but he suggested in passing that institute director Boris Nikolayevsky might have been responsible for the secret of the archive sale. He then summoned Etienne and Lola to meet him in a café at noon. Etienne recounted their conversation in a letter he sent back to his handlers in Moscow.

Lev noted that only four people knew the location of the archive: himself, Lola, Nikolayevsky, and Etienne. The first three were, of course, beyond suspicion. "We have only known Etienne for two

* The first time the institute reported the fault, one of Etienne's colleagues came to fix it. Etienne created a new fault and this time was called to make the repair himself. Just as he was leaving, having both mended the fault and examined the locks on the front and back doors, he was given a five-franc tip by Nikolayevsky, a Menshevik émigré.

† Those involved were each awarded the Order of the Red Banner, but the archive itself was operationally insignificant—consisting of lots of press cuttings but little that shed a light on the workings of the Trotskyist organization. Given that Etienne was, according to Trotsky's biographer Isaac Deutscher, guarding the most important documents at his own home at the time, it's possible that the NKVD staged the whole event to try to bolster his credibility.

years," he said, then paused. "But I trust him 100 percent." He went on to say how important it was to ensure that the second archive remained secure. Scrawled in the margin of Etienne's letter is a note that shows how futile this wish was: "We have already photographed this archive."

As always with the French Trotskyists, a round of ferocious denunciation and counter-denunciation followed. Suspicion fell on Boris Souvarine—who they believed was a "dangerous Communist." When Etienne was, inevitably (and, of course, correctly), suggested as the culprit, Lola leaped to his defense: "No way, you'd have to be a genius to play a game like that for two years. I remember very well the way he reacted to the executions in Moscow."

Etienne repaid Lola's faith. When Victor Serge accused her of being the spy, Etienne threatened to break Serge's neck if he didn't stop spreading the rumor.

After Reiss's friend Walter Krivitsky finally made his own break with the Soviet Union later that year, he also approached the Trotskyists in Paris, looking for their protection. Sedov asked Etienne, who had been ordered by the NKVD to track the defector's movements, to act as his bodyguard.

Krivitsky's arrival on the fringes of their group provoked another wave of destabilizing paranoia and infighting. On a rainy November day, with darkness already falling, he came to Gérard Rosenthal's office to issue Elsa Reiss, Sneevliet, Lev, and Pierre Naville a warning.

Shrunken, with an ashen face and hollow eyes, he explained that the NKVD had intercepted the letter he had sent to Elsa to arrange their encounter. "It was in their hand before it reached Amsterdam. I denied having written it, and denied knowing who might have done so. From that minute on I broke off all my attempts to manoeuvre to save time, and went into hiding. But who had that letter? How did it travel? There is a dangerous agent in your party. This proves it."

They all turned to Rosenthal, to whom the letter had been entrusted. "I gave it to Victor Serge to post to Amsterdam."

There was a moment of silence, broken by Krivitsky repeating his warning: "You have an agent in your midst."

At this, Sneevliet turned pale and began shouting violently, his features distorted. "An agent? Why, you are an agent, and agents see agents everywhere! Why did you come to us? You are a miserable N.K.V.D. agent, that's what you are!"

Krivitsky left abruptly, neither shaking anybody's hands nor giving Elsa, the wife of his oldest friend, a second glance.

In the days that followed, Sneevliet tried to put the pieces of the puzzle facing them together. He talked to Serge and asked him whether he had shown the letter to anybody. For him, there was only one conclusion: "There is an agent and it is that little Polish Jew, Etienne. . . . I say and I repeat that this secretary and right-hand man of Sedov's is an N.K.V.D. agent."

"If you are convinced of this," Serge replied, "then it is your duty to bring the matter up immediately with Sedov and insist on a full investigation."

Sneevliet followed his advice and spoke to Lev, who did not act on the warning. Three months later, Lev would be dead.

# 14

# Walking in a Graveyard

When he replaced Yagoda, Yezhov had brought with him three hundred officials, who were all given posts as assistants to NKVD department heads across the USSR. He explained that changes were necessary to satisfy the Politburo's demands for greater efficiency. Next, Yagoda's former deputies and department chiefs were told that the Central Committee wanted them to "investigate personally the political reliability of regional and local party officials and organizations" across the nation.

Each left for their specified destination. None arrived. At the first train stop, they were arrested and driven back to a Moscow prison. Weeks passed before anybody started to feel suspicious. By that time, Yezhov had already changed all of the Lubyanka guards as well as the officers commanding the NKVD troops stationed in the capital.

Only four department chiefs, including the broad-minded, intelligent Abram Slutsky,* head of the Foreign Department, were spared—mostly because they had close connections to Stalin.

---

* On one occasion, Slutsky deliberately withheld orders to detain one of his colleague's daughters until after he knew that she had crossed the border out of the USSR.

Yezhov buried himself in the heavy security of his third-floor office, and his purge of what he called his "secret sect" began in earnest. He often came to Politburo meetings straight from the torture chambers, dried blood on the hem and cuffs of his peasant blouse.

In 1937 alone three thousand operational NKVD officers were killed. Few felt safe. It helped if you were not an old Bolshevik, with any sort of "pre–Stalin Party history" that could link you—even tangentially—with the opposition. Equally, those who had a useful technical job, such as cipher clerks, or were junior enough not to excite envy or have connections with senior officials whose downfall might implicate them, were safer. But not safe.

Some officers, unwilling to face the treatment they had themselves inflicted on so many others in the Lubyanka's basement cells, threw themselves out of their office windows. There were so many victims that the death toll could no longer be hidden from passersby without sparking rumors of an imminent revolt.

Disturbing reports soon spread out across Europe. Orlov recalled, "Officers of the Foreign Department of the NKVD who arrived in Spain and France told weird stories of how armed patrols scoured the NKVD apartment houses and how sometimes a knock on the door of one apartment house caused a suicide shot to be fired in an adjacent house."

He was right to be alarmed. The Foreign Department was, inevitably, the subject of the greatest suspicion. There was a perception that it contained more "enemies of the people" than any other element of the Soviet secret services. Yezhov initially proceeded with care, aware of the logistical challenges of "cleaning up" the NKVD agents working overseas.

This was why Slutsky remained untouched. It was put about that the Foreign Department did not need the same rough treatment as their corrupted counterparts at home. Seeing this, many of its agents decided that it was safe to return.

Still, disturbing stories seeped out of the USSR. Word got out that the NKVD *rezident* in France, Dmitry Mikhailovich Smirnov, had been executed. Yezhov initially suggested that he had simply been sent as an underground agent to China. This claim's authority melted away when the wife of another officer revealed that she had by chance seen him arrested at the precise moment that she had arrived to visit him at the Hotel Moskva.

In response, Yezhov accused Smirnov of having been a French and Polish spy. His colleagues recognized this as an obvious lie. There had been no change to the cipher for communication with Moscow; Smirnov's network of agents continued to operate. Had they really been compromised, neither would have been left untouched.

As time passed, Orlov and his colleagues were presented with even more examples of officers on foreign assignments who had been recalled to Moscow and then disappeared entirely. Some of those summoned embraced their impending martyrdom. Others returned convinced they'd be able to prove themselves innocent once they had learned what they were accused of. They all met the same fate.

Those agents left in place were quick to respond. When they received reports about the show trials, they had to be careful not only about what they said about them but about their facial expressions and body language. Moscow would soon learn who had not responded with sufficient outrage.

The ambassador in Berlin, Yakov Surits, reported on the head of the legal residency in his embassy, B. M. Gordon:

> On 2 February a Party meeting was held in the Berlin embassy. Gordon, B. M., the rezident and Communist Party organizer, delivered a report on the trial of the Trotskyite Center.
>
> Gordon did not say a word about the fact that his rabble of bandits had a specific program of action; he did not say why this scum hid its program from the working class and from all working people; why it led a double life; why it went deeply underground.

> He did not dwell on the reasons why after all the enemies managed to cause damage for so many years.
>
> He did not deal with the question why, despite wrecking, sabotage, terrorism and espionage, our industry and transport constantly made progress and continue to make progress.
>
> He did not touch on the international significance of the trial.

But Surits did not know that he was also being denounced by one of his secretaries, who had written her own note to the Center:

> To this day the office of Comrade Surits is adorned with a portrait of [Nikolai] Bukharin with the following inscription: "To my dear Surits, my old friend and comrade, with love—N. Bukharin." I deliberately do not take it down, not because I greatly enjoy looking at it, but because I want to avoid the cross looks which Comrade Surits gave me when I removed the portrait of [Abel] Yenukidze.
>
> I am waiting for him to remove it himself, since if Bukharin was indeed once his close friend, he must now be his enemy, as he has become the enemy of our Party and of the whole working class. The portrait should immediately have been thrown in the fire.
>
> That, really, is all that I considered it my Party duty to report to you. After the adoption of the Stalin Constitution [of 1936] which has granted us great rights and put us under great obligations, calling us to exercise discipline, honest work and vigilance, I could not remain silent about these facts.

The same tragedies that civilians experienced in Moscow played out in NKVD stations across Europe. Alexandre Barmine, who made a more successful attempt at escape than other agents, called the purges against his fellow officers "The Nightmare Years." When working with

Victor Serge to produce a memoir, he remembered feeling as if he were "walking in a graveyard. All my friends and life associates have been shot. It seems to be some kind of mistake that I am alive."

And yet most of the NKVD's operatives continued to function as they had before: they did not run, or quit, or hide. They followed orders; they carried on spying, running agents, smuggling, and killing in the name of the Soviet Union. Some of this was due to the fear they all felt; some of this was because they could attribute the arrest of friends to unfortunate mistakes made by the party's leaders; some of this was the esprit de corps that came with being an agent, "the heady experience of working inside an invisible and seemingly invincible operation" as part of "the elite of humanity."

But more than that, most of them still *believed*.

The Russian Revolution had been a "revolt against a polluted society." It had already abolished private ownership, the greed for power, social distinctions, and sexual taboos. And the future felt still brighter. Communism, once achieved, would create a "nationless" paradise in which ethnic and religious differences, notably anti-Semitism, would be rendered obsolete. While the West was sclerotic, decaying, and decadent, riven by strikes and social unrest, the Soviet Union was being transformed by the First Five-Year Plan. Before the revolution it had been one of the most backward nations in Europe; now it was on course to become the most advanced: a utopia built in steel and concrete.

One fellow believer described the ecstasy he felt after his conversion to this cause. There was a "mental explosion" followed by "intellectual rapture":

> new light seems to pour in from all directions; the whole universe falls in pattern like the stray pieces in a jigsaw puzzle, assembled by magic at one stroke. There is now an answer to every question; doubts and conflicts are a matter of the tortured past—a past already remote, when one had lived in dismal ignorance in the tasteless, colorless world of those who *don't know*.

None of them were naive. They all knew it was not possible to sweep the old bourgeois order away without bloodshed: the enemies of the revolution remained too numerous, too adamant in their desire to crush everything that was being built in front of them. They had only to look at the barbarities of the Third Reich and Mussolini's Italy, or even at the cruel indifference to poverty and injustice that was the defining feature of capitalist nations such as Britain and France.

So, although the agents often heard of, or witnessed for themselves, things that had the potential to challenge their faith, they could always hold on to the promise of the future. They might see ragged, starving peasants shivering in the cold, many on the verge of dying from typhus, and surrounding them were the agents' own comrades from the NKVD, who were about to transport the peasants away from their homes and to the gulag. The agents might be so horrified by this that they began to hallucinate and convince themselves that they had seen bats flying over the poor victims' heads. And yet at the same time, they were reminded that "Fascist machine guns were mowing down the Austrian workers in their last desperate stand for socialism. . . . Everywhere Fascism was on the march. Everywhere the forces of reaction were gaining ground. The Soviet Union still seemed the sole hope of mankind."

It was this faith in their country's unique historical destiny that allowed most agents to find a way to reconcile their belief in a human communism with the absurdity and horror of Stalinism. Most but not all.

# 15

# Our Little Lyova

As 1937 wore on, Etienne's reports to Moscow noted Lev's deterioration. He was overworked, penniless, and anxious for his father, who, nonetheless, was as hard on him as ever. Lev was also drinking heavily and playing roulette.

In response to one fierce rebuke in which Trotsky threatened to move operational control of the Trotskyist movement away from Paris, Lev wrote another despairing letter to Natalia, listing all his hardships and ending with an oath of "complete and absolute fidelity to Trotsky and Trotskyism." He was lonely and desperate, he said, but at least he had Etienne.

His relationship with the complex, demanding Jeanne had deteriorated even further and he'd begun an affair, conducted on trips to Antibes, with Hélène Savanier, with whom he and Jeanne had stayed when they first arrived in Paris.

He was also shaken by what he had learned from the police investigation following Reiss's assassination. It revealed that one of the gang of assassins had applied for a Mexican visa and had already begun studying detailed plans of Mexico City. Lev sent a warning to his father, and the French police were sufficiently anxious that they assigned Sedov a special guard.

He had not realized how much Moscow knew about his life. Who was sharing his plans with them? All of this led to yet another round of speculation within the ranks of his closest friends about the presence of an agent provocateur. Although once again suspicion was directed at Etienne, Lev was unwilling to doubt his "best and most reliable comrade."

And yet he could not rid himself of the strange conviction that a noose was tightening around his neck. Convinced he was surrounded by enemies, he went to bed each night feverish with anxiety.

The sense that, in any room he walked into, there was always someone who was spying on him, perhaps plotting against him, made it hard to trust even those who had given repeated demonstrations of their loyalty. This, in turn, frayed relationships and deepened his loneliness. On one occasion, he felt moved to apologize to Victor Serge for refusing to give him his address when he went away to Antibes for a rest. "I am giving it only to our contact-man," he explained. "I really have to become frightened of the least discretion."

This queer paranoiac feeling was strengthened by everything he learned about what was happening in the country he had left behind. Each betrayal, each murder, each fresh example of a man's public humiliation broke something new within him. His most cherished memories were intimately bound to the men he saw being crushed by Stalin. Kamenev had been his uncle, Bukharin his affectionate playmate. He had once looked up to figures like Rakovsky, and his former supporters Ivan Smirnov and Nikolay Muralov—men he had seen as exemplars of courage and revolutionary virtue. He waited, in vain, for one of them to rediscover the spirit that had once distinguished them and expose the lies that swirled around the courtroom.

Some nights, he and Victor Serge lingered till dawn on the streets of Montparnasse, trying to "comb out the mad tangle of the Moscow Trials." Occasionally, one of them would step under a streetlamp and exclaim aloud, "We are in a labyrinth of utter madness."

Lev could repeat increasingly empty slogans about Stalinist bureaucracy, or Trotsky's withering denunciations of Stalin's flaws, but he worried that these mattered little ranged against the brute force of the regime his father's enemy had built.

TROTSKY'S PRIMARY CONCERN during his exile had been for those family members who had already been arrested or were at risk of it. He was less worried about Lev, who had legal residence in France and who he believed knew how to look after himself.

This began to change once he had moved to Mexico, partly because Lev was now the only one of his children who he knew, for sure, was alive. Trotsky started to send him a stream of urgent warnings about his safety—in particular urging him to exercise prudence when meeting new people, especially those over whom the NKVD might have a hold, like nostalgic exiles—and he drew attention to Lev's plight in public. In the aftermath of the assassination of the economist Dmitri Navachine, stabbed to death while walking his fox terrier in the Bois de Boulogne, he wrote, "Lately GPU agents stole my archives in Paris. Yesterday they killed Navachine. Now I fear that my son, who is considered public enemy number one, will be their next victim."

At the same time, Lev's friends also tried to persuade him to leave Europe. Lev hesitated. This reluctance was not because he felt safe. He knew he was being followed and expressed anxiety about the presence of an "outsider" in his circle. He also knew that he was tired and possibly dangerously ill. And yet he was convinced that he was irreplaceable. It was he who held all the threads linking his father to the oppositionists left in Russia.

He asked his father for advice, but Trotsky, who was living off advances for books he hadn't yet written, could offer little practical help. Again, Trotsky was helpless, stranded on the wrong side of the world, unable not just to save the revolution but also unable to reach out to his own son.

Ultimately, in November 1937, Trotsky wrote, giving his opinion that Lev should stay in Paris. Lev was unlikely to be allowed into the USA and his father thought he would be in just as much, if not more, danger in Mexico. Trotsky didn't want to restrict his son to the prison he found himself in, and he didn't believe that their constant disagreements would get any better if they were under one roof. He was also concerned about straining the hospitality of Rivera and Kahlo.

This prohibition left Lev in a state of mental collapse. Etienne's report on this development was passed on to Moscow:

> On the occasion of his son's birth "Mack" [Etienne] invited "Sonny" to dinner. "Sonny" spent the entire day over the bottle at "Mack's" and drank a lot. . . . Having drunk a great deal, but without passing out, "Sonny" felt terribly upset. He apologized to "Mack" and almost in tears begged his forgiveness for having suspected him of being an agent of the GPU when they first met. At the end of all these "revelations," "Sonny" said that right from the start in the [Soviet] Union the opposition struggle had been hopeless and that no one had believed it could succeed, that as early as 1927 he had lost all faith in revolution and now believed in nothing at all, that he was a pessimist. The work and the struggle that was going on now was nothing but a continuation of the past. Women and wine were more important to him.

A similar pessimism crept into Lev's communications with his parents. His conviction that he was irreplaceable made him postpone an operation for appendicitis, despite recurrent attacks of crippling stomach pain that left him barely able to eat. He was clearly troubled by his body's revolt against him, and he moved slowly, every limb drooping. Writing to Natalia, he asked: "What is left of my old strength?" In the same letter, he also mentioned, almost in passing, that he would soon need "a small operation." Lev was unwilling to add to the burden of his parents' cares.

Yet there was defiance too. Fears that the NKVD might seek to capitalize on his well-known struggles by staging "his" suicide led, in January 1938, to him writing an article entitled "Accused, I Accuse": "I want to warn public opinion that despite all that I have been through lately, I have in no way lost my moral balance and my confidence in life. I am therefore in no way inclined to commit suicide or to disappear. If something happened to me, it is on Stalin's side and not elsewhere that the cause should be sought."

Things started to feel more positive in the first days of February. Dieting had relieved the abdominal pains he'd been suffering. Finally he could publish the latest edition of the *Bulletin*, which carried news of the Dewey Commission's verdict proclaiming Trotsky's innocence. In a happy letter, he reported this to his parents, enclosing a copy of the proofs and an outline of his next plans.

In this, his last communication to Coyoacán, he made no mention of his health.

On 8 February he worked, with Etienne by his side, through the day. He ate nothing.

That evening he suffered his most severe attack of abdominal pain so far. His doctor placed ice on his stomach but it was clear that Lev could no longer delay an operation. He wrote and sealed a letter, which he handed to Jeanne with the instruction that she was to open it only in the event he was the victim of an "accident." He then began to discuss his next steps with Etienne. Both agreed that he could not register in a hospital under his own name—it would be too simple for the NKVD to find him.

He and Jeanne made their choice in secret, keeping the location from all but a tiny circle. On 9 February he entered the Clinique Mirabeau, a small hospital east of the Bois de Boulogne that was owned by a Dr. Boris Girmounski and staffed by White Russians. He was anxious enough about what might happen that he wrote his will and testament that day: Jeanne Martin would be left everything. It is not clear whether he was aware that Girmounski had previously worked for the NKVD, had left the USSR legally, and had bought the clinic for a "bargain price." Any of these details should have been a cause for alarm.

Lola Estrina's sister-in-law had recommended a surgeon called Dr. Simkov, and here too there was reason to be anxious. Simkov's impressive reputation belied the fact that in recent years a number of his patients had died after undergoing relatively simple operations.

Etienne arranged the ambulance that took Lev to the quiet Rue Narcisse-Diaz in the sixteenth arrondissement. He was then carried on a stretcher to the fifth floor. For as long as it took to enter the hospital, he masqueraded as Monsieur Martin, a French engineer. Although Simkov had agreed to help maintain his cover, the attempts at discretion were undermined when the two men spoke in Russian in front of staff.

Simkov and his colleague Dr. Thalheimer diagnosed an intestinal occlusion and recommended immediate action. They completed their operation by eleven p.m. that evening.

At first it seemed like a success. Sedov was well enough to be visited by Jeanne, Lola, and Etienne. He seemed cheered by these encounters, in which they resumed their conversations about politics and logistics. He asked Etienne to return as soon as he possibly could.

But 13 February saw a deterioration. Lev left his bed in the middle of the night, and as if gripped by a terrible agitation, he "tottered naked, febrile and delirious along the corridors." He entered an adjoining room and tried to grab an orange. When Jeanne dashed to the hospital, she was appalled by the sight of a wide purple bruise on his abdominal wall, not far from the scar left by the surgery. Thalheimer suggested that there had been a "postoperative accident that I can't explain." He asked whether her husband had made any recent attempts to take his own life. No, Jeanne told him, before bursting into tears and, for the first time, accusing the NKVD of having poisoned her husband.

Lev's temperature, previously stable, began to surge capriciously; his pulse was irregular. On 14 February, the doctors tried a blood transfusion. Although the comforted Lev joked with those around him during the procedure, there was no improvement. In the evening, Etienne, defying the instructions to keep Lev's location secret, notified the French Trotskyist Jean Rous. Another operation, on Lev's heart (without anesthesia due to his condition), followed on 15 February. Rosenthal caught his last sight of his old friend as he was "transported on a trolley through the whitewashed hallways to the operating room. . . . He was lying there, pale and inert, his gaze lost, his hands clasped on his chest and his breath panting. There was no indication that he recognized us. His eyes only blinked when the cart entered the brighter room." The operation made no difference. It was clear that his body was in the grip of something that the doctors did not understand. Their efforts to mitigate his distress were based on guesses. What was indisputable, however, was that his intestines were by now in a state of paralysis. The following morning, at dawn, he slipped out of consciousness and into a coma. More transfusions were tried, without effect. He died at eleven a.m.

THE TROTSKYISTS IMMEDIATELY sent a telegram to Coyoacán to inform Trotsky of the tragic news, but it did not reach him because he had temporarily removed himself from the Blue House.

Diego Rivera was prone to bursts of imaginative overexcitement, yet he was also a vigilant host. Over the previous days, he had noticed suspicious comings and goings in a nearby house and had persuaded Trotsky to seek temporary shelter in the home of Antonio Hidalgo, an old revolutionary. On 13 February Trotsky slithered into a car, in which he lay down on the floor until they had reached safety. While he was away, Natalia arranged the pillows in the bed at Coyoacán to make it seem as if he was still there. The servants were instructed to keep away from the room, and occasionally Natalia took tea up to her "sick" husband.

In the sun-flooded rooms of Hidalgo's beautiful house, Trotsky set about writing the "strangely vitriolic" pamphlet *Their Morals and Ours*, in which he justified "with extraordinary violence" the right for revolutionaries to attack the "rotten and obscene" morality of the bourgeoisie. "Only that which prepares the complete and final overthrow of imperialist bestiality is moral, and nothing else. . . . The welfare of the revolution—that is the supreme law."

At some point during the day, Rivera, who had heard the news on the radio, rushed into Trotsky's room.

"Leon Sedov is dead."

"What? What did you say?"

Rivera, suddenly conscious of how shocked his friend was, repeated himself. "Get out of here!" The artist found himself pushed rudely out of the door. Trotsky needed to be alone before he could lose control and collapse. He stayed there for a while "sunk in numb despair."

An hour later he arrived at the Blue House, where Natalia was sorting through old pictures of their children. She was surprised when the bell rang and her husband emerged before her. This was followed by another shock. She was suddenly aware that he was more bent over than she had ever seen him, his face ash gray. He appeared to have become an old man overnight.

"What is it? Are you ill?"

"Lyova is ill," he said in a low voice, "our little Lyova . . ."

For eight days Natalia and Trotsky sequestered themselves with their grief. When, at last, Trotsky emerged from his room, his "eyes were swollen, his beard overgrown, and he looked like a haggard, quivering ghost of himself." He struggled even to speak, and yet he was keen to start work again.

He released an affecting obituary for his son that was suffused with regret that while "our ideological solidarity had penetrated our very flesh and blood," his own "pedantic and exacting attitude" had caused him to treat Lev more harshly than any of his other collaborators.

> His mother, who was closer to him than anyone in the world, and I, as we are living through these terrible hours, recall his image feature by feature; we refuse to believe that he is no more and we weep because it is impossible not to believe . . . he was part of us, our young part. . . . Together with our boy has died everything that remained young in us. . . . Your mother and I never thought, never expected, that fate would lay this task on us . . . that we should have to write your obituary. . . . But we have not been able to save you.

The question as to how exactly a routine operation had led to Lev's death loomed over everybody. Trotsky accused the clinic and its doctors of being instruments in hands of the NKVD.

Lev's comrades believed, without proof, that he had been assassinated. They guarded the corpse until an autopsy could take place. The posthumous examinations attributed death to a postoperative complication (an "intestinal occlusion"), heart failure, and low resistance. Given Lev's physical decline over the past months, this was plausible. A toxicological analysis showed nothing. Furthermore, Jeanne had been almost constantly at her partner's bedside, and she hadn't seen anything suspicious, nor had any of the external experts brought in by the hospital's regular doctors to help explain why Lev had not responded to treatment.

There is no question that the NKVD would have been able to arrange Lev's death. According to the writer and communist apostate Arthur Koestler, the NKVD had a saying: "Any fool can commit a murder, but it takes an artist to commit a natural death." And Etienne had, of course, made sure that they knew where Lev was being treated.*

But there was no press release gloating about the assassination of a dangerous counterrevolutionary (and no subsequent evidence, either in

---

* There are rumors (undoubtedly fanciful) that Etienne finished Lev off with a poisoned orange.

documents or memoirs, suggests direct involvement). Lev also remained more useful to them alive than dead. As one NKVD source later argued, "His liquidation would have lost us control over information about Trotskyite operations in Europe."

Still, when Yezhov read the telegram telling him that Leon Sedov had died of "natural causes," he exuded professional satisfaction: "A good operation. We did a good job on him, didn't we?"

Elsa Reiss saw Etienne in the days after Lev's death; she thought he looked "defeated" and "profoundly shaken." Inside, however, he claimed to be elated. The day Lev died was the happiest of his life: "I did not have to spy on him any more. I did not have to denounce him. My job was finished, or so I thought."

This was either disingenuous or naive. The NKVD had its foot on the throats of the French Trotskyists; it was hardly likely to let go now.

Etienne suggested trying to further disorientate his grieving comrades. Immediately after the death, he proposed that Moscow should call for an autopsy; he believed that this would send Lev's former assistants into a panic. He also recommended spreading rumors that Krivitsky was implicated. At the same time, he did what he could to obstruct the police, presenting himself as Lev's closest friend and dismissing the idea that there had been any foul play. Sedov had been too weak, he informed them; his constitution had been too feeble. His death had been no surprise.

Etienne had been part of the organization long enough to have worked out how best to ensure that he could supplant Lev as the heart of the Trotskyists in Paris. And yet he was faced with the awkward fact that he had lost his protector against the suspicions of his comrades. Before even a week had passed, Etienne was writing to Trotsky indignant letters accusing Sneevliet of spreading the "slanderous rumor" that Sedov had been responsible for the death of Reiss.

He followed this up by asking Trotsky himself for his advice as to how he should deal with the suspicion that, he said, emanated purely from the jealousy over his close relationship with Lev. He also drove home the point that he was now the only person who knew enough to carry on the organization's work. Trotsky's response was to set up an investigatory committee so Etienne's accusers could present their charges to someone they trusted to judge them: "Comrade Étienne should take this step; and the sooner, the more categorically and firmly he does it the better."

Nothing came of this, and Trotsky soon found Etienne was as indispensable to him as his son had ever been. Etienne became the publisher of the *Bulletin*, Trotsky's most important European correspondent, and the point of contact for those who had fled the Stalinist terror and wanted to approach Trotsky.

It didn't matter that both Sneevliet and Serge were so sure that Etienne was an agent that they talked about their suspicions openly. When Trotsky needed the sorts of data and other information that were inaccessible to him while writing his biography of Stalin, it was to Etienne he turned. Etienne was the man who ensured that the paper published a suitable tribute to Sedov on the first anniversary of his death.

All the while he carried on deftly exacerbating the rifts between the leader and his followers. A measure of his success was that eventually even Trotsky refused to support Jeanne Martin's application for a new official inquiry into his son's death.

THIS WAS NO reflection on the depth of Trotsky's grief or on the impact that Lev's death had on his understanding of his situation. The tragedies that had befallen his two sons were what finally convinced him that he would never see Russia again.

Once Trotsky had written, "I do not measure the historical process by the yardstick of personal fate. . . . I don't recognize personal tragedy.

I recognize the replacement of one leader of the revolution by another." But now he realized the true extent of the nightmare that had overcome his family.

Trotsky knew nothing of the fate of his granddaughters, who had disappeared after the arrest of his first wife. Sitting inside a concrete fortress thousands of miles from the country he had been born in, he was torn apart with guilt for his failure to connect with Zina, for his failure to persuade Sergei to leave the USSR, for his failure to encourage Lev to leave Paris.

And all of this was a reminder of something else. The executions in Moscow, Siberia, Turkestan, and the Ukraine, the assassinations in Barcelona, Lausanne, and Paris had all had one target: him.

Trotsky appeared to shrink into himself. His communications with his entourage dwindled. One of his aides, who'd spotted unanswered correspondence on his desk, felt moved to make discreet apologies on his behalf.

Natalia too struggled to recover. For many months to come, she was apt to disintegrate into tears without warning. She felt imprisoned in the Blue House—too aware that while their guards and supporters were only ever passing through, she and Trotsky were trapped, perhaps for the rest of what remained of their lives.

As it turned out, this wasn't quite true.

# 16

# The Citadel

The biggest surprise about the relationship between Trotsky and Rivera is not that it came to an end; it's that it lasted as long as it did.

It was inevitable that the qualities in each of them that had once fascinated the other would come to seem grating and unbearable. Rivera disliked Trotsky's martinet behavior, his petulance and arrogance. Most of all he hated the expectation that he should stay quiet while the Russian talked. Trotsky struggled with the painter's mythomania and waywardness.

Things grew even harder when Kahlo, the only person who could moderate her husband's behavior and the person best placed to mediate between the two men, left for Paris in January 1939. The lonely Rivera immediately felt dejected and irritable.

Still, on 2 November, Day of the Dead, he turned up at the Blue House full of mischief and carrying a large purple sugar skull that had "STALIN" spelled out in white sugar on its brow. Trotsky acknowledged neither the gift nor the joke that had inspired it. As soon as Rivera left, he ordered Jean van Heijenoort to destroy it.

If before they were able to act civilly toward each other despite their political differences, now they exploded.

Their disagreements included everything from the class structure of the Soviet state, to Rivera's relationships with the trade unions, and his support for, in Trotsky's view, the bourgeois candidate General Juan Almazán in the race to succeed Cárdenas as president.

But below it all was the erratic, incoherent nature of Rivera's Trotskyism. He was too prone to announcing, "You know, I'm a bit of an anarchist," even as he was equally capable of suggesting, behind Trotsky's back, that Trotsky was a Stalinist.*

He was also increasingly frustrated by the Fourth International itself, which he saw merely as a futile and "vainglorious gesture."

In January 1939 Trotsky told the Mexican press that because he no longer enjoyed any moral solidarity with Rivera, he felt bound to leave the Blue House.

The break still wasn't final; Trotsky was still writing to Kahlo, asking her to help. Whatever their disagreements, it was clear he was deeply pained by the loss of a man who had done so much to make Mexico a friendly home for him.†

His appeal fell on deaf ears. Writing to Ella and Bertram Wolfe from Paris on 17 March 1939, Kahlo said, "More gossip: Diego had problems with the IV and seriously kicked *'piochitas'* Trotsky out of his life. I will tell you the problem later. *Diego is absolutely right*."

Trotsky offered to pay Rivera rent while looking for a new place to live. Rivera refused, then accepted, then changed his mind again, adding more sourness to the last stages of the break.

The Russian's last act before walking out of the house was to place

---

* The Mexican Trotskyists didn't like Rivera (who sometimes gave the impression that he believed only one person was actually capable of applying the doctrine in Mexico: himself) and resented his attempts to involve himself in the cause. When they attacked the painter, he asked his tenant to expel them from the organization. Trotsky calmly pointed out that he didn't have the authority, which prompted a disbelieving response: "But you are the leader!"

† When Stalinists accused Diego Rivera of having "sold himself to reaction," Trotsky defended him and expressed his own continued admiration for a "genius whose political blunderings could cast no shadow either on his art or on his personal integrity."

on his empty desk some of the objects he had been given by Frida and Diego, including the *Self-Portrait* and a pen she had given him; she had—without his knowledge—got a sample of his signature to have it engraved on the barrel. Trotsky had used these items for a long time, but they were no longer part of his life. The two men never saw each other again.

IT WAS JEAN van Heijenoort who, in March, found the little band of Trotskyists their new home on the muddy, unpaved Avenida Viena, just a couple of blocks away from the Blue House. The gloomy-looking mansion, built thirty years before, was surrounded by modest raw brick or wood houses interspersed with a few luxury villas; it was owned by the Turatis, a family of storekeepers from Mexico City who used it as a country retreat.

The mansion met many of Trotsky's requirements. It had lots of rooms and a large garden with ancient trees that came alive with birdsong every morning and was situated in a neighborhood consisting of mostly low-rise buildings, so surveilling the surroundings was easy. Its walls might have been roughly built, but they were also thick and almost impossible to scale, and the proximity of the Churubusco River meant that pretty much the only way of getting into the mansion was through the main gate. And yet it had barely been lived in for a decade; to some it seemed like a "ghost house." It was unfurnished and some of the floors had caved in. Alongside this repair work, a great deal needed to be done to enhance the mansion's safety.

Nevertheless, on 15 April 1939, the property was officially registered in Natalia Sedova's name. (Almost as soon as the rental contract was signed, rumors spread that the NKVD was going to buy the property, so Trotsky had to borrow money to complete his one and only real estate deal, commenting wryly, "I am not, by birth or inclination, a house-owner.") They moved into their new home in early May. A watchtower was built over the main gate. Access doors were reinforced with iron bars, sandbags placed next to walls to act as trenches, and an alarm installed. Keys were left in the cars parked in the garage in case the vehicles were needed for a hasty escape. These changes all complemented the security notionally offered by the policemen who were on duty day and night outside the building and by the ten or so Trotskyist guards inside it.

Trotsky immediately felt at ease. The mansion's forbidding exterior belied an attractive, spacious interior that was arranged so that he and Natalia had ample privacy. Trotsky started planting the cacti he had traveled specially to the lava wastelands of Pedregal to choose—a source of great delight—and building rabbit hutches. And, of course, he still had a revolution to inspire. But moving homes did not solve the central problem he faced. Stuck in Mexico, an ocean away from where his interests lay, he was too far from the world he wanted to be in, and at the same time, Stalin's agents remained too close. The file on Trotsky at the NKVD's headquarters was five inches thick and stuffed with photos that could have been taken only from inside his fortified villa: they showed guards, fences, and courtyards; Trotsky and Natalia; Trotsky having tea with his friends; even Trotsky's dog.

IT WAS EASY to find Trotsky or arrange a meeting with him. You just had to look his name up in the phone book.

Most of the visitors who arrived unannounced—like the publisher Cass Canfield, who, while he was on a trip to Mexico City, decided on a whim to see him—were benign. Very often they were welcomed. Trotsky enjoyed meeting leftists who had made a pilgrimage to visit the old revolutionary; he even began to relish the chance to spar with foreign journalists.

But there were many strange, uncomfortable encounters too. Within weeks of moving in, the inhabitants of the house on the Avenida Viena could not help but notice the proliferation of unknown faces in the area. What had looked like innocuous digging on a neighboring property turned out to be an observation point. Three or four men at a time were spending more time watching Trotsky's house than working on the trench.

In October 1939 a man who said he was called Manuel Fernandez Barrechena tried to gain entry. He claimed he was a member of the Communist Party who had flown in the Spanish Republican Air Force. He was now a refugee and had an urgent message for Trotsky.

It was clear to the guards that something wasn't right about the man or his story. They asked him where he lived. He told them the Hotel Moderno. Then they sent him away. The following day a call came from someone who introduced himself as General José Miaja, the commander of Madrid's defenses. Manuel Fernandez Barrechena was not just a great fellow, he said, but a rich one. He wanted only to give Trotsky a car.

Trotsky thanked him and telephoned the actual general, who was also in exile in Mexico, and who in short order confirmed he knew nothing of either Barrechena or his gift.

Anxiety in the house rose and one of Trotsky's secretaries was dispatched to the Hotel Moderno, where he confronted Barrechena, who was evasive, nervous, and unforthcoming. He was plainly not Spanish and had no documents. And yet because he had committed no crime, the police could not take any action against him.

There were other perplexing incidents like this. Each contributed to the sense of fear and threat that pervaded Trotsky's home: every fire, every accident, every unexplained event instantly seemed sinister. Even small or confusing incidents might presage the attack that they were sure was coming. This had an impact on everyone who lived in the little citadel. Seva said that in the year he lived with his grandfather, he became "addicted to adrenaline. . . . There was always an atmosphere of emotion, of tension. All the comrades wore pistols."

---

THE MEN CHARGED with keeping the compound safe were a mix of dedicated European Trotskyists and fresh-faced American college boys.*

There were, among others, the German Otto Schüssler† (small, blond, and Jewish), who had come with his wife, Gertrude Schrotter; the Englishman Walter Ketley, aka "O'Rourke"; Harold Robins (born Harold Rappaport in New York); the chief of the interior guards, Charles Cornell; Jake Cooper, Joseph Hansen, and Alexander Buchman, who was replaced by Robert Sheldon Harte on 7 April 1940.

It was difficult to challenge their commitment. They were risking their lives to protect a man they believed was going to change the world (again). In return they were paid nothing, slept in cramped quarters, and were hated, or scorned, by nearly everyone who wasn't a fellow apostle. As Jean van Heijenoort noted: "We were political outcasts; *comme des chiens lepreux*."

The guards lived under a constant sense of siege, had almost nowhere they could escape to, and were oppressed by their understanding of the great stakes they were playing for. It was inevitable that even small incidents could lead to impossible levels of tension and sometimes outbreaks of petulance and anger. Every tiny difference of opinion was amplified by the suffocating nature of their world and by the more routine human passions, jealousies, and flaws.

It didn't help that they were charged with defending someone who often made it clear that he didn't want to be defended. Trotsky repeatedly said of the Avenida Viena to van Heijenoort: "It reminds me of

* Working-class Trotskyists could not afford to drop everything and move to Mexico. The most proletarian members of the household were all Mexican: Carmen Palma, cook; Belen Estrada, maid; and Melquíades Benitez, handyman.

† Schüssler was Trotsky's assistant and clerk while they were in Turkey, and he continued to work for Trotsky in France, Germany, and Switzerland; he had come to Mexico because Trotsky asked him to.

the first prison I was in, at Khirghizan. The doors make the same sound when they shut. It is not a home; it is a medieval prison."

Trotsky was apt to wander out into Mexico City without an escort; this became almost completely insupportable when he started trying to look inside his poverty-stricken neighbors' homes to see how they lived and discover their opinions on Cárdenas's land reforms.

The guards knew that it was impossible to prevent him from seeing visitors but tried to create systems that allowed everyone who entered to be searched for concealed weapons. They also wanted to introduce a rule that their charge should never talk alone with anybody in his study.

Trotsky fought back hard against both. He believed that either people should be trusted sufficiently to be brought into the house without turning their pockets out, or they should not be admitted at all. He hated the idea of his friends being subjected to what he regarded as an indignity and knew too that many of his guests had personal problems that they would not discuss with a guard looming in the background. So the attempt foundered.

Ultimately, Trotsky was "the builder of the political party and a worker in the field of ideas. He preferred to trust his friends rather than to suspect them." And he preferred that his guards spent their time learning how to organize political movements rather than devoting themselves to protecting him. For him, mutual suspicion was far more inimical to an organization than the presence of a spy.* More than this, he knew that there was something futile about any attempt to protect him. The guards could build the walls higher and introduce ever more elaborate security measures, but one day someone would get

---

* Some elementary measures had been taken to ensure security. Pseudonyms were used in letters to other Trotskyists because it was believed, correctly, that they were being read by Kremlin agents. The Trotskyists might, however, have employed more secure names than "Old Man" or "Uncle Leon." "Crux," "Onken," "Vidal," and "Lund" were better, though they still offered little enough protection against the NKVD's cryptographers.

through. All these things could ever do was create a false sense of security.

Looking after Trotsky was a strange job. Secretaries like van Heijenoort, who had been with him throughout his exile, had become used to constantly having to falsify passports, use aliases, and trick others into believing Trotsky was where he was not.

Packages were opened carefully in case they contained bombs, and every day brought letters from cranks quoting from the Bible or making recommendations for how Trotsky could either save his soul or stay healthy. It was exhausting.

The secretaries had to be as knowledgeable about the finer points of Marxist doctrine as they were skillful at eliciting the sorts of small favors that made life in exile even vaguely bearable. They also had to be good at getting along with Trotsky and Natalia, which relied upon the ability, inter alia, to keep "unsolicited opinions to oneself." (Van Heijenoort's first wife left Coyoacán after a vicious row with Natalia.)

By trade, most of the men who came forward were writers or thinkers (with the exception of Robins, a tough son of Russian-Jewish emigrants who spent time in Sing Sing Prison after becoming embroiled in a scuffle in the aftermath of a strike by New York City hotel workers. He passed the time behind bars lecturing some of the roughest Prohibition-era gangsters on English poetry before becoming a taxi driver).

No great effort was put into establishing the men's suitability. They were rarely asked for formal documents or identification. Usually, it was enough for someone close to Trotsky to write a recommendation letter or vouch for them.

Few had experienced violence outside of the brawls that were such a feature of political meetings during the thirties, and some were painfully unsuited for the work. One guard had so much trouble with the gun he'd been issued that he turned it in. Another was asked to help build a barricade but stopped when it started affecting his sinuses. The tall, muscular Harold Robins was shocked, on arrival, to discover that although Joseph Hansen was an accomplished marksman, none of the other guards working under his supervision had fired a single practice shot in twelve months and they seemed to know nothing about handling firearms. He was also troubled by the point Hansen made of introducing new guards to the local brothels.

Guards rarely stayed for long. The work was often dull and was always demanding. Many guards gave in to exhaustion and boredom and became sloppy; when this happened, they were replaced. The other danger was that whatever spell Trotsky was able to weave over them usually wore off.

The relationships he established with his guards, whose political formation was of great importance to him, were intense but unidirectional. Trotsky was not interested in the men for themselves; for him, each new guard was a blank canvas upon which he could inscribe his own personality. Events usually followed a similar trajectory. The acolyte began regarding Trotsky with awed reverence, even imitating his attitudes and mannerisms. Jean van Heijenoort said of the early months he spent at Trotsky's side, "I was in love." No other word could do his feelings, and their intensity, justice. He, like so many others, had thrown his life over to join the comrades, in his case giving up a promising career in academia. When his mother objected, telling him about everything he would sacrifice, he replied, "How can you compare that with the chance to change *everything*?"

The experience of meeting Trotsky could be overwhelming. One British visitor wrote:

> I felt I was sitting in the 18th century trying to mark down the thoughts of Danton or Robespierre, and failing! I was amazed, I don't know why, at his spotless suit of white linen, at his shock of fine, carefully combed, silky gray hair, such hair as I have never seen, it looked as if he, or his secretary, spent hours

> brushing it and burnishing it. He wore spectacles behind which glowed his enormous, penetrating, all-embracing eyes. One felt he could see through everything, his eyes seemed to assimilate one and one's thoughts into their depths, one's faint personality sparkled for a second then he blinked, swallowed one and appeared not to have noticed it; rather like a snake swallowing a couple of rabbits or six chickens once a week for dinner, without mastication or any appearance of discomfort.

How exciting to have the chance to sit at the feet, to learn from, to help a world-historical figure!

But eventually the men all came to find Trotsky's "way of living and thinking an unbearable moral strain." Reverence and awe metastasized into uneasiness and doubt, then weariness, then opposition, then hostility. The man they had once seen as a god now only seemed to be a pitiable, arrogant collection of flaws and delusions.

Jan Frankel, who had joined group in February, moved out of the house in April; he found that his master's tempestuous behavior had become insupportable. In 1939, even the gentle, composed van Heijenoort finally had to put some distance between himself and the man he had served loyally for years.

Trotsky remained almost absurdly sensitive and demanding, allergic to anything even resembling a "Bohemian" atmosphere. He had, after all, been famous as the owner of the only punctual car in Moscow. The story was told that during the Civil War he'd been kept waiting several times by his chauffeur, whom he'd eventually threatened with dire punishment. These threats were ignored, so the next time the chauffeur was late, Trotsky simply picked up his revolver and shot him dead.

This passion for order and control spread into every aspect of Trotsky's life. "Trotsky was certainly the neatest man who ever led an insurrection. He was immaculate, and so was his office." He possessed an "innate fastidiousness and a horror . . . of slovenliness in dress, as in all other matters."

He was a man capable of being put off his stride by the way that his shirt cuffs protruded too far out of the sleeves of his suit after he'd been waving his hands around during a speech.

On one occasion in Coyoacán, Trotsky offered to help with the dishes after dinner. He was so painstaking, wiping each glass or dish with extreme care, that the whole process lasted well into the night, exhausting everyone he was supposed to be helping. The experiment was not repeated. (He relished doing dirty jobs around the house. If the plumbing went wrong, he'd fix it.)

Everything within the building's walls was, at least in theory, designed to allow him to go about his work with the minimum of friction. The household was guided by its inhabitants' understanding that, as Natalia noted, "L.T. in general was extraordinarily sensitive to physical breakage in his organism; the slightest bout of illness destroyed his equilibrium. He demanded total order and total well-being in his organism."

There were numerous spoken and unspoken expectations and rules. He would not allow dirty stories to be told in his presence, and he loathed anybody swearing in front of women and children. He could not tolerate women smoking or wearing makeup. He hardly used the familiar form of address with anybody.

And yet this was a household with few arguments. Trotsky almost always got his way, so why would he raise his voice?

DAYS WERE "RUN with the regularity of a metronome." The schedule was informed by Trotsky's desire to combine maximum effort with minimum exhaustion. And once his timetable was created, he followed it slavishly and expected everyone around him to do the same.

He knew that time was an increasingly precious commodity and did what he could to hoard even the smallest particles of it, which spilled over into seething resentment at "pointless conversations, unannounced visits, disappointments or delays." He woke early, while the air was still cool, completed his "farm" chores (his main relaxation), then worked in his office until lunch. This was a perfect space for him: a room in which he could think unhindered, with views out into the garden with its cacti and beautiful trees.

After lunch he retired to his study for a rest, during which nobody was allowed to disturb him, even if an urgent cable arrived. He read fiction or other nonpolitical books and devoured newspapers—including *The Times*, *The New York Times*, and *Le Temps* as well as titles from Mexico and Russia—underlining in blue or red pencil anything that interested him. After this, he took a nap for twenty minutes. At four p.m., he was ready to go again. There was group work, a spell of solitary study, and a return to his office, followed by a communal dinner in the dining room. Trotsky then worked in his study—drafting innumerable articles and dictating endless letters as well as trying to make progress on his biography of Stalin—before retiring to bed at nine or nine thirty. He slept so badly that he often had to resort to sleeping pills.

It was a demanding, often tedious life, which saw him work with the same ferocious focus he'd displayed in his armored train during the Civil War.* Trotsky spent as little time as possible at meals. He took almost no pleasure in the food before him. One secretary said, "I could not say that I ever noticed on his face any mark of enjoyment for what he ate and drank." Jean van Heijenoort, who for seven years, three times a day, watched Trotsky at the dinner table, said that he never heard him comment on food once. Trotsky himself once talked of "[e]ating, dressing, all these miserable little things that have to be repeated every day."

* When the weather suited, Trotsky worked in the garden, accompanied by the sounds of clucking chickens, the clack of his dictating machine, and the ringing of alarm bells accidentally set off by the pigeons that sometimes flew into the garden.

It was only at supper—a light family meal during which he was joined in the dark (the windows facing onto the street were bricked up), narrow dining room at the top of the house by guards and secretaries—that he unbent, telling anecdotes about his time in the Kremlin and leading the discussion, which was almost always about politics because, of course, there was no escape from politics. Trotsky's obsession with Marxism meant that he could find illustrations of it in daily life. Once, in a small park in Lyon, after he had watched a mother slap her child's face, he announced: "That's the dialectic of love and hatred." Coming out of a Mexico City dentist's office, he complained: "There ought to be a synthetic mode of treating a tooth." Even his birthday cake had written upon it: "Long live the Fourth International!"

More than anything, though, Trotsky was lonely. Fewer and fewer people were willing, or able, to visit him. Sometimes he could be seen walking up and down his study, talking to himself. He would have long conversations with the ghosts of old comrades like Kamenev, who had been shot long before. Or he'd speak the names of the men whom he had loved and who had betrayed their consciences: Smirnov, Lev Sosnovsky, once a leading Trotsykist, and Muralov. (Natalia noted that Muralov "had written that the waters of the Irtysh would have to flow back to the sea back to their source before he would recant.") Trotsky could not bear that a man like Rakovsky, whom he had admired so much, ended his life in prison, struggling desperately with his conscience.

Surrounded by acolytes, Trotsky desperately missed the company of equals. He knew that, cut off from them, he'd produce only inferior work. "He had truly no one around him," recalled Serge, except "[d]evoted and narrow-minded bodyguards." The only other person of real intelligence in the little "Citadel of ghosts" surrounded by soaring mountains and radiant sky was Natalia, who was herself worn out after Lev's death. At one point the Peruvian exile Juan Luis Velásquez brought Trotsky a poem he had written titled *"Soledad de Soledades."* Trotsky had it translated word for word and spent days reading it over and again. He was especially struck by one line: "Terrible to be so strong, so great, so alone."

Anger was one of the few ways Trotsky could relieve these feelings of frustration and impotence. He snapped at his family and staff. Sometimes he slammed doors so hard that windowpanes across the house fell out.

But a weary defeatism ran beneath this defiance. Occasionally, Natalia heard the old revolutionary heave a deep sigh when alone in his study and say, "I am so tired, so tired. I can't take any more."

# PART FOUR

Sylvia Ageloff

17

# I Like to Act

Sylvia Ageloff believed that she was a good person. Just like her father. She had never been involved in a crime. She did not drink, smoke, or use drugs. She was an avid reader. The FBI noted, almost grudgingly, that she was "extremely intelligent and well spoken."

Ageloff was frail and nervous, with a small, heart-shaped face, a long nose, and shortsighted blue eyes that blinked incredulously behind thick gold-rimmed specs. Her hair was dark blond and fine-textured, and her heavily marked eyebrows and eyes seemed too big for her head. Lots of people thought that even though she was just months shy of her thirtieth birthday, she looked like a child.

Clothes were not important to her. She generally appeared disheveled. Politics, however, was. She knew that some might look askance at her involvement with communist organizations but she was so absorbed in their attempts to improve the lives of America's working poor that she had little time to worry about what they thought.

For some years now, Ageloff had been part of the outer fringes of the American Left. She had first become interested in Trotskyism in college, she said, as part of an "academic study." She "did not think that democracy and capitalism were as ideal and beneficial as they should be" and could not "countenance Stalinism." For her the Soviet Union was an example of Bolshevism perverted.

She joined tiny factions that merged with other factions before splitting into numerous, equally opinionated new factions. A family friend said that he knew that she was interested in the Trotskyist movement: "[S]he always manifested Trotskyite Communistic beliefs and casually tried to interest him in the Trotsky Movement, by telling him what was going on, leaving literature with him to read." But she was not someone to ever press the issue.

Ageloff's sisters, Hilda and Ruth, were also traveling on the same route. Hilda had visited the Soviet Union in 1931, nominally to learn about alternative forms of teaching preschool, which gave her reason enough to see Nadezhda Krupskaya, Lenin's widow and the deputy minister of education. Ruth was inspired by radical young New York University professors like James Burnham and Sidney Hook.* It was this world that brought her into contact with the American Socialist Workers Party.

Not all of Sylvia's family, who were Russian Jews who spoke Russian at home, shared her politics. Her father, Samuel Ageloff, was a successful real estate agent in New York. Samuel had built a large apartment building at Fourth Street and Avenue A known as Ageloff Towers.

His daughters did not seem to hold this wealth, or the fact that he had remarried after the death of their mother, against him. This might have been because of his generosity. Sylvia's annual salary of $1,500 was supplemented by an allowance of between $150 and $200 monthly from her father, who expected her to spend it on house expenses—she shared an apartment in Brooklyn with Hilda—and food. She and her sisters also had use of a car.

The sisters were unusually well traveled. Sylvia had already been to Spain, Germany, Switzerland, France (at least twice), Britain, Mexico,

* Later, leading figures in the neoconservative movement.

Italy (with her sister Hilda), and Canada. In 1935, her sister Ruth, having finished her education in the USA, moved to Mexico City. Later, following an introduction by James Cannon, a leading American Trotskyist, she worked for five months as a typist for Trotsky in Coyoacán. She assisted him during the intense labors of the Dewey Commission, helping with translation, typing, and searching for documents. For a few weeks she had been a daily visitor, sharing in the comrades' life and work. But, notwithstanding Trotsky's "considerable affection" for her, she never became part of his permanent entourage and returned to New York.

In between her trips abroad, Sylvia had majored in dramatics and French at the Washington Square College, New York University. In 1934 she took an MA in psychology at Columbia University. Her thesis was on the concept of suggestibility: how the ideas of others can influence an individual. She was particularly interested in prestige suggestion, which takes into account the social relationships between multiple actors that determine a single question: *How easy is it for me to trick you?*

Sylvia used her research to make the case that both sex and race can determine prestige suggestibility. If you can establish the nature of people's social standing in the world and the nature of the relationships that surround them, it is possible to articulate their vulnerability to deception by others. Women, she believed, were better at resisting the deceptions of those in authority than men.

After graduating she had worked for the Jewish Children's Clearing Bureau as a volunteer at the Jewish Hospital, Brooklyn, and as a clinical psychologist at the board of education. She was now a social investigator for New York City Department of Welfare,* an office that oversaw the researching of the needs of the poor.

Sylvia's life was quiet and ordered. She lived with her sister, spent

* A source told the FBI that Sylvia was one of the eight highest-ranking applicants of the twenty-five thousand who took the civil service exam.

summer holidays traveling, and continued to devote a great deal of her spare time to political work. She did not want to become embroiled in espionage or assassinations. The fact that she ended up doing so was largely the result of a misjudgment by NKVD officials. They knew that the Fourth International's first conference was due to be held in Paris in the summer of 1938 and assumed that she would attend. Etienne was already providing them with a flow of information from inside the Trotskyist movement in France, but thus far they'd struggled to insert anybody into Trotsky's entourage in Mexico. Sylvia seemed to present them with an opportunity: if one of their operatives could begin a relationship with someone like her who was known and trusted by Trotsky and those around him, then that operative would be in a position to provide invaluable intelligence about the group's internal workings and potentially be able to indicate vulnerabilities in the little fortress's defenses.

The problem was that the NKVD had made a considerable overestimation of both Sylvia's position and participation in the Trotskyist movement. She was sympathetic to the work, but not in any serious way involved in it. And though she was indeed visiting Europe that summer, it was for a holiday, not to play a role in the forthcoming conference.

Nevertheless, the NKVD's plot began to gather pace. Its priority was to arrange a "politically impeccable" introduction between Sylvia and the agent who had been designated to seduce her. They needed somebody who was committed to communism and who could also provide the agent with information about Sylvia's habits and character.

A young associate of the Ageloffs, Ruby Weil, an employee of the Federated Press, was given the role of Cupid in this strange romance plotted on two continents for a couple who remained unaware of each other's existence. She was recommended to Louis Budenz, editor of the *Daily Worker* (who worked from a "guarded, locked, soundproof room," a sign that his remit extended way beyond just seeing his paper to press). Budenz had been charged with approaching Weil by the man responsible for secret work in New York, Comrade Chester, because she had the "requisite conservative background to act as a courier and in other secret capacities. She came from a respected family in the Middle West, successful in business and well regarded in community life." Ruby's "air of casual sophistication" also counted in her favor, as did the fact that she had attended a secret training school for those who might be asked to perform underground services.

Sylvia and her sisters had met the "quiet, soft-spoken . . . not really shy but not really effusive, either" Weil in New York early in 1938. They were all members of the AWP, and they became, Sylvia said, "friendly." Friendly enough to go to the movies together from time to time, but not so friendly that they kept in touch after Weil "disappeared"—not even Hilda, who had been closer to Weil than anyone else. Sylvia heard rumors that "she was joining the Communist Party, or was interested in it," but did not seem inclined to try to find out more.

Weil was a "militant Stalinist." At the same time, she was reluctant to betray her friend in this way. She was persuaded only when it was argued that "we were engaged in stopping Trotskyite plottings against Stalin's life."

Weil was even uncomfortable when given "a considerable sum of money" to buy clothes and fund telephone calls. Again, this reluctance had to be overcome. The next obstacle was more practical. Weil was no longer in close contact with the Ageloffs, so a cover story was hastily assembled to explain why she was suddenly so keen to take a long trip with one of them.

In June 1938, a few weeks before Sylvia was due to leave for Europe, Weil reappeared. She told Sylvia that her sister, who lived in England, had sent her money for the passage, and "since she had free time or was unemployed, wasn't it wonderful," could she come along?

Nothing about this alarmed Sylvia. When Ruby asked her, she simply said, "That's all right with me." Her trip was no secret: she'd been telling everybody she knew that she was saving up money for it. Ruby's sudden return to her life did not appear to discombobulate her.

"I knew her well enough that I wasn't surprised when she said could we go together." Nor did she seem to think that the difference in their politics would be a problem. "She was what I would call a sympathizer," Sylvia said of Weil. "She never forced her opinion. She was never very rigid about it. We would have discussions. One could talk to her. She didn't give the impression of being such a hardened Communist as being an agent of the OGPU. She gave the impression of being sympathetic."

Ruby's last task before leaving for Europe was to meet a Comrade Gertrude in Greenwich Village. This was a last-minute change to the plan that had been outlined to Ruby, who had become increasingly disturbed by the elaborate, mysterious scheme she was helping to facilitate. Nevertheless she kept the rendezvous, and she was given instructions that on arrival in Paris, she should proceed to a certain address where she would meet again with Gertrude, who would give her further orders and connect her with the Stalinist agent whom she was to introduce to Sylvia.*

WHEN RAMÓN WAS fighting in Spain, the qualities Eitingon had valued him for were his bravery, his daring, his ability to lead others. Now other, more subtle skills were needed. It helped that his political passion was allied to a highly developed theatrical facility. He loved card tricks, sang revolutionary songs with gusto, and was a gifted actor. Psychologists who examined him were amazed when he performed an impromptu satire—a comic pantomime in which he played all the parts, changing his voice and manner for each.

And he knew how to play a role. In Barcelona he had been an ele-

* In the statement he gave after his arrest, Ramón said that one of Weil's sisters, whom he had met a year before Sylvia's arrival in Paris, sent to him a recommendation letter vouching for her sister and her friend. This could be a fabrication. If true, it suggests that the NKVD was anxious to create as convincing a legend for its agent as it could.

gant and reserved employee at the Ritz, then a teenage revolutionary, and now, having disappeared from view in the summer of 1937, he reemerged as a well-dressed playboy. His affinity for clothes was useful here: he had the ability to appear studied *and* careless in his dress at the same time. This, after all, was someone who, even in prison, had been noted for wearing a beautifully tailored suit, waistcoat, and hat.* One man who met him later noted that he had a strong beard, but was always close-shaven, "like an actor."

There is a gap of several months between his disappearance in Spain and his reemergence in Paris. It's possible that he spent time in the Soviet Union, or fought as part of the Republican rearguard, or was simply given a few months in the French capital to accustom himself to a new city and a new identity.

Either way, at some point during this period, he learned to stop being Ramón Mercader and become somebody else: Jacques Mornard.

RAMÓN MERCADER AND Sylvia Ageloff met for the first time on 1 July 1938 at the Ritz bar.

Sylvia and Ruby were staying at the modest Saint-Germain-des-Prés Hotel in the Latin Quarter. They were joined by Ruby's sister, Corinne, and the trio went sightseeing.

Two days into their stay, Ruby suggested a drink at the Ritz. Almost the second they sat down, she stood up again, giving every appearance of being extremely surprised.

She then ran up to the bar and greeted a tall, handsome man in beautiful clothes. He was wearing a hat and had a camera looped around his neck. Weil greeted him effusively, then brought him back

* Ramón had theories about style, noting, "Elegance is that quality which makes it possible for those who know how to do so to dress well, but it is very difficult to be elegant."

over to introduce him to Sylvia, explaining that she had met him the day before while walking by herself in Paris.*

He was, he said, an occasional photographer for the sports pages of the communist newspaper *Ce soir* and the son of a Belgian count who, before his death, had worked as a diplomat.†

Sylvia's first impression of Ramón suggested that he was everything that she, an ascetic socialist, might have been expected to despise. He was, she said, a "playboy type who seemed to have plenty of money and never worked . . . he read little and did not appear to care anything about the problems of the world." The sparkling new car he'd left outside seemed to confirm this.

But she also found him easy to get on with, generous, and warm. Whatever her reservations about some aspects of his character, she enjoyed his company; one thing almost everyone agreed on was that Ramón had "magnetic charm." And he was physically attractive: athletic, well-built with an "animal vigor." So the women were quick to accept when he invited them to accompany him to the racetrack—he said he had to take photos for *Ce soir*—and then on a moonlight stroll through Paris.

For the next few days, Ramón, Sylvia, and Ruby went around Paris together, rarely out of one another's company. Ramón knew the city well: where to eat, what to drink, which cabarets were amusing. And he quickly began taking Sylvia out on car rides, to galleries, or on sightseeing trips.

He appeared to possess large quantities of money—wherever they went, Ramón paid—and there were few demands on his time. If he did work, it never interfered with his courting. He told Sylvia that he was combining studies at the Sorbonne with sports journalism. This,

* As ever, there is an alternate account of how the encounter was manufactured. At some point, Ruby mentioned that "she had a sister Gertrude who knew somebody in Paris that she had been friendly with, who was a young student and used to visit Gertrude at her house in Paris, and she was going to get in touch with him."

† Ramón later denied this, but it's what Sylvia told her sister.

plus an allowance from his mother, was what kept him rich.* But she never saw him writing, never went to any sporting events with him after their first encounter, and never witnessed him meeting athletes. The Tour de France came and went without him seeming to show any interest in it at all.

Sylvia enjoyed this treatment, even as she continued to be baffled, almost impressed, by Ramón's indifference to politics of any sort. He didn't even read ordinary news articles. Instead, he talked about music, theater, celebrities, sports, "things of that kind." She delayed telling him what he, of course, already knew about her own political beliefs. Perhaps she felt that this aristocrat would be put off by them.

After just two weeks, Sylvia had moved into the apartment of the man she had started calling "Jac." It was already understood that they would marry.

By this point, Ruby and her sister had returned to the United States. On her return, Ruby telephoned Hilda Ageloff. "I guess you want to know all about Sylvia?"

"Sure."

Weil proceeded to tell Hilda that her sister was having a lovely time and had met a nice man. A little later she called to say that Sylvia had been to a doctor with a slight cold and been told she had tuberculosis, so was going into Bedford Hills Sanatorium.

Over the weeks that followed, "Jacques Mornard" filled in more of his story. He claimed to have been born in 1904 in Tehran, Persia, the son of a Belgian diplomat, Albert Mornard. His brother, Roberto, was a diplomat with right-wing sympathies. In the years that followed, the family moved between Brussels and Paris. He had been taught by Jesuits before being bullied by his father into joining the army at the

* He also said that his father, who had died in 1926, left his family an inheritance of three to four million Belgian francs—money that remained untouched.

age of seventeen. He had "hated the military" so much that he managed to obtain a three-year leave from it in order to study: first at the École Polytechnique in Paris, then at the journalism school of the Sorbonne. The leave had long since elapsed, but he would not be returning.

In the time before he completed his journalism degree, he worked at *Ce soir* newspaper. Along the way he had married. The union, to Enriqueta Vanprouscht, began in 1934 and lasted just three months. He claimed that she was "a stupid girl" who had been "all right until we were married, then she changed." He was convinced that she had married him only for his money. In 1938, he said, he had deserted from the Belgian army, which explained his presence in Paris.

Beyond that, he was just a "average young man" who woke at six every morning to swim and was in bed by ten every night. He always seemed restless and moved all the time. His long limbs lent his gestures an exaggerated, almost theatrical quality. Sylvia was impressed by his abstemiousness. He never drank, though he did smoke, greedily, inhaling one cigarette after another.

Still, as a friend of Sylvia noted, they led "an easy, luxurious life." Ramón told Ageloff that as well as his responsibilities for *Ce soir*, he worked as a journalist for the Argus Press, writing its rugby reports, and for a magazine called *Auto* and for a handful of Belgian newspapers including *La Nation Belge*, *Les Sports*, and *Les Dernières Nouvelles*. Ageloff rarely saw Ramón working on his articles, nor did she see any published. (This was partially explained when he said that his work appeared under the pseudonym "Catsú.") He appeared to be ignorant of the basics of reporting, like how to write or dictate a story, and looked blank when asked even the simplest question about how a paper was put together. Nevertheless, he said that he earned three thousand francs a month.

There were other odd events that were difficult to explain away. Once a man called the apartment wanting to speak to Sylvia's boyfriend, who was away. The man refused to give his name. When told that Ramón was traveling, he requested that Ramón should call him as soon as he returned, then hung up. Asked about this later, Ramón told Ageloff that the man was his boss at *Auto* magazine.

Still stranger was the lucrative arrangement Ramón made for Sylvia to translate psychology articles from French into English for the Argus Press when she started to talk about returning to New York. She was tiring of Paris and running short of money, but reluctant to leave her lover. Within days he surprised her with the publisher's proposal. There were oddities in the agreement. She wasn't allowed to deal with the company directly and would never be told which of its papers—which were scattered across the globe—had printed the pieces she'd worked on.

Again Sylvia allowed herself to be convinced. She had no reputation in the field, either in France or elsewhere in the world. She wasn't a professional writer, and nobody at Argus could have had any idea whether she knew anything about the subject. And yet they were willing to pay her a rate higher than any leading French psychologist could have expected to receive. She ignored this and chose to see the weirdness of the arrangements as evidence of Ramón's delicacy and savoir faire.

She had, after all, seen the company's name on the envelopes containing the payments that were sent to Ramón. And accepting the arrangement meant that she could stay with him in Paris without feeling like a kept woman.

Each night she lay in the darkness of their bedroom next to a man whose body was a map of scars. Some were innocuous enough. There was the large one at the back of his tongue, which he had received climbing a tree. One on his scrotum had been inflicted during a game of football, and several on his fingers were courtesy of a dog bite. But others were harder to explain. Two sat on his upper lip, his skin damaged by a stone and the recoil of a rifle. And then there were the livid marks on his right forearm, evidence of the wound he had suffered while fighting on the Aragon front. Each was a question begging to be asked; Sylvia does not appear to have taken the opportunity.

Sometimes a new friend, Maria Craipeau, a native Pole who had arrived in Paris with just a bundle of clothes seven years previously, helped her with the typing. Maria remembered Ramón as "a rather bland, pleasant, elegant fellow, who fitted in socially everywhere. He spoke of his father's numerous diplomatic postings, of his mother whom he adored and who was a great horsewoman. Ramón wasn't interested in anything much, least of all in politics. When we came to talk to Sylvia, he would leave the room. He was sweet, generous, charming. An inoffensive type."

He was the sort of person who wanted everyone around him to be happy and to have a good time. When Maria fell ill, Ramón and Sylvia immediately came by taxi to pick her up and take her to their house. For two days Ramón cared for Maria "with unfailing devotion." He administered her medicines and sat by her bed, telling her a stream of stories. On the day that her illness turned into a fever, he described to her "the struggle of red blood cells and white blood cells marching in close ranks, in military fashion. He wanted to make me laugh."

But nevertheless something about the arrangement unsettled Maria. One day, as Sylvia and she worked, she stopped suddenly, with her fingers on the keyboard of her typewriter, and turned to her friend. "Listen, Sylvia, there's something wrong with this; this kind of job doesn't usually pay so well."

They sat on the bed, Maria lit a cigarette, and both tried to make sense of the situation. Who was Ramón? What exactly did he want? His lack of interest in politics reassured them, as did the fact that he absented himself from their conversations. They knew he was lying about certain aspects of the arrangement, perhaps the whole thing, but why? Sylvia's hypothesis was that he had invented the job because he wanted to give her the money she needed to stay in Paris, as well as the illusion that she was earning it. Perhaps the best answer was also the most obvious one: maybe he was madly in love and just didn't want to lose her.

---

Ramón did not appear to have any friends of his own. When they socialized, it was with Sylvia's acquaintances, "Manni, Waltha, Naty, Frank, and Elizabeth." The group roamed beyond the capital to visit tourist sites: Château-Thierry, Verdun, Metz, Tours, Blois, Chartres, and Deauville.

Ramón was the perfect companion on these trips. He spoke French and English impeccably. Nobody he talked to ever remembered a single word of Spanish crossing his lips. Nor did he ever mention Spain or indeed anything else that might have revealed anything of the man he had once been. This doctrinaire Stalinist, whose political opinions read like Kremlin propaganda (prostitution was "one of the ulcers of capitalist society"; religion "the opium of the people"; Jesuits "lackeys of the capitalist class") and who was used to a "rigid . . . categorical way . . . of expressing himself," kept quiet even as his companions offered opinions that repulsed him. He existed in his new friends' eyes as a sort of bland but pleasant blur. Maria Craipeau thought he "didn't have a firm opinion on anything, everything he said was insipid. He seemed to have no culture."

We do not know what this man—who had spilled his own blood and taken the lives of others in defense of cherished ideals and who only months before had been fighting in a civil war—made of the necessity of posing as a class enemy, nor what it cost him to leave the woman he loved, Elena Imbert, and instead share a bed with somebody he had been directed to seduce.

His brother Luis saw how the life Ramón had chosen, or had been chosen for him, was antithetical to who he really was. "Ramón was a man of integrity," Luis said. "He was not a liar, nor frivolous. He was serious and precise in every aspect of his life and relationships with others. He had . . . the psychology of a soldier. For him, black was black, white was white."

But now Ramón was being forced to lie promiscuously about every aspect of his existence. He was cultured and widely read, and now he had to pose as a bored, ignorant playboy. He could not show the part of himself that was "cynical, sarcastic, impertinent."

It was an extraordinary act of self-erasure made possible by the control he was able to exert over his will. He directed his energy to suppressing inconvenient thoughts and emotions. He would not shout or scream when something angered him, although his real feelings might have leaked out in ways detectable to those watching him closely: his skin would go pale and his fingertips tremble.

There was just one occasion when he lost his composure. During a discussion between Sylvia and Maria about Picasso, it was clear Ramón wanted to say something—to reveal something of himself. "You don't know anything about it, it's not all that . . ." he exploded. His eyes, which usually smiled, flashed with anger; his fists clenched. But the desire to assert himself passed quickly. Maria, who was watching him, thought: "He never allowed himself to be himself in front of us."

# 18

# He Couldn't Be Forgiven

Stalin never stopped thinking about Trotsky. He thought about Trotsky during the day as he paced the corridors of the Kremlin in his much-darned party tunic and baggy old trousers, smelling of old tobacco and the talcum powder his bodyguard Karl Pauker used to fill in the pockmarks on his face. He thought about Trotsky at night, in the last moments before the book he was reading slipped out of his hands and he fell asleep on one of the large, hard divans that were in every room in his residences.

His great peasant's head, with its irregular black teeth, was full of hatred and fear that left him frantic. While Lenin was safely embalmed, Trotsky remained at large and was producing millions of words that were almost exclusively directed at challenging the myth Stalin was making such assiduous efforts to build.

Individual articles were capable of driving Stalin into a frenzy. Trotsky was making increasingly wild-sounding accusations, such as the one that Abel Yenukidze had been shot for trying "to stay the hand that was raised above the heads of the old Bolsheviks."* In the spring

* The same January 1939 issue of the *Bulletin* was supposed to have an article commemorating the anniversary of Lev's death, but Trotsky couldn't face writing it. In-

of 1938, accurately anticipating the devil's pact that the Soviet Union eventually struck with Nazi Germany,* Trotsky suggested, "Over the last three years, Stalin has labeled every one of Lenin's comrades-in-arms agents of Hitler. He has destroyed the flower of the command staff, shot, replaced or exiled around 30,000 officers [actually nearer forty-three thousand]—all on the same charge, namely that they were agents or allies of Hitler. Having destroyed the Party and decapitated the army, Stalin is now openly advancing his candidature as Hitler's chief agent."

Stalin received reports on every aspect of Trotsky's behavior and activity from his embassies in Moscow and Washington as well as from intelligence units on the ground. Every report he read from the New World inflamed Stalin's hatred and underlined his conviction that the Foreign Department and the Secret Political Department of the NKVD were failing to do their jobs properly. Yezhov in particular didn't seem to be able to exert sufficient control over his "mission" abroad.

And now, Stalin learned, the enemy who knew more about him than anybody else and who was actively seeking more information, was writing a biography of him. Stalin didn't want to read any more. He was tired of failure after failure and, with a European war looming, increasingly sensitive. When, he angrily asked his intelligence chiefs, would "they end this slander of socialism?"

In 1937, at the Central Committee Plenum, he had accused his special services of spinelessness and indecision. "The one thing we lack is the willingness to liquidate our own carelessness, our own placidity, our own short-sightedness."

The same year, Yezhov wrote a report noting that that the NKVD Security Directorate had squandered the chance from 1932 to 1933 to

---

stead, he asked Etienne to do it: "You are doing a great service in publishing the *Bulletin* so punctually and with such care. This is to your credit."

* Trotsky was one of the most acute observers of the unique menace posed by Nazi ideology.

expose "the Trotskyist conspiracy" and eliminate it. The sinister implication was that they had allowed him to stay alive. Yezhov's report went on to discuss extant connections between Trotsky's son Lev and Soviet officials in Berlin and the "criminal" relationship between Georgy Molchanov, chief of the NKVD's Secret Political Department, and members of the Trotskyist opposition. And since then, Reiss and Krivitsky had tried to defect, with varying degrees of success.

No Soviet official operating abroad could mistake the message: they were being watched. Hunting down enemies of the people had become a greater priority for the NKVD than, for instance, intelligence collection. By 1938 so many officers had been recalled or liquidated that a number of NKVD residences ceased to function. Those in London, Berlin, and Tokyo did not quite close but each had one, at most two officers in place.

People were so afraid of messages recalling them that the Center realized that it needed to use subterfuge. This was backed by compulsion. On 8 June 1938 Stalin signed a law decreeing that close relatives of Soviet officers who fled were liable to be deported to Siberia. NKVD officers were informed of a secret addendum to the law stipulating an automatic ten-year prison term for wives and close relatives of defectors. They could be executed if it was discovered that state secrets had been betrayed.

But simple failure could also have lethal consequences. In February 1938, Yezhov gave his deputy Mikhail Frinovsky the order "to remove Slutsky without noise." He had outlived whatever symbolic value he'd once enjoyed, and his men had failed to land even a glove on Trotsky. Slutsky was summoned to Frinovsky's office. Hiding in an adjoining room was M. S. Alekhin, head of the Operational Techniques Department. Once Slutsky entered, Leonid Zakovsky, another Yezhov deputy, followed him into the office, pretending to be waiting for the others to finish.

Then, without warning, Zakovsky threw a mask of chloroform over Slutsky's face.

As soon as he had passed out, Alekhin emerged and injected poison into his arm. Frinovsky brought in a doctor, who found Slutsky "slumped awkwardly across an armchair with an empty tea glass at his side." The doctor duly certified death by heart attack, an analysis that was loudly shared elsewhere in the building by Frinovsky. Nevertheless, at the funeral, NKVD officers who were familiar with the symptoms of cyanide poisoning noticed telltale blue spots on Slutsky's face when they filed past his open coffin.

Shpiegelglass was next. He and his men had identified Trotsky's location a number of times but never acted quickly enough. Moscow had been left frustrated and angry by Trotsky's escape from France to Norway. Then Shpiegelglass failed to organize the infiltration of his entourage into Mexico. In June 1938 he was summoned home. It was alleged that he, along with Yagoda and others, had "penetrated the NKVD agencies as Trotsky's accomplices." For a while he was still allowed to analyze Etienne's reports but there was no doubt that he had lost his superiors' trust. By the time his arrest eventually came, it had long seemed inevitable.

New bodies were needed in the hunt for Trotsky.

Pavel Sudoplatov was poised and intelligent with a face dominated by great dark eyes. He was solidly built, with thick hair swept back off his forehead, and there was something about him that recalled a prosperous man of business. This genial, humorous carapace concealed a subtle, creative intelligence, a passionate belief in communism, and an adamantine ruthlessness.

Years later, Sudoplatov told another officer about his recruitment philosophy.

> Go search for people who are hurt by fate or nature—the ugly, those suffering from an inferiority complex, craving power and influence but defeated by unfavorable circumstances. . . . The

> sense of belonging to an influential, powerful organization will give them a feeling of superiority over the handsome and prosperous people around them. For the first time in their lives they will experience a sense of importance. . . . It is sad indeed, and humanly shallow—but we are obliged to profit from it.

Like Eitingon, Etienne, and Reiss, Sudoplatov was another creature of the old empire's distant fringes. Born in Melitopol, Ukraine, in 1907, he had entered the Red Army at the age of twelve. He served as a telephone operator and a cipher clerk in his unit's Intelligence Department, then ran agents in his home city, before joining the Ukrainian NKVD's Secret Political Department in 1927.

In 1934 Abram Slutsky, then head of the Foreign Department, asked Sudoplatov to become an illegal officer serving abroad. This, Sudoplatov said, was a "fascinating and challenging" prospect. He was sent on crash courses in German, hand-to-hand combat, and weapons and introduced to other members of the hierarchy, such as Shpiegelglass (whose cover for his Parisian operations was a fish store specializing in lobsters near the Boulevard Montmartre).

After eight months of training, he was ready for his first trip abroad. He was sent to Germany to infiltrate the ranks of Ukrainian nationalists and was so successful that they invited him to attend a Nazi-run training school.

During a brief visit back to Moscow, Sudoplatov met Stalin for the first time. The experience overwhelmed the thirty-year-old. Stalin, whose senses were "ferally acute," noticed this and tried to calm him. "Young man, don't be excited. Report the essential facts. We have only twenty minutes."

"Comrade Stalin," Sudoplatov replied, "for a rank-and-file party member to meet with you is a great event in life. I understand I am summoned for business. In a minute I will control my emotions and report the essential facts to you and Comrade Yezhov."

They chatted for a while about what he had learned about their enemy. Stalin showed a particular interest in Yevhen Konovalets, the leader of the Organization of Ukrainian Nationalists.

What are his personal tastes? asked Stalin. "Try to exploit them."

"Konovalets," said Sudoplatov, "is overly fond of chocolate candies."

Within days, the director of the NKVD's technical bureau, Mosiev Paulkin, had been ordered to create a bomb disguised as a box of chocolates. Sudoplatov was charged with delivering it.

As Shpiegelglass waved him off to Rotterdam, where the assassination was to take place, he reminded him: "You are supposed to act as a man if the attempt fails." Sudoplatov did not need to be told that he was expected to use on himself the Walther pistol he'd been supplied rather fall into enemy hands.

Sudoplatov also heard in passing that the man who'd brought him to Moscow, Abram Slutsky, had suffered a heart attack. For the moment this did not strike him as sinister.

At eleven fifty a.m. on 23 May 1938, a day on which warm sun had succeeded rain, Sudoplatov left a small parcel wrapped in brown paper with his target in a restaurant called Atlanta, on the Coolsingel, the city's main thoroughfare.

Half an hour later, as he left a shop carrying a newly purchased hat and light raincoat, he heard a "bang that sounded like the blowout of a tire." He saw people running toward the restaurant but did not stop. Instead, he rushed to the railway station, where he boarded the first train to Paris. While there, he took the opportunity—he did not think he would be returning to the West anytime soon—to order three fashionable suits and an overcoat as well as a number of shirts and ties. They would be picked up from the tailor once completed and then sent back to Moscow in the diplomatic pouch.

This important work done, Sudoplatov—who had a passport identifying himself as a Dutchman, Josef Novack, who had arrived from Germany a few days before—then traveled to Barcelona, where he stayed for three weeks posing as a Polish volunteer in an NKVD-run guerrilla group.

Here, he linked up again with Eitingon,* whom he had first encountered five years before when he headed the section for illegal operations in the Foreign Department. On Moscow Center's instructions, Eitingon escorted Sudoplatov to Bordeaux, where he caught a Soviet ship. He returned to warm, admiring congratulations. His assassination of Konovalets—which was considered "a classic by generations of KGB officers: elegant, efficient, and politically expedient"—had made him a celebrity.

It was exhilarating for Sudoplatov to be able to resume his life. When he thought about what he had done, he could reassure himself that "my assassination of Konovalets was justified in every way"; he also took pride in his belief that "no innocent people were hurt by the explosion."†

And yet his account of this time is shadowed by events he couldn't, or perhaps didn't want to, understand. During the course of a brief holiday in Ukraine he took with his wife, relatives revealed "rumors of atrocities." They learned that Mendel Khatayevich, the secretary of the Ukrainian Communist Party, was "an enemy of the people." It was alleged that he was involved with Polish communists, though Sudoplatov was inclined to ascribe his fall from grace to "some mistakes in their practical work," perhaps relating to ways in which he had bent rules to help feed his neighbors during the "desperate years of hunger." As hard as Sudoplatov worked to explain these developments away, he was left with an unshiftable sense of discomfort.

This anxiety was compounded when, on his return, he discovered

* Sudoplatov also claimed, almost certainly in error, that he met Ramón Mercader, who had just returned from an operation behind enemy lines. Sudoplatov said that he found the young lieutenant "charming" and eagerly listened to accounts of his brother's death in battle—Ramón apparently told Sudoplatov that Pablo had tied grenades to his body and thrown himself under a German tank—and of how his mother had been wounded during an air raid.

† This was not true: several bystanders had been injured in the blast.

that he would be joining the *nomenklatur*, having been appointed special assistant to the director of the Foreign Department. He couldn't be quite sure what was going on, but the atmosphere felt increasingly ominous. Mikhail Shpiegelglass, who knew that his own arrest was only a matter of time, "grew more grim with each passing day" and stopped spending weekends with Sudoplatov and other friends from the directorate.

That same summer, Yasha Serebryansky was recalled to Moscow and arrested. He had been awarded the Order of Lenin in recognition of his efforts at the helm of the AST, efforts that had increasingly been directed against men who were supposed to have been serving the Soviet Union.* The AST had played its part in the terror, and now Serebryansky had been caught by the dogs he had unleashed.

Under torture he supplied the names of alleged French and British spies. The report that followed his arrest concluded that he'd built a network containing "a large number of traitors and plain gangster elements." He was sentenced to death, and his wife to ten years in the gulag for failing to report him.†

A little while later, Alexander Orlov defected, eventually escaping to the United States. Unlike Reiss, he had no moral disillusionment, simply a cool calculation of his best interests: he was convinced that if he returned as ordered to Moscow, he would be liquidated.‡ Yezhov was so afraid of how Stalin might react to the news that he tried to hide information about it from him.

---

* Aside from the moral repellence of the work of the AST, its members contributed to a marked diminishment of the effectiveness of Soviet intelligence. The flow of information to the Center dried up, but even if there had been more, there was almost nobody left capable of analyzing what they received.

† Luckily (at least for him), by the time his case was heard, in July 1941, events had rendered him more useful alive than dead. He was swiftly readmitted to both party and secret service.

‡ After Orlov's disappearance Eitingon became acting chief of the NKVD in Spain. In his first report back to Moscow, he wrote: "In my opinion, we should put an end, once and forever, to misleading our chiefs and must teach our officers to report things as they are in reality. I stress once again that indulging in fantasies is dangerous in our business."

Then in September Sudoplatov and his colleagues heard that Yezhov's secretary had shot himself while boating on the Moscow River. That same month, the Georgian Lavrenti Beria was given operational control of the NKVD—even Stalin had grown tired and sickened by the wild frenzy unleashed by Blackberry. Yezhov quickly vanished into a decadent limbo, drinking and holding orgies.

Beria's appointment was initially welcomed by the NKVD. One agent, Mark Laskin, recalled: "We were overjoyed by the appearance of this pure and ideal figure."

This did not last long. Beria was clever and irreverent and could work for a week without sleep. He was a kind parent who could be moved to tears by a Rachmaninov prelude. But this man who wore pince-nez that in photos always seemed to reflect the light back, obscuring the "snake eyes" beneath, was also a rapist, a flatterer, an intriguer, and a murderer. One Bolshevik said that when Beria came into a house, "he brought darkness with him."

Beria came flanked by his own swaggering acolytes from the Caucasus and quickly expanded the Terror to anyone connected to Yezhov. A constrained, fearful atmosphere pervaded the Lubyanka. Sudoplatov could sense his colleagues' reluctance to discuss anything and realized that people had stopped gossiping or making jokes. Rumors rushed in to fill the space that they left.

On the eve of the anniversary celebrations of the October Revolution, the moment that he had feared arrived. At four a.m. his phone rang. It was the head of the secretariat of the Foreign Department.

"Pavel Anatolievich," he said, his agitation unmistakable, "you are immediately summoned to Comrade Merkulov, first deputy director of the state security administration. The car is waiting for you. Come as soon as possible. Shpiegelglass and Passov have just been arrested."

Sudoplatov regarded this development coolly, noting of Shpiegelglass: "He didn't carry out the job of killing Trotsky. So he couldn't be forgiven."

Sudoplatov arrived, expecting to be shown into a prison cell.

Instead, he was told to take over as acting director of the Foreign Department. Later that day, as he idly looked through the contents of a safe owned by the former head of the department, Zelman Passov, he encountered two shocks. The first was a recommendation, signed by Yezhov, that he be awarded the Order of the Red Banner. The second was an unsigned order to make him assistant director of the Foreign Department.

Sudoplatov took the documents to Vsevolod Merkulov, who smiled and gave Sudoplatov another shock. He tore them to pieces and threw them into a wastebasket. Sudoplatov was puzzled by this behavior. He also felt cheated: he'd risked his life and now his rewards were lying in shreds at the bottom of a bin.

Three weeks passed before Yezhov was charged with plotting to overthrow the government. The Politburo then passed a resolution denouncing all senior NKVD officials as "politically unreliable." It was at precisely this moment that Sudoplatov realized the unsigned promotion could have been his death warrant.

This knowledge softened the blow of his demotion to assistant director of the Spanish section (as did the fact that all other intelligence service veterans were also demoted to assistant chief of section). Still, in the days that followed, Sudoplatov's nerves were stretched even further.

He and his wife were both interrogated by Beria, who wanted to find out if they were double agents.* Emma Kaganova started warning her husband that there was something evil about Beria. He was, she said, a "man without feeling." Making the (almost certainly correct) assumption that their apartment was bugged, they started to speak in a form of code. When they needed to talk about Beria, they referred to him as "Shadiman," the hero of a novel about war in Georgia in the Middle Ages. (Prince Shadiman ends up falling victim to a power struggle between feudal lords.)

* "Are you German or Ukrainian?" he asked Emma, impudently looking her up and down. "Jewish," she replied, enjoying the surprise on his face.

But it was clear that even these precautions were not enough. During an interview with another party official, Sudoplatov was reminded that he'd been brought to Moscow by the now disgraced NKVD official Vsevolod Balitsky—"an enemy of the people, who had been executed." It was suggested that he was still on friendly terms with other recently exposed enemies; the only solution was to set up a commission to investigate him.

A man who Sudoplatov described as a "good friend" asked him "stupid questions," arguing that he was defending his innocence as a "typical Trotskyite double-dealer." Whatever Sudoplatov said in his defense was not enough, and a resolution was passed calling for his expulsion from the party as a result of his connections with enemies of the people and his failure to expose Shpiegelglass.

It was now December. The expulsion needed to be endorsed at a general party meeting of intelligence services that wasn't scheduled until January. So, in the meantime, all Sudoplatov could do was turn up at his office, sit at his desk, and do nothing. New members of staff were so afraid of contamination that they refused to talk to him. Even old comrades were wary about asking him questions. Sudoplatov fell into deep, paralyzing depression. He also began to grapple with the senselessness of what appeared to be happening.

At no time before had he feared extermination by the system to which he had given so much. He had agreed with the "the brutality and stern order that characterized our centralized society"; it was the only way of preserving a country surrounded by enemies.

Things were unarguably different now. And yet he still tried to rationalize what was happening. The arrests of his friends could have been only the results of mistakes or incompetence, which were even more likely now that their places had been taken by inexperienced people like Vladimir Dekanozov, the new chief of the Foreign Department. It was too uncomfortable, too impossible to believe that anything else was going on.

These attempts to comfort himself were not enough to prevent him from feeling a kind of stunned disbelief. The meeting that was supposed to be ratifying his expulsion kept on being postponed, but this was just a minor inconvenience; he expected to be arrested at any moment. All he could do was remain watchful, keep on going to his office in the Lubyanka, and try to nurture what little hope he had left.

# 19

# CHILDISH GAMES

By March 1939 the Terror's grim momentum started to slow. Beria suggested to Stalin that it was time to pause and take stock; otherwise there would soon be nobody left to arrest.

That same month, Sudoplatov's fate took another lurch in a strange direction. He was summoned to Beria's office, where Beria, wearing the pince-nez that made him look like a Jesuit priest, accused him of indolence. Sudoplatov argued that he had just been obeying orders. Beria ignored this and told Sudoplatov that he needed him to come to an important meeting. Sudoplatov assumed that they were probably going to a safe apartment to meet an agent Beria was running personally.

It was only as the car transporting them entered the Kremlin through the Spassky Gate and then stopped at a dead end off Ivanovsky Square that Sudoplatov realized that he was being taken to see Stalin.

They walked down long, polished floors with red-and-green carpets, and past offices with high doors. On either side of them was wooden paneling up to their shoulders; gloomy drapes hung from the windows. A guard offered them a military salute and the traditional greeting:

*"Dravia zalayu, Tovarich Beria"* (Good health to you, Comrade Beria). Otherwise, the corridors were empty. Everything had the hushed, antiseptic quality of a hospital.

Sudoplatov began to feel convulsed by a mixture of apprehension and excitement. By the time Beria opened a door into a reception room so vast that it made the three writing desks it contained look like doll's toys, he could hear his heart beating out loud.

They were greeted by a short, thickset man in a green tunic like Stalin's who talked to them in an affectless voice. "It appeared to me," Sudoplatov thought, "that there was a strict unwritten rule banning emotions in this room."

The man led them into Stalin's office and closed the door behind them silently as they sat at a long table covered in green baize cloth. The files on the desk were arranged in perfect order. When Sudoplatov looked up, he saw that they were overlooked by portraits of Lenin, Karl Marx, and Friedrich Engels, a communist Holy Trinity.

Stalin himself was "focused, poised, and calm." As Beria began the conversation, Sudoplatov was struck by Stalin's self-confidence and ease—he made his visitors feel as if he was listening carefully to everything they said.

"Comrade Stalin," Beria said, "having exposed on the party's orders the NKVD Foreign Department's former leadership's treacherous attempt to deceive the government, we suggest that Comrade Sudoplatov be appointed a deputy director of the NKVD Foreign Department [the thirty-one-year-old Pavel Fitin would head it] in order to assist recently mobilized party activists to comply with the orders of the government."

Stalin frowned, a pipe filled with tobacco in his hands. Then he struck a match and moved his ashtray closer. When he eventually started speaking, he appeared to ignore the nomination. Instead, he asked Beria to outline his priorities for intelligence operations abroad. As Beria spoke, Stalin heaved himself up and started to slowly pace up and down in soft Georgian boots that made no sound. At no point was there any hint that his attention had slackened.

He reacted simply and, to Sudoplatov's mind, naturally. "It was hard to imagine," he later wrote, "that such a man could deceive you."

After a brief tour d'horizon, Beria turned to what he believed was the major problem: the Left abroad was in disarray because of Trotskyist infiltration. Trotsky and his supporters were competing with Soviets to be the "vanguard of the world Communist revolution."

In response, he suggested that Sudoplatov be made responsible for all the NKVD's anti-Trotskyist operations, which involved a number of priorities, none more pressing than the liquidation of "Trotsky, the worst enemy of the people."

Stalin agreed: "There are no important figures in the Trotskyite movement except Trotsky himself. If Trotsky is finished the threat will be eliminated."

With this, he returned to his seat and talked about how unhappy he was with previous attempts to kill Trotsky. He'd first assigned the task of liquidating Trotsky to Shpiegelglass in 1937! Then he "stiffened as if giving an order."

> Trotsky should be eliminated within a year, before war inevitably breaks out. Without the elimination of Trotsky, as the Spanish experience shows, when the imperialists attack the Soviet Union we cannot rely on our allies in the international Communist movement. They will face great difficulties in fulfilling their international duty to destabilize the rear of our enemies by sabotage operations and guerrilla warfare if they have to deal with treacherous infiltratons by Trotskyites in their ranks.
>
> We have no historical experience in building the industrial and military might of the country while we consolidate the dictatorship of the proletariat.

Stalin ended his disquisition with an order: Sudoplatov would head a detachment of *buyeveke*, shock troops, who would carry out the murder of Trotsky in Mexico. If Sudoplatov and his team were successful, the members of the party would never forget those who were involved. They would ensure that not only the participants, but every member of their families was looked after.

For Sudoplatov there was no "moral question" when it came to

> killing Trotsky or any other of our former comrades who had turned against us. We believed we were in a life-and-death struggle for the salvation of our grand experiment, the creation of a new social system that would protect and provide dignity for all workers and eliminate the greed and oppression of capitalist profit.
>
> We believed that every Western country hated us and wished to see our doom. Therefore, anyone who was not for us was against us.

This meant that they could "take vengeance on our enemies with cold self-assurance."

Instead, Sudoplatov expressed his anxiety that he was not fit for the job because he didn't speak Spanish. With Stalin remaining impassive, Sudoplatov asked for permission to recruit veterans of the Spanish Civil War.

"It is your job and party duty," Stalin replied, "to find and select suitable and reliable personnel to carry out the assignment. You will be provided with whatever assistance and support you need. Report directly to Comrade Beria and nobody else, but the full responsibility for carrying out the mission remains with you. You should personally make arrangements to dispatch a task force to Mexico from Europe and report it only in your own handwriting."

The meeting was over. They shook hands and took their leave.

---

Things continued to move precipitously. Sudoplatov's promotion was confirmed and he was given a new office in room 735, on the seventh floor of the Lubyanka. Its previous occupant was his unfortunate old boss, Abram Slutsky. Emma was anxious that his new position might leave him exposed—she worried that his precipitous rise had led to his denunciation. Sudoplatov felt that too much was happening too quickly for him to brood.

Two days later he learned that the party had reconsidered its decision to expel him. He would merely be reprimanded for his failure to expose hostile elements in the directorate. Then, the following day, he got a call from Eitingon, who had returned from Spain to report back on a war that was almost lost (about this time, the writer Ilya Ehrenburg saw him in Madrid tossing files onto a bonfire—a job he appeared to be enjoying more than Ehrenburg thought he should) and to seek new instructions.

"Pavlusha," Eitingon started, dispensing with formalities, "for ten days I have been in Moscow doing nothing but being under close surveillance by the Operations Department. I am sure my telephone is tapped. You are one who knows my real work, so please report immediately to your superiors that if they decide to arrest me they should do it now without these childish games."

Sudoplatov invited Eitingon to his office. Eitingon's fate had been entwined with Trotsky's ever since, ten years before while he was the NKVD's *rezident* in Istanbul, he had been assigned to watch Trotsky. Now, however, his relationship with this man whom he had only ever observed from a distance was about to enter a new, more deadly phase.

To execute his orders and exterminate the man who was codenamed STARIK, or "Old Man," by the Center, Sudoplatov knew he faced two complex challenges. The first was how to find a way into a strongly defended compound. Planning for this could be deferred until they had secured more information. The second problem was ensuring that the assassination could not be blamed on Moscow.

The early conversations between the two men did much to shape the operation that followed. Eitingon suggested the name of UTKA, which means "duck" but also "disinformation." ("When the ducks are flying" means "press publishing disinformation.") This was presumably a reference to what those loyal to Stalin believed Trotsky was doing.

Sudoplatov was also familiar with the agent networks in the US and Western Europe, and he began suggesting people they could rely on. Maria de la Sierra, their "best agent," who had been placed with Trotsky as a secretary in Norway and had traveled to Mexico with him, was known to the traitor Orlov, so she had to be recalled. Eitingon suggested relying on agents who hadn't already been involved in operations against the Trotskyists in Paris and Mexico City. It's possible that he already had the Mercaders in mind. Ramón had been charged with securing Sylvia Ageloff's trust. Could this be parlayed into something more? Eitingon also recommended maintaining a distance between their grouping and the local NKVDs in the US and Mexico. Instead, they would use NKVD agents operating under "non-official cover"—"illegals," as the Soviets knew them.

They estimated that they would need $300,000 to set up, equip, and establish cover for their operations in the New World. To present their options, they arranged a meeting with Beria in which they emphasized that they had nobody in Trotsky's entourage capable of carrying out the assassination, so they would probably have to storm his residence.

Beria suggested employing Orlov, who was now in America. Eitingon objected, pointing out not only that they hadn't gotten on very well together in Spain, but that the defector was likely to interpret an overture from the NKVD as a prelude to an assassination attempt. Next, Beria dragged up other personal connections. "He had a string of Georgian princes in the West who fed him rumors about unbelievable treasures in remote hiding places in the Caucasus." Beria also mentioned two of his wife's exiled uncles—one a Bolshevik and one who had served in Georgia's Menshevik government.

But even as he spoke, Beria realized that he needed a network that wasn't vulnerable to betrayal. He approved Eitingon and Sudoplatov's proposals and told them not to worry about money. By early August, Stalin had also signed off on the plan.

Trotsky's death drew closer.

# 20

# So Funny

Early in 1939 Sylvia wrote a letter to her sister Ruth. *I am living a fairy tale,* she said.

Ramón continued to be an evasive, vague, affectionate puzzle in her life. The fantasy was maintained by his skill at deception and by her unwillingness, or inability, to interrogate the strange lacunae and contradictions in the picture he had painted of his life. When she asked about being introduced to his family, he told her that neither parent would consider her a suitable daughter-in-law. She wanted to believe in him, so she did.

What did begin to change, however, was his interest in politics, in particular in the Spanish Civil War. By now Sylvia had told him that she was a Trotskyist, though she had said little, if anything, of her connections to the movement's leader. After a lengthy conversation about Marxism, he started to engage with political ideas, albeit only gradually.

Ageloff did not introduce him to any "important" member of the Fourth International, nor did she invite him to any of the party's private conferences, but they did attend several public conferences. Most significantly, although Sylvia was not a formal delegate at the founding conference of the Fourth International in September 1938, she was at some sessions as an interpreter.

The conference itself was held at the home of the French stalwart Alfred Rosmer in Périgny, just outside Paris. At the forefront of the minds of everyone attending was another tragedy that had befallen the movement. In August, the headless body of Trotsky's former secretary and translator, the German Rudolf Klement, washed up on the banks of the Seine; he had been the designated secretary of the Fourth International.

He was a "self-effacing, studious and hard-working young German refugee, tall, thin, and stooping, with a pale face and sharp eyes"; he had embraced the grueling nature of life in exile—the lack of money, the fact that his papers were never in order—without complaint. One morning in July he had been kidnapped from his room in Paris. His breakfast was found untouched on a table. This event coincided with Ramón disappearing briefly from Sylvia's life, on a visit, he said, to his family in Brussels. A little afterward, Trotsky received a strained, tremulous letter "from" Klement. In it, the German broke with Trotsky, claiming that his final disillusionment had come when he learned that Trotsky was in negotiations with Hitler.

Nobody fell for what was clearly a clumsy NKVD ruse, and the death set off a fresh round of suspicion and accusations among the French Trotskyists. Nevertheless the conference went ahead. Sedov, Klement, and Erwin Wolf were posthumously elected honorary presidents and the event was presided over by Max Shachtman, who had been furnished with documents designed to guide the conference by Trotsky. Sitting in Coyoacán, almost six thousand miles away, Trotsky impatiently waited for results.

Huge efforts were expended to guarantee safety and security for the twenty-one delegates from eleven nations who attended. The venue was changed at the last minute by Pierre Naville to protect it from the NKVD; only one plenary session was held over the course of a single day; and it was agreed that afterward to ensure "deepest secrecy," the delegates would issue a communiqué talking about the "congress held at Lausanne."

These efforts were in vain. It was not just that in the lead-up to the conference a great deal of significant documents, including reports of Trotskyist work in other countries and the draft of the Fourth International's statues, vanished.

Etienne was elected to the International Secretariat and to the Executive Committee as the representative of the Russian section. (There were no members who actually lived in Russia; they had all been exterminated.) Reporting to his handlers in Moscow, Etienne gave details of a special commission that had been set up "to combat the police and the GPU," as well as lists of attendees and resolutions passed—which included a call to try to infiltrate Trotskyists into various mass organizations.

Ramón came too. Mostly he lurked aimlessly outside the conference room, doing his best to suggest that he had no interest at all about what was happening on the other side of the door. But casually, careful not to draw too much attention to himself, he introduced himself to prominent Trotskyists, such as the American James Cannon; without any fanfare, almost without anyone noticing, he was edging closer toward the man at the movement's center.

In February 1939, Sylvia returned to New York to see her family. Before she left, she confided to her friend Maria her doubts about what would happen if her boyfriend were to follow her there: "I can't easily imagine him with me in New York. What will my family and friends think of him? He is not from our background, is not interested in politics. . . . I don't know how he will adapt, and, for my part, I am not sure that his company will be so pleasing to me in the context of my own city. But, we will see." Perhaps aware of these anxieties, Ramón wrote to her from time to time; it was important that she continued to believe that his feelings for her were as strong as ever.

Ramón's accounts of his life in Paris gave her the impression that his days were empty. He had no job, even if he had enough money to live on. His time was spent in cinemas or strolling around parks.

In truth, Sylvia's absence freed Ramón. He could see his mother, who in her mid-forties remained a vivid presence—speaking rapidly with a slight Catalan accent, lighting a cigarette from the stub of the one she had just finished. He also saw his brother Luis and Elena Imbert, although they did not stay for long: Elena, who was suffering from tuberculosis, and his brother were sent to Moscow, where it was thought they'd be safe in the event of another war.

It also meant that when Eitingon and Sudoplatov—bearing false papers provided by George Miller, the Austrian head of the NKVD's forged passport office—arrived in Paris in June 1939, Ramón was free to see them. The pair had traveled from Moscow to Odessa, then taken a ship to Athens, where they changed identities and got on another ship for Marseille. From there they took the train to the French capital.

They had devised a plan that involved two discrete groups that would each be kept unaware of the other's existence. The first, MOTHER, comprised Caridad (KLAVA/CLAUDIA) and Ramón (RAYMOND).

The most significant figure in the second group, HORSE, was the painter David Alfaro Siqueiros (KONE), who had traveled to Paris to meet with Eitingon and Sudoplatov. The pale-skinned Siqueiros had a shock of curly hair that he swept dramatically from his forehead and gray-green eyes that stared violently into any camera pointed in his direction. He had been variously a mine union organizer, a senior figure with the Mexican Communist Party, and a delegate to various conferences, and he had led Mexican volunteers in the Spanish Civil War, during which he was known as "the little colonel." This restlessness meant that he had spent most of the last decade moving around constantly: Buenos Aires, Moscow, New York, Los Angeles, Madrid, and several prisons.*

Siqueiros possessed gigantic levels of energy and "sparkling theories [fizzed] out of him like bubbles out of newly opened champagne," but he was also fickle, undisciplined, and prone to abandoning his murals in favor of following a lightning impulse to rush off to organize workers in remote mining districts or to recruit new members for a revolutionary cell in the provinces.

He was a sometime friend, sometime ally, more often rival of Rivera's (Kahlo called him "that damned Siqueiros") whose work was striking and unconventional—he favored using implements like a spray gun that he felt were "untainted by traditional artistic preciousness"—but also heavily political.

When the NKVD first made contact, Siqueiros had been working hard—his eyes red, his hands always covered in paint—on a giant mural on the staircase of the Mexican Electricians Union building. The painting, titled *Portrait of the Bourgeoisie*, showed capitalist monsters with diabolical machines, soldiers wearing gas masks and their tortured victims, and crows marching blindly to war while a parrot screeches into a microphone. Siquieros unhesitatingly abandoned the project to focus on his new task. Other hands would finish the job.

There was also a third group of assassins led by "one of the most remarkable of all Soviet illegals." Josifas Romualdovičius Grigulevičius—aka Pedro and Padre, MAKS and FELIPE—was known within the Illegals Directorate of the NKVD as Iosif Romualdovich Grigulevich and to his friends as Grig.

Grigulevich was cosmopolitan (he spoke Spanish, Portuguese, German, English, and Russian), louche, and so good at assuming false

* Siqueiros had met Caridad on her visit to Mexico in 1936, and she introduced him to her son when he came to Spain the following year. Laura, Ramón Mercader's daughter, had in her apartment a lithograph by David Alfaro Siqueiros signed by the artist with the following dedication: "To Ramón, our Ramón, with my eternal friendship, the love of families and the memories of Spain."

identities that a decade later this Lithuanian Jew could pass himself off as a Costa Rican diplomat serving as the country's ambassador to both Italy and Yugoslavia.*

Another agent who was attached to the AST, he had started out liquidating Lithuanian police informers and then made his name in Spain, under the alias of José Ocampo, leading NKVD operations against suspected Trotskyists. It was this work that recommended him to Beria and ensured that he wasn't caught in the Terror's meat grinder.

Grigulevich acted as a cutout, coordinating, from his base in New Mexico (Zook's Drugstore in Santa Fe†), with the Siqueiros group so that Eitingon could stay at one remove from the operation. Once he was satisfied that everything was as ready as it could be, he would enter the country posing as a French citizen.

The conversations with the two groups reassured Sudoplatov that the operatives Eitingon and he had chosen were reliable and had experience of "high-risk" military operations. But he also suggested that Eitingon devote a month to training Ramón and his mother in tradecraft: the basic skills of how to spot surveillance, how to change their appearance, how to work sources, how to recruit new agents.

Alongside all this, Ramón made a curious attempt to contact Frida Kahlo.

The painter remembered how:

> In Paris I had met Mornard . . . and he went around insinuating to me that I should take him to Trotsky's house. "Not me, because I am quarreling with the old Trotsky," I told him. "I only ask you, please, to find me a house near there." "Well look for yourself, because I am too sick to look for houses for anyone,

---

* He was ordered to organize the assassination of Yugoslavia's leader, Josip Tito, a plan that was abandoned only when Stalin died.

† Currently a Häagen-Dazs ice-cream store.

and I cannot give you lodging in my house, nor can I introduce you to Trotsky, I never will introduce him to you."

Ramón himself relayed a version of this to Sylvia's friend Maria Craipeau. He was so animated as he did so that at one point he laughed until he cried. "I'm going to tell you something so funny. Really I have never been in my life so ridiculed. Listen: I learned about the arrival in Paris of Frida Kahlo, the wife of Diego Rivera. I bought an enormous bouquet and went in search of her."

He told Craipeau that he then followed Kahlo from place to place, still carrying his massive collection of flowers, before finally catching up with her at an exhibition opening.

Kahlo rejected both his flowers and his requests. Ramón's response to this was to walk into the street and offer the bouquet to the first woman he encountered; she fled in terror, leaving the flowers in the gutter.

"Can you see me, holding the bouquet?" he asked Maria, suddenly puzzled that she didn't share his amusement. "But why aren't you laughing?"

Craipeau, who knew that the Trotskys were staying at Kahlo's house in Mexico and was troubled by an element of the story that she couldn't quite understand, asked him why he had gone to such efforts to meet the Mexican painter when she meant nothing to him. He immediately stopped laughing and said, "It would have amused me to meet her," then left the room.

Beyond this, he limited his activities to paying occasional visits to French Trotskyists. He gave them money but appeared diffident and incurious about what they might do with it. In parallel, he began to prepare to travel to the United States. He told Sylvia that the main obstacle to him being able to join her was obtaining a US visa: the Belgian authorities would not let him go because he'd absconded from his military service.

---

THE PROBLEM WITH creating Jacques Mornard, the fictional son of Belgian diplomats, was that fictional sons of Belgian diplomats did not have the sorts of documents needed to travel to the United States.

Luckily, this was an area in which the Russian intelligence services excelled.

They had established a number of clandestine passport factories called *pass apparat* across Europe. These were staffed by skilled forgers who were known as "cobblers" because they employed the sorts of stitching, dyes, and eyelet machines normally used to repair shoes.

The drawback with these forged passports was that no matter how good they were, they could always be detected by reference to passport serial numbers held by the country of origin.

It was possible to obtain a passport by subterfuge, such as by getting a photostat copy of the birth certificate of a baby who had died in infancy but would have been of a similar age to the applicant. All that was then needed were two witnesses to swear notarized oaths that they had known the applicant for five years.

Theft was the other option. Soviet *rezidenturas* all had standing instructions to do what they could (fraud, bribery of officials from passport offices) to secure the real thing.

American passports were the most highly prized. They possessed prestige that generally prompted European police to treat their holders with respect, and the United States' status as a nation of so many immigrants meant that fewer questions would have been asked if somebody didn't speak perfect English.

The flood of idealistic volunteers who joined the International Brigades during the Spanish Civil War provided the NKVD with an unparalleled opportunity. They confiscated volunteers' passports on their arrival in Spain and almost never returned them. When a man was discharged, he would often be told that, sadly, his documents had been lost.

Instead, almost every diplomatic pouch that traveled from Spain to the Lubyanka contained another batch of passports. As soon as it was confirmed passport holders had been killed, the NKVD looked into their family histories. Once they were satisfied, it was straightforward to adapt the documents to their new bearers.

The solution to the Mercader problem came in the shape of a man called Tony Babich. Born on 13 June 1905 in Lovinac (which in 1939 was in the Kingdom of Yugoslavia and is now in Croatia), he had acquired Canadian nationality by naturalization in 1929 before applying for a passport in 1937, claiming that he wanted to visit his country of origin.

Instead, he traveled to Spain. At some point before May 1939, he was killed,* and his passport, number 31377, fell into the hands of the NKVD. Once the necessary adaptions had been made, Frank Jacson, a Canadian mining engineer, was ready to cross the Atlantic.

Ramón had carried on seeing Maria in Sylvia's absence. They'd meet once a week, he'd take her to dinner, and they usually ended up at the cinema, where they laughed uproariously at Marx Brothers movies. Then, suddenly, he approached her with an idea. "That's it, I've got the papers," he told her. "I'm leaving. Listen, I would like to make you a proposition. Please believe that I am doing this in a completely fraternal spirit. I've got a fair bit of money and I know you've always wanted to travel to the USA. Come with me, I'll pay for your journey."

Maria said nothing. What was strange, she thought, was that not only did Ramón seem to understand immediately that she absolutely did not want to come, but that he seemed relieved by her refusal. Quickly, he moved on to talking about other matters.

Ramón set off from Le Havre in August 1939. As he left Paris, he had hugged his French friends. "If only you knew what I'm about to do!" he told them. Caridad left the same port on a different ship a little later. Their timing was fortunate: had their departures been de-

* His death certificate is dated 12 May 1939.

layed by only a few days, they might have found it considerably more difficult to leave.

Eitingon had no such luck. The extra time he spent training his agents meant that his fake Polish passport was no longer valid. The declaration of war after Adolf Hitler had launched a massive surprise invasion of Poland two days previously, the beginning of World War II, on 3 September 1939, led immediately to tight restrictions on foreign travel for Poles. He was left with three options: mobilization into the French army, internment, or somehow obtaining a new identity.

While Eitingon went into hiding in a mental hospital run by a Russian émigré, Sudoplatov returned to Moscow, cursing himself for the delay they'd incurred and having ordered the Paris *rezident*, Lev Vasilevsky, who operated as consul general under the alias of Tarasov, to do everything he could to provide Eitingon with new travel documents.

A month later, Vasilevsky conjured up a forged internal passport identifying Eitingon as a Syrian Jew suffering from a mental illness. This had the virtue of establishing that he was clearly unfit for military service and that he had the right to residency, which could be used to obtain a passport.

The French officials had been bribed, so leaving the country wasn't an issue, but getting into the US was. The only connection they had was with a "respectable" Swiss businessman who was in fact an NKVD illegal, Maksim Steinberg. This presented a further problem. In 1938 Steinberg had refused to return to Moscow when recalled. Instead, he wrote a letter pledging his loyalty but noting his fear of being unjustly purged.

Vasilevsky sent a case officer to Lausanne. After a tense meeting in which Steinberg made it abundantly clear he was willing to shoot his visitor if he turned out to be an assassin, Steinberg agreed to help.

A week later, the visa arrived. Eitingon was free to cross the ocean, and Trotsky had less than a year to live.

# 21

# Pictures and Everything

Frank Jacson passed through Ellis Island on 9 September 1939, disembarking from the SS *Île de France*, which had left from Southampton. Immigration records registered him as a thirty-four-year-old, unmarried mechanical engineer who could speak and write English and who carried British nationality. He was five foot seven, with brown hair and eyes and a fair complexion. Reassuringly there was no record of his ever having been a criminal or an anarchist. He had paid for his own passage, and he possessed a ticket for an onward destination and approximately $50 in cash. The passenger had previously been in Mexico for the purpose of "recuperating from an accident."

The official also noted some additional information. Jacson, who was Serbian and had been born in "Lovinak, Jugoslavia," was traveling under an "executive order," which indicated that he had been cleared on the order of the Immigration Services, Washington, DC.

He gave as his home an address—1269 St. Denis Street, Montreal—that did not, and had never, existed, and he said he would be staying at 50 Livingston Street, Brooklyn, while in the city. He gave Sylvia Ageloff and the American Express Company (indicating that he possessed a "letter of credit there") as his references, along with a number of Mexico City residents—including Evelyn Reed and H. A. Schultz.

Once Ramón had cleared immigration, he made his way to the apartment on 601 West One Hundred Tenth Street Sylvia shared with her sisters, Hilda and Sophie. He waited there for her to return from work. So much about him had been unexpected. This unannounced arrival was just one more surprise.

He told Sylvia that he'd used money his mother had given him in Brussels to obtain his passport from a group of people who sold fake documents to those who wanted to flee from Europe; he didn't want to be conscripted into the Belgian army and fight. The passport had cost between eight thousand and ten thousand francs. This was the only time Sylvia saw the document identifying him as Frank Jacson.

As she had with everything before, Sylvia took this new development in stride. It sounded as plausible as everything else Ramón had told her before, and at least she could carry on calling him Jac without fear of slipping up and exposing his fraud. Hilda said that she had known about Ramón, because Sylvia and he wrote to each other constantly; she understood that they were "very good friends." Not long after he had materialized at their front door, he quit his hotel and moved into the apartment. Hilda also said that she and others continued to believe that the relationship was platonic.*

In the days that followed, he met more members of the family, including her brother Allan (who worked in the real estate office run by their father, Samuel, and brother Monte). Allan later recalled that he had encountered Ramón several times and thought him a "thorough gentleman." Sylvia's family appeared as uninterested as she was in asking him any question that might make him uncomfortable, even though they all knew that he was there illegally. Instead, "they took him at face value making no inquiries into his past." The whole family was "completely fooled."

---

* The couple told a different story to people outside the family. One FBI informant said that he'd spoken to a man called Thomas who had been in the Abraham Lincoln Battalion and had been introduced to Ramón by Sylvia. Thomas had planned to "make a play for her," but had dropped the idea once he found out she was with Ramón.

Hilda thought that the man who was now living under the same roof as them must have been wealthy because he was always in restaurants and theaters, and yet at the same time, it seemed that he had no job: he was free all day long and never spoke about a job or business. And Hilda, who was "personally" in charge of the mail, said that at no point did he ever receive any letter.

Sylvia suspected that Ramón had an undisclosed method for correspondence. On one occasion she saw among his effects a card bearing a flowing signature, "from Minni"; the card had been sent from Brussels through the Paris American Express office. There was also a compartment with a lock inside one of his suitcases. She believed that he used this to hide letters. Ramón said that he neither received nor sent any mail at any point in his time in the United States.

It is not clear whether Hilda was aware that Ramón had given Sylvia $3,000, which she kept in her bank account and would later return to him. It had been given to him, he said, by his mother in order to cover his travel expenses in the New World, once he had told her that "nothing could prevent him from going to the United States."

While in New York, he made further financial provisions. On 5 October he purchased a letter of credit worth $2,500 from American Express, using his Canadian passport to make withdrawals. He also obtained American Railway travelers' checks in the value of $1,000.

He and Sylvia moved into an apartment owned by a Trotskyist friend in Greenwich Village. During the day, while Sylvia worked, he went to the cinema or to parks. The only person she was aware of him meeting was a Costa Rican diplomat whom he said he had met on the boat. They went to the New York World's Fair together.

Ramón said that his false passport precluded him from attending any event of a political nature, and he continued to display limited interest in politics, although he occasionally showed an "eccentric human sympathy" toward Trotsky.

The couple, when they appeared in public, mostly went to a film or a show or a good restaurant. Sylvia had the curious impression that

Ramón had been to the city before. On one boat trip, he showed off, "telling everybody what was lower Manhattan, and so forth."

Sylvia asked, "How could you tell them, how did you know?" He replied, airily, that he had been so interested before he had left Europe that he "studied pictures and everything." Sylvia was not convinced. "I knew right away that he knew New York," she later told a friend, "despite what he said."

SYLVIA AND HER friends and family were not the only people Ramón saw in New York. He met with the NKVD *rezident*—the clever, cultured Gaik Ovakimian (known by the FBI as "the wily Armenian"), who had by 1939 become chief of scientific intelligence in the United States and was one of the Soviet Union's most effective spies. Ovakimian took receipt of instructions from Moscow Center, which he passed on to Ramón.

There was also his mother. Caridad was enthralled by the capitalist metropolis in which she had arrived. She loved the elegance of the shops on Fifth Avenue. Ramón shared this passion, telling Luis: "Don't believe what the propaganda says. New York is the most beautiful and electrifying city in the world." (Caridad, however, had reservations: "She didn't like the way they spoke English, the way they behaved. She found them rude, crude, very rustic." Caridad believed that Americans' scientific and artistic achievements were entirely due to the importation of Europeans. She also believed their houses were built shoddily.)

In October, Eitingon arrived in the city and opened an export-import company as cover for the communication hub he was establishing. This marked a shift in gravity for the operation. The New World, not Europe, was now the center of operations.

As he had in Paris, Ramón ensured that Sylvia was kept completely separate from these other elements of his life. There was a single exception to this. One night, as the two of them ate dinner in a restaurant, Eitingon sat watching at a table nearby. There is no explanation as to why he arranged this piece of voyeurism; perhaps he simply wanted to see his dupe in the flesh.

WITHIN DAYS OF Eitingon's arrival, Ramón announced that he was leaving New York for Mexico City and offered Sylvia a new set of fabrications.

He told her, without showing any proof, that he had obtained a job working for the head of the Allied Purchasing Company, a man called Peter Lubeck, an exporter-importer who had fled Belgium before the outbreak of war. He claimed that Lubeck was wealthy and important and that his business consisted of buying important commercial assets such as oil, copper, sugar, and iron for England and its allies. He was vague about where the operation was based, suggesting without sounding too confident that it might have offices in San Francisco, Los Angeles, and Mexico City.

Ramón explained that his mother had arranged the job through her connections and that he was to be employed in a "general capacity." He also indicated that his stay in Mexico would only be temporary—his firm was going to set him up in New York as its representative.

The Ageloffs, still enchanted by him, came as a group to wave his train off.

# Part Five

Leon Trotsky and Natalia Sedova

# 22

# *SÍ, NO, GRACIAS*

One day in September 1939, Bartomeu Costa-Amic was walking down a street in the center of Mexico City when he suddenly found himself caught in the middle of a demonstration—Mexican Stalinists were agitating against the presence of Trotsky in the country. Costa-Amic was a Catalonian journalist in exile and a former member of POUM. Three years previously, he had been sent by its leader, Andres Nin, to lobby the Spanish president to allow Trotsky asylum.

The protest itself was not unusual. In recent months they had become more and more frequent. What was strange, though, was the tall woman with a hard look on her face and a cigarette between her fingers who was clearly trying to avoid drawing attention to herself by remaining behind the front rank of protestors.

Costa-Amic recognized Caridad Mercader immediately: he had known her since the first days of the Spanish Civil War when, nominally at least, they were on the same side. Things were different now. He rushed over to confront her, raising his voice and pointing at her with his right forefinger raised as if to skewer her: "You bitch, you're in Mexico to prepare the Trotsky assassination!" Her only response was a loud laugh.

---

CARIDAD WAS THE first of the killers to arrive in the country. Her priority was assembling, discreetly, an arsenal of weapons for the assault planned on Trotsky's compound by buying guns from different shops.

A couple of weeks later, she was joined by Ramón. He had crossed into Mexico at Nuevo Laredo on 12 October 1939, carrying with him a large trunk and several suitcases filled with clothing, which included dinner clothes, two suits, a pair of riding breeches, a pair of slacks, twelve shirts, two silk scarves, hunting boots, spurs, two overcoats, multiple pairs of pajamas, and a cane.

Ramón was granted a tourist permit for five months, though he had presented himself as an exporter of oils and various raw materials, which justified frequent travel. He said he was supposed to be opening an import-export office for his employer, Peter Lubeck. In order to prove that he had the resources to support himself, he attached the application for a credit card from the American Express Company, number 41789.

He checked into the Hotel Guardiola and almost immediately bought a car, a Ford. Not long afterward, he returned to the same dealer saying he wanted to exchange it for a 1937 Buick. The Ford, he said, didn't suit him.

He wrote to Sylvia, telling her that he was still waiting for his boss, but that he looked forward to her joining him. She replied that she needed to give notice at work.

In the meantime, he contacted the men whom he had met during his time as a saboteur in Spain and who had traveled to Mexico under the guise of refugees from the Civil War. This included Vittorio Codovilla, who came fresh from liquidating Trotskyists in Calabria; Carlos Contreras, a specialist in executions; Pedro Cheka, whose surname spoke for itself; and of course Eitingon, who stashed his documents and cash at the apartment of Marta Meller, a Spanish émigré, and otherwise avoided appearing in the open. Very few of the Stalinists in Mexico even knew he was in the country. He would take a distant supervisory role, with Grigulevich and Siqueiros handling the majority of the day-to-day planning and administration.

They were also joined by Lev Vasilevsky, the man who had played such an important role in obtaining Eitingon's passport in Paris. He would be appointed first secretary of the USSR consulate in Mexico.

Once Grigulevich arrived (he was soon seen driving a "luxurious, dark colored car"), he moved quickly to expand his team, bringing in Siqueiros's former pupil, Antonio Pujol Jimenez (JOSE), to act as second-in-command for the assault. Also involved were the Mexican communist Laura Araujo Aguilar (LUISA), who would later marry Grigulevich; Luis Arenal, another painter; and his brother, Leopoldo.

They could draw on the wealth of information they possessed about the layout of the house and the organization of its defenses. This was supplemented in April when they managed to place an agent among Trotsky's guards.

In parallel, the raiders established how the police assigned to the Avenida Viena operated. Pujol arranged for two young communists, Julia Barradas Hernández and Ana Chávez López (the ex-wife and the girlfriend, respectively, of two of the attackers*), to rent opposite Trotsky's compound an apartment that could be used to conduct reconnaissance and entertain the police officers and seduce at least one. Slowly, remorselessly, the operation was gaining momentum.

But until Sylvia arrived, there was only a limited amount Ramón could do. He familiarized himself with the city, specifically the area around Trotsky's home on the Avenida Viena.

In order to maintain his cover story, Ramón carefully managed his use of Spanish. On his arrival he restricted himself to using the sorts of words anyone might have picked up from movies: *"mañana"* or *"ay ay ay."* But he let it be known that he was studying the language, which

* One of whom had a daughter called Sovietita.

he claimed reminded him of Italian. By the time Sylvia, who knew only that he spoke French and English, arrived a few months later, she saw him reading Mexican newspapers and appearing to understand them perfectly.

Antonio Arguimbau Parrfest, a waiter at the Hotel Montejo, where the couple would stay the following summer of 1940, served them breakfast in their room; he usually found them lying in bed together. He said that occasionally Ramón answered in simple phrases in Spanish like "*sí, no, gracias*" when he was asked about meals. What the waiter found weird was that Ramón could read and comprehend the menu, which was completely in Spanish.

Jean van Heijenoort noted that although Ramón claimed to be Belgian, the court records show that "his French was sprinkled with Hispanicisms."

Ramón also began mountain climbing. He made friends with Mr. Patino, an employee of Pan American Airways in New York. Ramón told Patino that he was a Canadian mining engineer with $5,000 deposited in a local bank account and that he had flown on private planes to mining missions in Central and South America.

He misrepresented his climbing experience, boasting that he had scaled Mont Blanc. In November Patino organized an excursion up Popocatépetl. Ramón had all the equipment he needed, but he got tired halfway to the top and remained at a way station.

Occasionally, Ramón broke out of character. Patino remembered how on the outbreak of the Russo-Finnish War, Ramón had dismissed the Finns and said in the boldest of terms that one day the USSR would rule the whole world.

# 23

## *Muerte a Trotsky*

Most evenings after their move to the Avenida Viena, Trotsky and Natalia went into the garden of their little fortress and sat on a wooden bench to watch the Mexican night fall. Sometimes they exchanged a word or two. More often, they were silent.

Trotsky's existence had shrunk further: compressed into the walls of his citadel. Threats to his life continued to mount. The previous year, the defector Orlov, calling himself Stein, had written to Trotsky, warning him that he was in danger and that the threat lurked in Lev's entourage in Paris. Stein identified a man called "Mark." Trotsky, who knew Zborowski only as "Etienne," ignored the attempt to alert him. Stein was insistent and telephoned from San Francisco. Trotsky refused to take the call. As far as he was concerned, it was just more NKVD mischief. He had more important things to worry about.

When Etienne was told of accusations made against him in the Orlov letter, one witness reports him giving "a hearty laugh." But he did not travel to Mexico after Lev's death—he knew he had come too close to being compromised.

Then there was the reality that shaded every second of Trotsky's and Natalia's lives. Trotsky knew he would be killed. He even predicted that the NKVD would time its attack on him to coincide with a dramatic phase of the Second World War in order to avoid attracting too much attention. Natalia shared this conviction. She said that ever since the first of the Moscow show trials, they had been "waiting, with sure inner knowledge, for the assassins."

In the last few months, the outings into the desert that had offered Trotsky such a welcome release had begun to seem more and more freighted with risk and were abandoned. He rarely left the house now except to go to the dentist or make even more uncommon trips to the mountains.

When traveling through the city's streets, he held a handkerchief around the lower part of his face in an attempt at disguise. This only sometimes worked and passersby excitedly recognized him and called out, "Trotsky! Trotsky!"

His only real exercise, apart from pacing around the yard, was the "melancholy chores" of planting exotic cacti in the courtyard and raising chickens and black-and-white rabbits that looked like pandas. He scrubbed their coops and hutches, inspected the animals for any signs of illness or parasites, and fed them "according to the most scientific formula he could obtain," grinding his own grain and carefully calculating exactly how much was needed to keep his rabbits healthy. It was an unexpected echo of his early life on his family's farm. Even when his health was poor and the commitment became a strain, "he could not give it up," said Natalia, "for he pitied the little animals."

Visitors from their past only confirmed how remote from it they were, how unrecoverable it was.

The arrival of Alfred and Marguerite Rosmer—who brought with them Trotsky's grandson Seva in August 1939—was a relief. Alfred Rosmer, whose face reminded Victor Serge of a "Gothic and harmonious sculpture," had been friends with Trotsky since before the Great War, then for a time "became his constant companion, in the Kremlin and in his armored train." In Prinkipo he had helped Trotsky's attempts to build international opposition against Stalin, but then in 1930, Rosmer had backed the wrong faction in an internal Trotskyist dispute and their friendship had been frozen. They had not spoken at any point during Trotsky's stay in France.

Now all was forgiven. Rosmer and his wife, Marguerite, who was short and squat with "a massive head and neck," were greeted warmly. They moved into the house and took all of their meals with the Trotskys. There were gatherings in which files were organized and old documents reviewed. As the two men worked, they talked, reminiscing with an intimacy that Trotsky could share with only a tiny number of those still living.

Trotsky was grappling with uncomfortable thoughts about the causes he had dedicated his life to. The working class had not been able to stop Hitler, Mussolini, Franco, or two world wars. Was this a fault of its leadership, or was the proletariat incapable of ruling and transforming society? If it were a question of blaming the leadership, then one could simply create new Marxist parties. But if the fault lay with the working class, then Trotsky had to contemplate the idea that the Marxist conception of capitalist society and socialism was wrong.

Russia was the only place in the world where workers had overthrown capitalism, and look at how it had degenerated. What if the proletariat in the West seized power before having to cede it to a privileged bureaucracy, as Trotsky had witnessed in the Soviet Union?

All his adult life, he had believed that the adamantine laws of science and history would lead unrelentingly to the establishment of socialism; now he was forced to consider the idea that a totalitarian bureaucratic system like that ruled by Stalin might, in fact, be "historically necessary." It was almost but not quite enough to shake his faith. While he still had this, there was no question of giving up. "Life is not an easy matter," he had once said. "You cannot live through it without falling into prostration and cynicism unless you have before you a great idea which raises you above personal misery, above weaknesses, above all kinds of perfidy and baseness." Perhaps he would not live to see the next revolution—a melancholy thought—but he was as sure as ever that it would come.

---

TROTSKY'S POOR HEALTH also played on his mind. Would his body give up before Stalin could get to him?

It was in this gloomy, fatalistic frame of mind that on 27 February 1940, not long after a checkup from his family physician, Dr. Zollinger, he started writing a longhand draft of his testament.

"My high (and still rising) blood pressure is deceiving those near me about my actual condition," it began. "I am active and able to work but the outcome is evidently near. These lines will be made public after my death."

Whatever his anxieties about his physical decline, it was a document full of fine words, defiance, and surprising tenderness.

> For forty-three years of my conscious life I have remained a revolutionist; for forty-two of them I have fought under the banner of Marxism. If I had to begin all over again I would of course try to avoid this or that mistake, but the main course of my life would remain unchanged. I shall die a proletarian revolutionist, a Marxist, a dialectical materialist, and, consequently, an irreconcilable atheist. My faith in the communist future of mankind is not less ardent, indeed it is firmer today, than it was in the days of my youth.
>
> Natasha has just come up to the window from the courtyard and opened it wider so that the air may enter more freely into my room. I can see the bright green strip of grass beneath the wall, and the clear blue sky above the wall, and sunlight everywhere. Life is beautiful. Let the future generations cleanse it of all evil, oppression and violence, and enjoy it to the full.

On 3 March he added that the progress of his illness probably meant

> that the end must come suddenly, most likely—again, this is my personal hypothesis—through a brain hemorrhage. This is the best possible end I can wish for. It is possible, however, that I am mistaken (I have no desire to read special books on this subject and the physicians naturally will not tell the truth). . . . [But if faced] with a long-drawn-out invalidism . . . then I reserve the right to determine for myself the time of my death. The "suicide" (if such a term is appropriate in this connection) will not in any respect be an expression of an outburst of despair or hopelessness. Natasha and I said more than once that one may arrive at such a physical condition that it would be better to cut short one's own life or, more correctly, the too slow process of dying. . . . But whatever may be the circumstances of my death, I shall die with unshaken faith in the communist future. This faith in man and in his future gives me even now such power of resistance as cannot be given by any religion.

Trotsky returned with new force to his work on the biography of Stalin, articles for the *Bulletin*, and various sallies against critics within the Socialist Workers Party. All of this boosted his morale. He started attacking his correspondence with vigor and his entourage stopped worrying about his mental condition. Trotsky began to say that his high blood pressure had actually given him a "surge of spiritual energy."

RAMÓN CONTINUED TO send loving letters and telegrams to Sylvia. Some of them, according to Hilda, were written "in a foreign handwriting" alien to the Americas.

Keen to join her lover, she obtained a doctor's note certifying that she had sinusitis, which required recuperation somewhere warm. On New Year's Day 1940, Sylvia flew into Mexico City, having obtained a leave of absence from her job as a social investigator at the New York

City Department of Welfare, where she had worked since May of the previous year. (Her colleagues all spoke highly of her but noted that she was out sick quite frequently.) "I was going anyway," she said, "and was anxious to see him."

As soon as she was settled, she wrote to her sister Hilda, explaining that she did not need any money because Ramón earned $15,000 per year. He was taking care of her now (although her father continued to send her small sums).

The couple lived first in the María Cristina Hotel, then in an apartment on Calle Humboldt. Sylvia noticed that her partner had acquired a mountaineering ax since she had last seen him. She thought nothing of it.* She also heard him speak Spanish for the first time: he told her he'd learned some while they'd been separated.

They led the same free-spending existence as they had in Paris, and Ramón remained disappointingly uncommitted to the cause that was so important to her. "When I was in Mexico from January to March," she said, "he showed a little more interest in politics as a concession to me, but nothing that would give a clue to his feelings." (When they attended a rally at the city's Palacio de Bellas Artes addressed by leading Stalinists such as the American James Ford, Sylvia wanted to interrupt and was dissuaded only when Ramón warned her that they were surrounded by a crowd of people who saw her as a political enemy.)

But what was strange was that for perhaps the first time since they had met, he was busy. His work at Peter Lubeck's firm had activated something in him. The man who had been so listless and vacant in Europe and New York was now enthusiastically quoting the prices of copra, sugar, and oil to her; explaining the difficulties he encountered with Mexican labor; and complaining about the slowness of shipping. This, as much as anything else, convinced her that he was bona fide.

---

* It was clearly new, and he kept it in a box. Its handle had not, at this stage, been shortened.

---

Although, just as in Paris, Ramón seemed to have few, if any, contacts in Mexico City, Sylvia had a network of Trotskyists she could quickly get in touch with.

In Mexico Sylvia met again with Otto Schüssler and Gertrude Schrotter, whom she had first encountered in 1938. They visited the flat she shared with Ramón and were introduced to him. He made a point of asserting that he had "no interest nor relationship to any political groups or parties" and left the others to talk about several political topics and issues regarding "The Organization" in another room. (At the same time, he, along with Sylvia, also let it be known that he had donated money to the Fourth International while they were in the USA.)

Three weeks later they all ran into one another at a picnic in the city of Toluca. This was the beginning of a sort-of friendship,* with the couples meeting up several times over the next few months.

Ramón cheerfully talked about his life. Sylvia, by contrast, was more cautious, stating only that she worked "in an office." She was similarly cagey about her family.

At some point Sylvia made herself known to Trotsky's household, and she was greeted warmly. Trotsky and his entourage retained fond memories of her sisters and were grateful for the messages she brought from comrades in New York. Natalia in particular seemed to go out of her way to be kind to Sylvia, asking solicitous questions.

Then there was a stroke of luck. Fanny Yanovich, Trotsky's secretary, fell ill and was forced to stay in bed at home. Sylvia knew French, Spanish, and Russian—which was good news for Trotsky, who used

* Questioned later, Schüssler was adamant that despite his and Schrotter's close relationship with Ageloff and Ramón, he didn't consider them his friends.

to moan that the lack of a Russian-speaking secretary left him "paralyzed at work"—so she was called in to help transcribe notes that Trotsky had spoken into a Dictaphone.

Ramón now had a reason to make repeated visits to the house. For the moment, his mission remained limited: he was there to find out about Trotsky's habits and daily life and his relationships with his followers as well as about the security system, the guard roster, and the arrangements of phone lines, power cables, and alarms.

His brilliant memory allowed him to retain pictures of the house, patio, walls, and guard towers; where each member of the household slept; where the police were stationed and what routes they patrolled. But he was careful not to seem too interested. He never tried to interrogate Sylvia about her experiences inside the house on the Avenida Viena, except once, when he asked whether Trotsky liked having picnics outside of his house. No, she said, he never left home.

Ramón dropped her off by car on the days she visited the compound, and then he waited, patiently, at the great metallic gate for her to come back out. He did not seem to mind how long he sat there.

To begin with, he did not attempt to address the guards; he was content to let them observe him from watchtowers or through peepholes in the doors. But after a while, they began to speak. Just a few words here and there to start with, then longer, more complete conversations. He offered them cigarettes, though he refused to enter the house, always staying in the courtyard. He was self-effacing and discreet and made a point of not asking any questions about Trotsky.

As time went on, he started to invite the guards out to restaurants or to let them borrow his car to take Trotsky out for his rare excursions. He started to open up and become more loquacious, even if he avoided politics in favor of talking about his clothes, money (he frequently praised Peter Lubeck's financial ability), and car. The guards come to know him as *el novio de la señorita* Sylvia (Miss Sylvia's boyfriend).

Ramón also began to cultivate Alfred and Marguerite Rosmer. In addition to Alfred's ties to Trotsky, Marguerite was very close to Natalia. Making a good impression on them could only help in his attempts to find out more about the household and its dispositions.

Luckily for Ramón, the Rosmers already had a strong family connection to the Ageloffs. They had stayed with Sylvia's sisters when returning from Europe with Trotsky's grandson.* Sylvia found Marguerite sympathetic and began to confide her anxieties about her boyfriend's false passport.† In turn, the Rosmers took to Ramón. Brief exchanges at the door to the house on the Avenida Viena grew into a more sustained relationship. Marguerite liked this handsome, kind, gentle boy. They accepted his invitations to lunch in a restaurant or to take a walk, and they occasionally asked for help with small favors. He was always happy to oblige, making himself available at any time to drive them wherever they wanted to go. According to Adolfo Zamora, who was a regular guest at the Avenida Viena in 1940, the Rosmers, especially Marguerite, became "infatuated" with Ramón. After he had given them a lift into the city, she told Trotsky that Sylvia had "a very sympathetic fiancé."

Ramón was equally charming with young Seva, who registered the sudden arrival of a smartly dressed man with a flashy car and, it seemed, plenty of money. (But Seva also thought that Ramón was the sort of man nobody paid too much attention to beyond recognizing that he was polite and the kind of man who took his comrades out for dinner.) Ramón accompanied Trotsky's grandson on an excursion with Sylvia, the Rosmers, and a handful of guards—a sign of the confidence people already had in him. This outing was felt to be so successful that

---

* Hilda let the Rosmers stay, without charge, in her home in Brooklyn. Ramón's lawyer, Eduardo Ceniceros Ríos, always claimed that his client had paid for the passage of Seva. This seems highly unlikely. They'd never met by this point, and it's hard to believe that Trotsky would have allowed someone whose credentials stretched no further than being a New York Trotskyist's boyfriend to play this intimate role.

† It's likely that the first time Trotsky heard the name Frank Jacson, or Jacques Mornard, was when, during a conversation with Sylvia, she confided that her partner had traveled to the country on a false passport. He said that personally speaking he was not worried, but that they should be careful about the Mexican federal authorities as well as about the police, who kept a record of everybody who visited the compound.

he was entrusted with taking the boy to school and on a trip to a natural park halfway between Mexico City and Toluca.

AND YET, FOR the second time, Sylvia grew anxious that her partner was not everything that he had claimed.

The unquestioning trust she had felt in Paris had given way to something unsettling, although difficult to place. Beneath the bluster about copra prices and shipping delays and beneath the generous gifts—in Mexico he bought her perfume, a necklace, and a lighter—she realized he had never clearly explained what his job was.

In March, she learned that one of her sisters was ill. Ramón had, she believed, gone to work that day in office 820 on the eighth floor of Edificio Ermita, so she went to see him—perhaps hoping she could make a call from his workplace.

She had the building's address on a handwritten note he had given her, but when she arrived, she discovered that the building had only six stories and that there was no office number 820. What she did not know at the time was that Edifico Ermita was also the residence of David Alfaro Siqueiros and his brother, Jesús. Though the brothers themselves had fled by this point, Jesús's family still lived in apartment 604.

There had been other strange incidents. One night, while the couple ate dinner at the One Two Three bar, Ramón greeted an "elegant" woman in her mid-thirties who Sylvia was convinced they had also once spoken to at the Café de Flore in Paris. But Ramón claimed that Sylvia was confusing her with a different woman, Mrs. Ceuponit, a Belgian socialite who was a friend of his mother's, and he pointed out that Mexico was a common destination for those who were fleeing from the war.

Was it usual that Ramón and his boss, Peter Lubeck, used code names in the letters they wrote to each other? On one occasion she asked him about this; in response he wrote some signs on a piece of paper that he shredded immediately.

Was this man she loved perhaps a British agent? She believed it was a personal matter, not something to bring up with Trotsky. She did, however, share her concerns with Marguerite Rosmer during a visit to Coyoacán, telling her that although she loved Ramón "selflessly," she was troubled by the contradictions and evasions in his life and the stories he told about it.

The older woman sought to reassure her friend by telling her that she would investigate Ramón's activities and background. Had Sylvia considered that perhaps he was hiding the true details of his job because he was ashamed of it? Marguerite had also been asking herself why a man who was in other respects so open should be so secretive about his employment. He was so vague about how, exactly, his boss was making so much money that she assumed he was involved in some sort of trade profiting from the war.

It's not clear what investigations Marguerite was actually planning to carry out, but soon afterward her husband fell sick and she devoted her time to taking care of him. Sylvia informed Ramón of her suspicions and the process she had set in motion. Keen to quell any doubts about his story, he shared more details about his employer and the business they were involved in.

Sylvia had little choice but to continue to accept what he told her at face value. Still, it is clear that some undigestible piece of suspicion remained. On 29 March, Ageloff and Ramón visited Trotsky's house prior to her return to New York—her leave had expired. Trotsky was busy, so they were able to speak only with Natalia. Later that day, Ageloff made her lover promise to stay away from Trotsky's house. She argued that if the authorities discovered that he had entered Mexico with a fake passport, they might create problems for Trotsky.

Ramón, as blandly pleasant as always, agreed. Almost immediately after Sylvia had left, however, he wrote to say that he had been forced to break that promise because he'd had to visit to help the ailing Alfred Rosmer. He did not tell her that on some of these trips, he was able to take photos, probably with a concealed camera. Copies were sent to the special dossier on Trotsky kept by the KI Registry of the NKVD.

On 11 April, Ramón moved to room number 65 at the Shirley Courts, a discreet boardinghouse consisting of several independent apartments furnished in the "American fashion." Lush flower beds and lawns added to the luxury feel. When he registered, he again offered the false 1269 St. Denis Street address.

He spent two months here, although he disappeared for five days (12 to 17 April) almost as soon as he arrived. There would be other mysterious absences during his stay. He'd vanish for three or four days at a time, saying only that he was traveling elsewhere in Mexico, to the ports of Tampico, Veracruz, or Acapulco. During these trips, he never left anything in his room and insisted on keeping a steamer trunk, which he said contained engineering equipment, in the manager's office until he returned.

The owner, James Shirley, kept a closer eye on him than on any of his other guests. There was something about Ramón that he didn't like. Ramón rarely left his room and was generally reserved in his manner. Shirley was so suspicious about the fact that his guest's car returned from the excursions coated with dust and mud that he inspected the mileage indicator to see if the distance traveled would offer any clues as to where he'd gone. But Ramón always reset the dial.

James Shirley remembered that Ramón received a handful of visitors and took frequent phone calls, including those from Madame Rosmer but also those from a man with a German accent and a woman with a French accent. These generally came between eleven a.m. and noon, because he went out in the afternoons.

One of his callers had a very pronounced Russian accent. On another occasion, two men who looked like Mexicans came to see him. Ramón hesitated before going out to meet them. First, he went to the garage where he stored his car. After a few minutes he began peering through an upstairs window at the men standing below. Finally, he joined them in the garden. They handed him letters, which evidently satisfied whatever lingering concerns he had; then they went with Ramón up to his room, where they stayed talking quietly for an hour and a half.

Ramón was permanently watchful. Whenever he spoke on the telephone or received a guest, he stood with his back against the wall of the hotel office, never taking his eyes off the front door. Sometimes he installed himself in the garden to watch comings and goings.

It was as if he was afraid of being watched or caught by surprise.

And yet at other times, this carefulness gave way to garrulity. He was clearly less anxious about revealing that he spoke Spanish here, announcing that he had learned the language when working as an engineer in the state of Chiapas, Mexico, but he had then been back in Belgium for twelve years.

On another occasion he claimed that he was one of only six men who knew the Bering Strait and Arctic Circle perfectly and that the Canadian government had offered him $1,200 a month to do surveying work in them. He also expressed "rabid hatred" for the Royal Canadian Mounted Police, saying that they'd killed his father and brother. Ramón, the upright, rigid communist, appeared to be enjoying the license his new identity gave him to litter his path with wild fabrications.

RAMÓN'S ARRIVAL IN Mexico coincided with a sinister change to the atmosphere in the country.

This was partly due to a wholesale revolution at the top of the Mexican Communist Party.

At the beginning of the year, the general secretary, Hernán Laborde, was visited by Vittorio Vidali, the famous "Commandante Carlos" of the Republicans' Fifth Regiment and a member of the Comintern. Vidali told Laborde that the decision had been taken to kill Trotsky and that he needed the general secretary and his party to provide all the help needed for the operation.

Laborde disagreed, as did his closest supporters, Valentín Campa and Rafael Carrillo.

Moscow moved swiftly. Laborde and Campa were expelled from the party and replaced by more pliant figures.

Trotsky followed these events closely. He was also aware of David Alfaro Siqueiros's plans to attack him, which were an "open secret" among Mexican communists. The painter was making his preparations with "great levity" and almost no attempt to disguise his intentions.

Calls for Trotsky's expulsion from the country grew. It became ever more common to see walls in Mexico City plastered with posters accusing him of being part of a conspiracy with reactionary generals aimed at replacing President Cárdenas with a fascist dictatorship.

On 1 May 1940, twenty thousand communists in uniform marched through Mexico City, brandishing banners that demanded "Out with Trotsky." His supporters began to worry that his right to asylum was under threat, especially if Cárdenas were to lose the next election.

Trotsky and Natalia felt the change in atmosphere keenly. The city that had been a mostly friendly home to them for the past three years now had filled up with sinister, malign figures. They watched as their guards stared impotently at the strangers and vehicles that made slow loops around their home. There was increased scrutiny of all visitors, and Trotsky asked the local authorities for reinforcements to the police guard that was supposed to be maintaining constant surveillance of his home. But they could do nothing to prevent the increased tempo of demonstrations against Trotsky, in which it was common to hear the cry *"Muerte a Trotsky"* ("Death to Trotsky"). Nor could they quell the growing virulence of the attacks against him in the communist press in such publications as *La Voz de Mexico*, *El Popular*, and *Futuro*.

"This is the way," Trotsky observed, "people write who are preparing to change the pen for the machine gun."

# 24

# Two Hundred Bullets

In April 1940 a new guard arrived at the Avenida Viena. Robert Sheldon Harte, just twenty-five, was cheerful and fine-featured. He'd come to take responsibility for the alarm system that had been connected to the local police station by Alexander Buchman, the American Trotskyist he had replaced.

While Harte's enthusiasm couldn't be faulted, sometimes his focus could. He had quickly fallen in love with Mexico. In his free time, he wandered around Coyoacán, collecting bouquets of field flowers, and he adored watching the brilliantly colored birds in the aviary. None of this was a problem in itself; however, on one occasion, while the house was being rebuilt, and Trotsky's guards had to open gates at fifteen-minute intervals to let a worker push a wheelbarrow out onto the street and then back in again, Harte was so completely absorbed by building a birdcage that he simply handed the key to a worker.

Trotsky warned him, "If you behave like this, you might prove to be the first victim of your own carelessness." This slip should have caused alarm. With the threat to Trotsky mounting month by month, even the smallest incidents of absentmindedness could have had fatal consequences. But no action was taken.

Some members of the household were troubled by other elements of Harte's behavior. There was a sense that he wanted to know too much. As April turned into May, Fanny Yanovich began to find some of his requests increasingly annoying. He asked ceaseless questions about Trotsky's biography of Stalin as he walked her home each night. How far had he got? What part was she writing? Sometimes he'd insist that he wanted to retrieve a fountain pen that he said he had left in Trotsky's study.

At five p.m. on 23 May, he interrupted Trotsky, who'd been working hard since seven that morning and was alone at the time. Harte said he wanted to check the wires of the alarm system. The exasperated Trotsky said: "It is not possible to work with these continuous interruptions. Leave me, please!" Sheldon obeyed immediately. Later on, after Trotsky had finished for the day because of a severe headache that could not be relieved by aspirin, Yanovich carried on working into the darkness, copying the document he had been composing. Sheldon Harte, who had appeared nervous all day, asked her insistently when she thought she would be finished. Later, she realized that he wanted her kept away from what he knew was about to happen. As he drove her back home from the Avenida Viena, she noticed a suspicious vehicle parked nearby. Everyone around Trotsky had learned to become hypersensitive to potential threats, yet Sheldon Harte seemed completely uninterested in this car.

THEN, IN THE early hours of 24 May, the NKVD finally struck. The night before, at ten p.m., Siqueiros and twenty of his followers assembled in an apartment on República de Cuba Street in the center of Mexico City. Siqueiros carried with him incendiary bombs. He provided the other men with ropes, rubber gloves, and abundant liquor, and gave them strict instructions to remain there until he gave them the order. They laughed and joked and drank as if it were a feast day.

At two a.m., he returned dressed in a major's uniform, his face disguised with dark glasses and a false mustache that made him look like Adolf Hitler. He was also wearing, somewhat incongruously, a "Kaiser" helmet from the Great War. His band of assailants greeted him with "great bursts of laughter." He posed for them, asking, "How does it suit me?" They replied in chorus: "Very well."

His right-hand man, Pujol, was in the uniform of an army lieutenant, and the other men were also supplied with uniforms, which were either cleverly tailored fakes or had been stolen from local soldiers and policemen. The only Soviet agent present was Grigulevich, who, because he had been sufficiently discreet, was known to most of the men simply as the "French Jew."

It was a night of heavy, warm rain. The group set off for Coyoacán carrying with them revolvers; at least two machine guns; a rope boat ladder with wooden rungs and a metal hook at one end; an electric saw; and a *Santo Niño* (Holy Child)—an iron bar routinely used by Mexican burglars to force open doors and stun anybody foolish enough to put up resistance. Another handful of men joined the group in a street near the Avenida Viena.

The first part of their task was the easiest. Of the five police officers on guard outside the compound, three were asleep. At approximately three thirty in the morning, two of Siqueiros's men dressed as police officers and another in a military uniform showed up at the sentry box. Struggling to contain their surprise at what appeared to be a visit from their superiors, the two men watching Trotsky's house went out to establish what was happening.

They were immediately disarmed, tied up, and threatened with death if they made any noise. The attackers shouted, "Long live Almazán!" and explained to their captives that policemen across the city had been arrested: it was a coup. Siqueiros and somewhere between fifteen and twenty men, all of whom except one were in uniform, woke and then bound with ropes the three remaining gendarmes.

With the perimeter of the building secure, the attackers cut the cables for both the alarm and the telephone. Next, Grigulevich approached the compound's gate, knocked, and when prompted gave a password.

The gate swung open. Waiting for them was Robert Sheldon Harte. As twenty-five men rushed inside to take up positions on the patio, Siqueiros signaled that Harte and Grigulevich should wait outside.

The raiders flowed through the garage and into the garden, where they divided into four groups. The first two approached the French windows of Trotsky's and Seva's bedrooms.

Another group raced into the dining room, which they knew led through Trotsky's study and up to a connecting door that led into Trotsky's room. The last group headed toward the guards' quarters. Siqueiros stood waiting with a machine gun ready to stop anyone coming to Trotsky's aid.

There was no attempt to stop them; the whole house appeared to be asleep.

At just before four a.m., the first three groups started firing. Natalia woke, followed by a befuddled Trotsky, who struggled to shake off the effect of the sedatives he had taken for his insomnia. For a few seconds the couple thought the noise was simply fireworks let off during a local fiesta. But as the acrid stench of gunpowder grew ever more oppressive, it became clear that they were under attack. Natalia reacted first, whispering to her husband, "They're shooting, they're shooting into the room. . . ." Then she pushed him onto the floor and slid on top of him.

They continued communicating silently, with Trotsky gesturing to his wife to stay prone on the floor. A frantic barrage came in from the two doors on either side of the room as well as from the French windows just above where the couple hid. They listened as bullets ricocheted off the walls and the ceiling, and shards of glass and plaster landed all around them. The darkness around them was punctured by muzzle flashes spitting light across the bedroom and garden.

Thoughts raced through Trotsky's mind: he wondered where the police were, pictured their guards already dead or tied up, and fretted about the safety of his grandson. Some of the shots were coming from Seva's room.

Natalia tried to move her body to protect her husband—it seemed to her that the bullets were getting closer with every second. She remembered thinking: "Why does no one come? Why does no one call us?"

Time passed. A moment of silence was followed by the dull thud of an explosion. The force blew Seva's door open, revealing flames. Natalia raised her head high enough to be able to see a figure silhouetted against the flames. His distorted face, helmet, and the metal buttons on his greatcoat all glowed red. The man looked around the bedroom as if inspecting it for signs of life. He raised his pistol, emptied it into the beds, then slipped away.

The couple stayed crouching in the corner of the bedroom.

Then a scream came from Seva's room: "Grandfather!" He seemed to be both warning and beseeching them.

"The voice of this child in the darkness, amidst the gunshots" was for Trotsky "the most tragic memory of that night."

"They've taken him," whispered Trotsky.

There were what seemed to both Natalia and Trotsky endless flashes and flickering shadows, which then stopped abruptly and were followed by "a deathly, total silence, an unbearable silence that chilled us through." Their first thought: *It is inconceivable that that our grandson Seva, our friends the Rosmers, the young American guards are not all dead.* And then another thought: *They're coming for us.*

Natalia was sick with despair. Frantically she considered where she could hide her husband. She knew that the attackers would slaughter him if he was discovered.

It was at this moment that "Seva's clear voice, quivering with joy" rang out, calling the Rosmers. "Al-fred! Mar-gue-rite!"

---

As soon as Seva heard shots, he'd rolled onto the floor and curled up. He watched as two assailants in uniform smashed his door down and then fired shots into his mattress.

He was struck by a bullet that came through the French window—it had been aimed at Trotsky, but missed and ricocheted, scratching the top of one of his toes as he lay huddled on the ground. It was a light enough wound that he did not register it amidst the chaos. The only other person who was wounded was Trotsky himself, who was bleeding from two small cuts on his leg.

When the firing stopped, Seva could hear a voice outside the door. He made out the word "*bombas*" and realized with a jolt that someone was about to toss a bomb into the room, evidently keen to finish what they had started. He dashed into the adjoining room before the first incendiary bomb ignited.

Then he followed a group of shadowy figures into the garden, before going into the secretaries' office, and finally into the dining room. A trail of blood showed the route he had taken. The attackers, having fired into every room and exhausted their ammunition, disappeared through the trees into the darkness where Siqueiros and Grigulevich were waiting for them. As they knew they would, they found that the Dodge and the Ford in Trotsky's garage were sitting ready with the keys in the ignition in case of an emergency. They sped off and later abandoned the two vehicles. One was discovered close to the house, stuck in the mud of the usually dry Churubusco River; the other made it farther, to Calle Mérida.

Trotsky's guards, woken from their slumbers, were not able to provide the protection that they had been brought to Mexico to give. Siquieros and his machine gun were sited on the patio behind a eucalyptus tree that sat between the house and the gardens. The guards were cut off from Trotsky and everyone else.

A barrage from the patio as intense as the attack inside forced the guards to shelter in their room. They could hear a voice speaking in perfect English above the gunfire: "Don't go out and nothing will happen to you." It was joined by another: "This has nothing to do with you, but if you dare to get involved, you'll be killed too."

None of the guards fired back.

One "leveled his gun at one of the assailants, drew back the hammer, and then torn by indecision lowered his weapon." Otto Schüssler, who had been taken completely by surprise, found that his machine gun had jammed. A parlormaid later said she saw him standing with his weapon in his hand, watching from the kitchen doorway.

Charles Cornell too was torn from his sleep by the first shots. He thought his comrades were fighting off an attack. But then he heard the same warning to stay inside as his comrades had.

He fumbled for his revolver, then remembered that he had lent it to Harold Robins the night before. Still, he started for the bedroom door. Then Robins spotted him and called out: "Look down, Charles! Don't show yourself!" Cornell ignored his comrade and extended his head far enough that he could make out three figures near the guardhouse. One was in a light suit; the others were in dark clothes. He picked up his rifle, put a dark garment over his light-colored pajamas to make himself less conspicuous, and made as if to head for the courtyard. Just as he was about to leave, Robins shouted, "Don't show yourself, Charles! Lower your head, good God!"

Cornell realized later that his fellow guard, who had a better view of the situation, had saved his life. Instead of rushing out, he stood at the door. He shot at and missed a man he did not recognize sprinting across the courtyard. When he saw Otto leave his room and go to Trotsky's, he yelled, "Watch out, Otto! You are in danger!"

And then it was all over. Otto and Charles discovered Harold in one of the guardrooms.

"Can I go to the old man's room?" Cornell asked Robins.

"Wait until we turn off the light."

They ran to the dark house, terrified of what they'd find. Trotsky's study door was shut, so they headed for the patio.

The iron gate gaped open, the police were trussed up, and their two cars had been stolen. On the concrete floor of the garage was an article of clothing—a Mexican serape that the two men had last seen draped over Harte's shoulders—and a revolver they also recognized as his. One of the policemen told them he'd seen Harte dressed in khaki riding breeches, brown riding boots, and a sweater under a brown coat; he'd been led by the arm to one of the cars, but he had seemed willing to go.

Cornell hadn't heard the cars start. Now he was preoccupied by Harte's disappearance. "Doesn't this disappearance seem suspicious to you? Do either of you still trust Sheldon?"

Natalia and Trotsky, who were still trying to work out why nobody had come for them, struggled with the study door. It had either been locked by their assailants or jammed.

Bullets had turned the door lacy, and Trotsky and his wife peered through holes at papers sitting tidily on the desk in the gentle light coming from a shaded lamp.

Natalia started hammering on the door with her fists. Otto Schüssler emerged from the other side to let them out. They stepped through the door and for a moment felt bewildered to find themselves in this immaculate room.

It was a shock to learn that the attack had not lasted for much more than five minutes. Perhaps even more shocking was the fact that they were still alive. There were bullet holes everywhere; Trotsky's bedroom door looked like a sieve. Several bullets had torn through the bolster and pillows where their heads would have been. Mexican police counted seventy-three bullet holes in Trotsky's bedroom wall alone; Trotsky thought that two hundred had been fired in total.

The men had stormed through the house, pumping bullets out of their Thompson submachine guns, and had hit nobody but Seva. It was clear that they had been familiar with the layout and yet they had not eliminated their target.

There were a number of reasons for the close escape. The Trotsky bed had been fitted with a steel plate that protected him and little golden-haired Natalia. The assault had been carried out in the dark, and the attackers were clearly somewhat anxious about hitting one another. Given the volume of gunfire and the fact that Trotsky's room had been surrounded on all sides, it was surprising that there had been no accidental injuries.

Most of all, with the possible exception of Grigulevich, nobody involved in the operation had been trained in close-quarter combat or in conducting room-by-room searches. The attackers were peasants, miners, and muralists who had been taught how to fight a guerrilla war. They had come drunk on tequila and adrenaline and then found that they were terrified by the violence they unleashed. Still, they must have left convinced they had accomplished what they had been sent to the Avenida Viena to do.

By the time Colonel Leandro Sánchez Salazar, the chief of police, arrived, the inhabitants of the compound all seemed strangely calm.

"The whole house stank of gunpowder, like a battlefield," Seva remembered. But they had put out a couple of fires—one on the lawn, the other in the entrance to Seva's room. There were also two improvised incendiary devices that had somehow not ignited, even though their casings had caught fire.

Natalia had extinguished one of the fires with a rug, suffering burns on her arms and legs in the process. A third unexploded bomb, containing enough dynamite to destroy the whole house, was discovered in the garden; it was a reminder that for Stalin the destruction of Trotsky's archives was almost as significant a target as Trotsky himself.

Seva, his left foot bandaged, was playing amidst the garden's smoldering grass. The police chief was struck by how much he resembled his grandfather. The guards also gave the impression that nothing serious had taken place, answering Sánchez Salazar's questions "in cheerful and even condescending monosyllables."

When Sánchez Salazar was finally granted an audience with Trotsky and Natalia, he found them still clad in pajamas and dressing gowns. Trotsky, as genial and polite as ever, was smiling—a little mockingly, Sánchez Salazar thought—and his eyes twinkled beneath his "Mephistophelian eyebrows" and tortoiseshell spectacles.

Trotsky put his right arm on the colonel's shoulder and took him across to the rabbit hutch, where the rabbits were feeding with the same sangfroid displayed by everyone else in the household. Trotsky, in a "calm and grave tone," told the chief of police, "Fate has granted me a reprieve. It will be of short duration."

He said that they had been saved by a "happy accident," and then his irrepressible sense of his own worth intervened. It was possible, he said, that "my wife and I came to the aid of the happy accident by not losing our heads, not flying around the room, not crying out or calling for help when it was useless to do so, not shouting when it was senseless, but remaining quietly on the floor pretending to be dead."

The only discordant notes in this peaceful scene came from some of the women who had been involved. The cook Carmen Palma and the maid Belen Estrada both seemed terrified. Palma, who shook with fear, could not even raise her head to look Sánchez Salazar or any of his men in the eye. And then there was Natalia, who could not suppress her anger. She said nothing directly but threw the colonel a fierce look when he saluted her while she was kissing Cornell and Schüssler and talking affectionately to them.

The whole encounter was so odd that Sánchez Salazar left wondering whether there had been an assault at all. Had Trotsky staged a fake raid in a convoluted attempt to discredit Stalin?

# 25

# Things Are Better as They Are

It was only once David Alfaro Siqueiros and his accomplices were in hiding that they learned from the radio that they had failed.

Eitingon, who had always kept his distance from the operation, receded further into the background. Grigulevich disappeared, presumably slipping across the American border and hiding out in Santa Fe at Zook's Drugstore.*

Siqueiros also tried to escape, though with less success. Several days after the raid, Mexican police, searching meticulously in scorching sunlight and with mosquitoes cutting them to shreds, discovered a man sleeping in the grass on a bend in a country road.

He was unshaven and wore dirty, torn khaki clothes, miner's boots, and a wide-brimmed straw hat. Nevertheless, the slumbering figure was unmistakably Siqueiros. He woke with a start and seemed so surprised to find himself surrounded by police that he offered no resistance. He carried with him no weapon, only a leather satchel containing sixteen hundred pesos in notes (more than $100), a moun-

* The Mexican police never discovered his identity. He spent much of the rest of the war running an illegal residency in Argentina, where, according to KGB files, he planted more than a hundred fifty mines in ships bound for Germany.

taineer's knife, a pen, a tube of toothpaste, a bottle of brilliantine, and corn tortillas wrapped in a napkin.

As soon as he was exposed as the ringleader of the assault, the Stalinist press quickly moved to dismiss him as "half-mad," "an irresponsible adventurer" who had sold himself to Trotsky, who had paid him to fake an attack.

But Siqueiros did not have to face the consequences of his actions for long. The Chilean ambassador to Mexico, the poet Pablo Neruda, worked hard on his behalf.* By the end of the month, Siqueiros and his wife and daughter had fled, via Cuba and Colombia, to Chile, where he painted and campaigned for art "at the service of the victory of the democracies."

They would not return to Mexico until 1944.†

ROBERT SHELDON HARTE did not get the same chance to escape. His corpse was found in a shack in the Desierto de los Leones on 25 June. It was covered with powdered lime that had bleached his skin and turned his head a red that, in the blue light of the police lanterns, "gleamed like molten metal." He had been killed as he slept.

It was discovered that he had been recruited in New York by Grigulevich under the cover name of CUPID and infiltrated into the house on the Avenida Viena. A search of his room gave up a key to room 37 at the Hotel Europa, which contained a suitcase covered in Moscow

---

* Neruda had a poet's attitude toward authority—he was suspended from his office for a month for having made commitments without securing permission from those higher up the chain of command.

† "They acted like firecracker makers," Frida Kahlo announced. "They killed a gringo called Sheldon Harte, they buried him in the Desierte de los Leones, and they fled. Naturally the police caught them; they put Siqueiros in jail but Cárdenas was his *cuate*."

Her asperity was, at least in part, caused by the fact that the botched assault had put her husband under suspicion. Diego Rivera had to be smuggled out of his San Ángel studio covered by canvas on the floor of his assistant Irene de Bohus's car. They drove right past Colonel de la Rosa of the police and the thirty men he had been given to detain the painter. Rivera spent weeks in hiding before a friendly government official arranged a passport for entry into the US.

stamps. When questioned by the police, some of the workers at the hotel remembered seeing an incredibly drunk Harte on the evening of 21 May, two nights before the attack. He was waving a wad of banknotes and was in the company of a prostitute.

Grigulevich had not told Sheldon Harte what would happen after he opened the gate. Eitingon explained that although the young American was keen to help the NKVD by providing information and opening the gate, he was shocked when he realized that he might be party to a massacre. "Sheldon appeared to be a traitor and brought the attackers to the room where there was neither Trotsky nor his archive. As soon as they started shooting he angrily told the assault group that being an American, had he known how they would behave, he would never have let them in."

This was a problem for the Soviets, as was the fact that Sheldon Harte knew Grigulevich's identity. They could not risk exposure. Sudoplatov said that a decision was taken on the spot to liquidate him: he was taken away and shot. "And what else could we do with him! To hide him away and then illegally transport to Moscow would be too complicated."*

THE TRUTH IS that Sheldon Harte was probably neither wholly one thing nor another, but simply "a mixed-up college boy with a social conscience who was torn between orthodox Communism and Trotsky's ideas."

Many wiser, tougher men than Sheldon Harte, who had a portrait of Stalin hanging in his bedroom in New York, had found themselves seduced by Trotsky's charisma and authority. Perhaps he was trapped by competing loyalties. Perhaps too he learned that beneath the progressive Stalinist rhetoric about a better, more equal world lay terrify-

* After Trotsky's assassination another guard opened the Spanish-English dictionary he had borrowed from Harte's library. His wife pointed out to him that the volume bore the signature of David Alfaro Siqueiros.

ing violence, and he was unwilling to countenance the consequences. But by the time he opened the gate to the smiling Grigulevich, it was already too late.

Trotsky had never shared his other guards' suspicions about Sheldon Harte. He then closed his ears to anything that suggested that the young American had gotten into the car willingly or that he had been allowed to go by himself on walks from the farmhouse where he and the other attackers had retreated to. Trotsky believed that if "Harte had been a G.P.U. agent he could have stabbed me on the quiet," and the murder only strengthened his conviction. "Bob perished because he placed himself in the road of the assassins. He died for the ideas in which he believed. His memory is spotless."

The last decade had been, among other things, a relentless parade of evidence that Trotsky's judgment of character could sometimes go awry. He had been shocked and hurt by the way that men who had once been steadfast allies crumbled so quickly under Stalinist pressure. There were countless examples of people who had infiltrated his inner circle, earned his trust and even love, and then betrayed him. Still, Trotsky could not accept his fallibility. When Yanovich told him all the things about the young American that had troubled her, he listened politely before shaking his head. "Don't keep on. That's completely impossible."

She realized that he could not admit to himself that he'd missed an agent provocateur.

It was Trotsky who composed the dedication on Sheldon Harte's tombstone.

For many of the inhabitants of the "little fortress" on the Avenida Viena, the weeks after 24 May were characterized by a paralyzing feeling of doom.

Trotsky remained dynamic—perhaps overly so. He tried to interfere in the police investigation, writing letter after letter to both the police and the press and angrily trying to challenge what he described as the "absurd idea of self-assault." (The Mexican police chief Sánchez Salazar had briefly suspected that Trotsky had staged the attack.)

Trotsky was also energized by the rush of visitors that arrived immediately after the attack, with sympathizers, police, and journalists all trying to force their way into the house.

One of the guests was Ramón, who came on 25 May saying he'd read about the assault in the papers. He appeared anxious to display a mixture of solidarity and indignation, reserving particular concern for Robert Sheldon Harte, whom he referred to as "my friend Bob," a phrase he used repeatedly during his visit. The disappearance of one of the household's cars and the damage sustained by the other gave him an opening. Suddenly his Buick became extremely useful.

On 27 May, three days after the raid, he offered to drive Alfred and Marguerite Rosmer the three hundred miles along winding mountain roads to Veracruz, where they would embark for Europe. He told them it was no inconvenience; he had to travel there on business a couple of times a month anyway.

At seven fifty-eight a.m. on 28 May, Ramón was allowed to come beyond the courtyard for the first time. He had arrived at the agreed time, and the secretaries asked him to go into the garden while the Rosmers finished packing their luggage. Emboldened, he made his way farther into the compound and found Trotsky feeding his animals. They shook hands and talked about rabbits for a while. Trotsky observed that from a scientific perspective, it was difficult to get the correct food. Ramón agreed, saying that unless you got it right, you risked the rabbits' stomachs becoming distended.

As before, he was careful not to linger too long with the Old Man. Spotting Seva, he trotted over to him to give him a toy glider. The young boy, excited by his gift, played with it on the lawn where only four days before an incendiary had smoldered. It was at this point that Trotsky, as always at pains to appear courteous, suggested to Natalia that they should invite "Sylvia's husband" to breakfast.

Ramón sat down at a table in the courtyard with Trotsky, Natalia, the Rosmers, and two of the guards. As he drank coffee, he talked about his time in Paris, saying that he had been friends with Rudolf Klement. Natalia, keen to find a way to relieve the tension that had infected the last few days, asked if she could accompany Ramón and the Rosmers on their expedition to Veracruz. Reba Hansen, the wife of one of Trotsky's guards, also decided to join them. Ramón agreed and there was cheerful commotion as the car was loaded and the Rosmers bade affectionate farewells to everyone who was staying at the Avenida Viena.

The drive gave Natalia a chance to get to know Ramón better. He was, she felt, "shy and likable." Months later, she remembered how, as they drove through the busy streets of Veracruz, Ramón had pulled up outside a building to ask a passerby how to get to the port. She noted this only briefly. She was surprised because she recalled him telling her how often he visited the city. But she let it go, just as she dismissed another ambiguous recollection from the past few days. When he had come to see them on the day after the assault, he had been shown the bullet holes that riddled the walls. He had remained almost completely indifferent, an attitude that she thought was "not natural" given how close she and others had come to death.

She was unwilling to devote her entire life to suspicion. Perhaps if Trotsky had been more concerned himself, she might have listened to the nagging doubts that were forming inside her, but he attached little importance to this "strange and self-effacing" man who had appeared on the fringes of his life.

This does not mean that they did not discuss him. Natalia says they did so multiple times, often in the company of the Rosmers. Ramón was weird and they found his personality difficult to puzzle out. At one point, while Sylvia was still in Mexico, Trotsky had appeared to want to get to know Ramón better. He toyed with inviting the couple for coffee, but then dismissed the idea, saying, "Things are better as they are."

As always, he was far more interested in the vast impersonal forces of history than he was in living, breathing human beings.

Over the next week, Ramón made several more visits to the Avenida Viena. On 30 May he entered for half an hour, from three forty-two p.m. to four twelve p.m., long enough to drop off Natalia, whom he had brought back from Veracruz. Trotsky, who was taking a nap, saw him for only a moment. Ramón was there again on 4 June, from two thirty-one p.m. to two fifty-five p.m., and on 7 June, from four thirty p.m. to four forty-five p.m.

It was clear that he had gained the trust of everyone in the household. "From then on," Natalia observed, "our comrades on sentry duty opened the gate freely to him."

## 26

# Shipping Documents

On 13 June, Ramón went to the house on the Avenida Viena to announce that he was going to the United States later that day for two weeks to "transfer" the businesses of his boss to New York. He offered to leave his car with its residents during his absence; he insisted it might be useful. His abrupt departure was not unusual; the comrades were accustomed to the slightly erratic pattern of his comings and goings.

Jake Cooper, one of Trotsky's secretaries, decided to accompany Ramón to the airport, where they had lunch before his flight to Brownsville, Texas, left. As they ate, Cooper asked him about his career as a journalist as well as about his political activities. His tone was friendly; like everyone else he was more intrigued by the newcomer than he was suspicious. Ramón happily explained that he hadn't tried to make contact with the Mexican Trotskyists on arriving in the country, but that he had actively campaigned in the French section of the Fourth International. He said that he knew its central figures well and had been close to Rudolf Klement and Lev Sedov. These lies went unchallenged. Warming to his theme, he began to lament the death of Robert Sheldon Harte, before exclaiming at Trotsky's luck in escaping death: "I hope," he said, "that the police will soon arrest the aggressors and that the working class of the whole world will make Stalin pay dearly for all his crimes!"

THE RETURN TO New York reunited Ramón with Sylvia. Instead of staying in an apartment, they paid $15 a week to occupy room 737 of the Pierrepont Hotel.

Ramón explained his presence in New York by telling her that he had to "attend to some financial details for Lubeck at the British Consul's Office" and that his firm was losing money on account of a drop in the value of the Mexican peso, which they could buy more cheaply in New York. Beyond that, he said little. He confirmed what he had already told her in a letter: he had met Trotsky without her, though did not say who had effected the introduction.

Each morning, he left their hotel to go to his "office," located in the Chase National Bank building on Wall Street. Nobody bothered to check if this was true. The only tangible financial action he took was canceling his credit card on 27 June. In the evenings, they saw Sylvia's sisters as well as the Rosmers. At some point during the time he did not bother to account for, it is possible that he saw Gaik Ovakimian, to obtain further instruction from Moscow Center.

Sylvia observed him send and receive a number of sealed packages. He kept a few packets sealed with red wax in the hotel's office safe. When Sylvia asked him what they contained, he told her "shipping documents." This was puzzling, although what truly unsettled Sylvia were the suitcases full of dollars in his possession. She found this "scary"; what could he possibly need the money for? He never explained.

On 17 June another suitcase arrived in New York. Ramón had arranged its shipping, but did not try to recover it. This job was left to a man identifying himself as H. Christie, who claimed to be staying at the Pennsylvania Hotel (although there was no record of him ever having visited); however, the forwarding agents refused to release it to him because the consignee had not obtained a customs declaration from the port of entry.

The forwarding agent who spoke to the mysterious Christie was puzzled by the arrangement. Their impression was that "CHRISTIE did not know very much about JACKSON [*sic*] but seemingly was merely doing a favor for an acquaintance."

When it was finally opened, it was found to contain an incoherent range of objects that were more curious than they were incriminating.

Alongside a number of books in French (including a guide to Canada) and a Spanish-English conversational guide (*First Spanish Book* by Lawrence A. Wilkins, which had been well used by its previous owners, a school in Daytona Beach), there was an English translation of *The Good Soldier Schweik*.

There were a copy of the magazine *Todo*'s 21 March 1940 edition, which carried an article by Trotsky; various items of photographic equipment; a range of footwear (including sandals, evening pumps, and riding boots); an empty machete scabbard; a retractable steel pocket ruler marked in meters; a full-dress suit; and the sorts of winter clothes that would have found little use in Mexico City.

Together, the contents of the trunk gave the impression of somebody who was closing one phase of his life and ready to make a fresh start somewhere else.

THEN, ALMOST AS soon as it had begun, Ramón's time in New York was over. On 30 June he set off from LaGuardia Airport with three bags weighing fifty-seven pounds, including a large suitcase full of what he said was Mexican currency but absent the trunk he had guarded so jealously at the Shirley Courts.

Where before, his journeys had been fairly direct, he now took a circuitous route. He flew first—via a plane that stopped in Washington, DC, Richmond, Greensboro, Charlotte, Greenville, Atlanta, Montgomery, and Mobile—to New Orleans, where he spent the night of 1 July in the St. Charles Hotel. The next morning he caught a seven thirty Eastern Air Lines flight to San Antonio, via Houston, arriving at 12:05 p.m. He was clearly doing his best to be discreet: at no point was he observed making any phone calls or establishing contact with anybody. All his tickets were bought with cash. Nobody, from bellhops to people working on ticket desks, remembered seeing him.

The only exception was a Mrs. Roy Clark from Houston, who shared a taxi with him from San Antonio airport into the city. Ramón, who did not speak a single word to her through the journey, got out of the cab at the Gunter Hotel. The only records of his stay here were the meals charged to his room, one to the value of fifty cents and another to eighty-two cents.

From San Antonio he took a train to Laredo, then walked across the International Bridge and caught another train to Mexico City. He would have known that as long as he possessed the correct documents, the border guards would not have made a record of his reentry into Mexico. Officially, he had left the country in June and never returned.

He traveled through Mexico, spending a couple of nights in San Luis Potosi before arriving in Mexico City on either 5 or 6 July. Here he checked into room number 230 at the María Cristina Hotel, where he stayed until Sylvia joined him in Mexico. He slept during the day and went out at night, only returning to the hotel between four and five in the morning. He received no letters, took no phone calls, and met with no visitors. The only communication with the outside world he received was an unsigned telegram that arrived on 7 August; it read:

PLEASE COME BACK TO NEW YORK AT ONCE.

Alone in New York, Sylvia became increasingly anxious. She sent four telegrams, including one to Ramón care of American Express at ten twenty-six p.m. on 29 July; it read: “No letter for many weeks.

Worried. Wire immediately present plans. Sylvia." The sender was given as "H. Ageloff."

Finally, on 7 August, the same day that Ramón received the unsigned telegram, he called Sylvia long-distance from Mexico City. He told her he'd been taken sick in a village outside the Mexican capital. Would she join him immediately? Ramón overcame her initial reluctance—he had indicated that he'd be back in New York in September—by saying that his plans looked as if they might change and he wanted to see her in Mexico City.

Taking no luggage and giving her address as 191 Joralemon Street, Brooklyn, Sylvia took an Eastern Air Lines flight to Brownsville, Texas, at seven fifteen p.m. the following day. There she bought a ticket for a flight to Mexico that left at nine ten a.m. on 9 August. She had taken a vacation from work that was due to last until 23 August.

Upon her arrival, Ramón and she checked into the quiet, central Hotel Montejo, where they "lived as man and wife." They were unobtrusive, unremarkable guests. None of their conduct caused a complaint or drew any suspicion. The manager, Miss Noriega, noted that the couple dressed simply. She thought Sylvia was a rather "disorderly person," presumably referring to her clothes rather than to her demeanor.

Again, Ramón offered Sylvia vague explanations for his whereabouts and behavior in the time they had spent apart. He said he had made several trips within Mexico to Guadalajara, Veracruz, Torreón, and Puebla, but also reiterated that he had fallen ill.

Sightings of him were, certainly, fleeting. He had met his mother and Eitingon. One witness, an Alfonso Dufret Peralta, saw Ramón and a "woman who was not obese but had a good build" and fair hair arrive in an expensive-looking, very dark (perhaps even black) Buick twice at the "Watson and Philipps" house. Dufret Peralta heard Ramón ask the doorman in Spanish if Mr. Wolff was there. Mr. Wolff, apparently, was a German Jew who spoke German, French, Spanish,

Yiddish, and English and was involved, the witness claimed, in "suspicious business." On the first visit, Wolff and Ramón spoke for fifteen minutes while the woman remained in the car. On the second visit, Ramón and the woman left because Wolff was not in.

Ramón's aimlessness and seeming lack of direction were deceptive: he knew exactly what he was doing.

# PART SIX

Ramón Mercader

# 27

# FEAR

After the attack on 24 May, an encrypted telephone message was sent from Mexico to New York, where it was decoded. Then it was transmitted to Moscow the same day and delivered to Stalin: "Operation carried out. Results known later."

It was left to Eitingon to send the next message, which confirmed that the attempt had failed. But its arrival was delayed, because it was sent via a Soviet ship to New York, then on to Lev Vasilevsky in Paris, but he could not decipher it and did not realize its importance. Instead, Stalin and Beria learned of the failure through TASS, the Russian news agency.

On Sunday, 26 May 1940, Sudoplatov was summoned to Beria's dacha. He arrived to find Beria eating lunch with his deputy, Sergey Nikforovich Kruglov, and Ivan Aleksandrovich Serov, commissar of state security in the Ukraine.

Unwilling to talk in front of his other guests, Beria gestured for Sudoplatov to wait for him in a garden full of rare semitropical vegetation that he obviously hoped he could nurture through the harsh Moscow winter.

A little later, Sudoplatov was joined by his host, who interrogated him about the composition of the team he had approved in Paris and asked him what he knew of the plan for the attack.

Sudoplatov assured his indignant superior that while "the professional level of the Siqueiros team was low . . . they were devoted comrades and ready to sacrifice their lives," and that he was expecting a full report from Mexico within a day or two. They returned to the dining room, where Beria suggested that Sudoplatov should go back to his office immediately and inform him as soon as there were any developments.

Two days later Eitingon's report arrived. "Taking the entire responsibility for this nightmarish failure," he wrote, "I am prepared at your earliest demand to leave for Moscow in order to receive the punishment due for such a failure." But he also promised he would correct the error if he was given a few more weeks and another $10,000 to $15,000.

Eitingon wanted the Center's permission to adopt a new plan that involved using a single agent to carry out the assassination. This presented a risk with wider implications. For some time, the penetration of Trotskyist groups abroad had been a significant priority for Soviet intelligence. It was how they knew almost everything that was going on inside the Trotskyist movement.

If the agent was caught while trying to kill Trotsky, it could expose the whole network and render the NKVD effectively blind about the intentions of Trotsky and his followers.

Sudoplatov knew that it was "a decision too important to be taken by me and Eitingon; it had to be made by Beria and Stalin."

When briefed, Beria instantly understood the implications of the plan. He did not respond immediately, instead telling Sudoplatov to wait. Two hours later Sudoplatov was called to Beria's office and told: "Come with me."

They drove west, out of Moscow, arriving thirty minutes later at Stalin's dacha. The meeting was short. Sudoplatov explained the failure of the first plan and the risks of the second. Stalin asked one question: "To what extent is our agent network in the U.S. and Mexico under Ovakimian involved in the operation against Trotsky?"*

Sudoplatov reassured him that the two outfits were completely separate and that whatever happened, Ovakimian's espionage under the cover of the trading company Amtorg would remain uncompromised.

This was enough for Stalin. "The elimination of Trotsky," he said, "will mean the total collapse of the entire Trotskyite movement, and we will have no need to spend any money on combatting Trotskyites and their attempts to undermine the Comintern or us."

He approved the approach suggested by Eitingon and ordered a cable to be sent expressing full confidence in him. Sudoplatov prepared the cable, adding a postscript from Beria: "Pavel [Beria's code name] sends his best regards."

It was already eleven p.m. Stalin asked Beria and Sudoplatov to stay for dinner. Stalin, seeming relaxed and convivial, encouraged Sudoplatov to try some Georgian wine that he served mixed with Lagidze, a Georgian lemonade that Stalin had flown to him daily.

If Stalin was angry, Sudoplatov thought, he was masking it well. He was clearly not pleased about the failure thus far of the operation, but what Sudoplatov sensed more than anything was determination. Stalin was willing to risk his whole agent network in order to get what he wanted.

AT SOME POINT in 1931, when he was still *rezident* in Istanbul, Eitingon had sat up late into the night with two other agents, including a comrade he knew as Molotkovsky, who had lately played the same role in Greece.

Molotkovsky was pensive, while Eitingon appeared to be "more

* In addition to the support Ovakimian provided for the Trotsky operation, he was involved in handling material from the physicist and Soviet spy Klaus Fuchs relating to the US's development of the atomic bomb, and he recruited Julius and Ethel Rosenberg, who would both later be executed for passing atomic secrets to the Soviet Union.

interested in the gramophone which he wound up from time to time." Then Molotkovsky asked if Eitingon was interested in taking over the agency network in Greece: "[T]he people running the show in Moscow are bureaucrats rather than Chekists and are letting valuable sources go."

Eitingon looked up from the gramophone: "It's all the same to me. If you want I'll go to Greece. . . . I'm not scared of failure. . . . I have to say I'm fed up with all this work. . . . As soon as I go back to Moscow, I'll stop working for the OGPU, I'll go away somewhere."

Nine years later, Eitingon knew that this option was no longer open to him. If he failed or walked away, he would be liquidated. His family would likely be condemned to a similar fate.

As soon as he received the cable from Sudoplatov giving his plan approval, he summoned Ramón and Caridad to a safe house in Mexico City.

Eitingon's first proposals were ragged; they felt like a gambler's last throw. He began by floating the idea of poisoning Trotsky, but there was nobody suitable in the household who could be given this task, nor did they have access to a laboratory where a toxin might have been manufactured. Next, he suggested dropping a bomb on Trotsky's home on the Avenida Viena. This idea foundered quickly too. How would they find a sufficiently skilled pilot, and would it be possible to reach Coyoacán without being intercepted?

One plan remained. They needed somebody who was willing to operate alone. Brute force was not enough; it was time for something else.

Later, during perestroika, Grigulevich was asked what the major driving force for his work in the thirties and forties was. "Fear!" he said without hesitating. "Fear of possible repercussions for not doing something, for not fulfilling an order."

Ramón understood that if Eitingon went home without completing his mission, he would be killed. Ramón knew that if you were given an order, it was expected that you should follow it unquestioningly or face the consequences. He had seen plenty of his comrades in Catalonia disappear for less.

Ramón and Eitingon were personally close.* Ramón understood what was happening in Moscow. Eitingon and Sudoplatov had both passed through their own spells under suspicion. Shpiegelglass and Serebryansky were under arrest. Many others had disappeared into the gulag or been terminated on foreign streets. The message was clear.

There was one more thing. This was the chance to be personally responsible for eliminating the man Ramón understood to be perhaps the single greatest threat to the future of the revolutionary project. If Trotsky was guilty of even a tenth of what he had been accused of, then surely no killing could ever have been more justified. And what better way for a Spanish communist to express his gratitude to the Soviet Union, the only major nation to have lifted a finger to help the doomed Republicans?

The young Spaniard would simply be, as Eitingon put it, "carrying out a just sentence" that had already been delivered in Moscow. The person given the honor of performing this task would become one of the revolution's greatest heroes.

Ramón had not joined the NKVD as an assassin. For the last two years, he had drawn on his talent for deception, not violence. But he knew what he was capable of. He had been hardened in the crucible of the Spanish Civil War. He was physically strong and brave and could contemplate taking another man's life with equanimity. He was no stranger to hand-to-hand combat: once he had stabbed to death a sentry who was guarding a bridge his comrades were going to blow up. And he was only twenty-seven. If he was caught and imprisoned, he felt sure he'd be able to sit the sentence out and begin his life anew once released. Eitingon, who was in his forties, did not have this lux-

* Again, there is debate as to exactly how close this connection was. One author has argued that Eitingon had become a father figure to Caridad's children, living with them for a few years in France and paying for their education, and that he was actually Luis's father. There is no evidence for this.

ury. Somewhat slyly he informed the younger man, "Mexico is the ideal country for an act of vengeance. They don't even have the death penalty."

Perhaps too Ramón realized that circumstances were narrowing his options.

Sylvia Ageloff later confided to her friend Maria Craipeau that after the failed May assault, Ramón had reacted violently. She was so frightened by his expression that she flushed down the toilet any papers, like her party membership, that she worried might have been compromising. She was not able to articulate to herself why she was so afraid. And then events took their course and she finally understood: at that moment Ramón had realized that it was *his* turn.

All of this would have been swirling around in Ramón's head at the moment that he stepped forward and told Eitingon, "Don't worry. I'll do it."

Caridad consented to her son's role. All that was left was to establish the details.

The plan that Eitingon hoped would allow Ramón to complete his task and then walk out "quietly and unmolested" was also the most brutal.

Ramón was "prepared for three alternatives: to shoot Trotsky, stab him, or beat him to death." The NKVD typically executed its victims with a bullet fired into the back of the neck, severing the spinal cord. But a knife or a club would be easier to hide from Trotsky's guards and, used correctly, would be far less noisy. It might be possible to murder Trotsky without anyone finding out for some time. The year before, an NKVD agent armed with an iron bar had liquidated an ambassador who was contemplating defecting.

Eitingon and Caridad were anxious to give Ramón the best chance possible of escaping safely. They proposed that they, along with a team of five guerrillas, would try to storm the villa while Ramón was inside, which might lure the secretaries away from Trotsky and allow the assassin to work unencumbered. However, it was decided that it was far more likely that the guards would gather round Trotsky rather than run into the street. Ramón's response was blunt. He did not agree with the plan. He would carry the death sentence out alone.

The Center agreed to provide a getaway car and chauffeur. A private plane would be waiting at Mexico City's airport, and Ramón would be able to travel on a false passport secured in a deal struck between Soviet agents in Mexico and communists working in the country's foreign office.

Ramón would get Trotsky alone in his study—the conspirators knew that he continued to disregard his secretaries' efforts to ensure that he should never see a guest without a guard present—and then Ramón would kill him with one crushing blow. Ramón would also carry a pistol in case this failed, though it was not clear how likely he was to escape a shoot-out with the guards and police.

He would then leave the study and walk out of the house and across the patio to the exit, where he would get into his car and drive around the corner. Here he'd be met by a new car that would contain his mother and the chauffeur. Eitingon would be sitting in another car a block away.

If everything went according to plan, by midnight Ramón would be in a different country with a new name and nationality.

In the meantime, they worked on providing a plausible motive for Ramón's assault. They knew suspicion would immediately fall on the NKVD if he was captured, whether or not he managed to kill Trotsky. But if this suspicion could not be dispelled completely, they knew how valuable it would be to offer an alternative explanation that would create just enough uncertainty and give Ramón a story he could cling to.

# 28

# OTHER METHODS

In the weeks after the raid on 24 May, Trotsky met several times with the Mexican journalist Eduardo Téllez Vargas, an admirer of the old revolutionary who wrote for *El Universal.* Téllez Vargas's final visit was on 17 August; he came away troubled by the encounter. It was clear that Trotsky trusted nobody; something had shifted in the Old Man. At one point, without naming anybody, Trotsky said: "I will be killed either by one of them in here or by one of my friends from the outside, by someone who has access to the house. Because Stalin cannot spare my life."

There was another visitor to the compound that day: Jacques Mornard.

At this time, many of Trotsky's other visitors, who believed he was too easy a target, tried to persuade him to escape to another country—perhaps France, or the United States, or elsewhere in Latin America—and go underground.

He rejected their entreaties. He was too old, he said, too tired of running. He could not spend the rest of his life as a hunted fugitive; he had to live and work in the open, to endure the "hell-black night" until the end.

This defiance ran parallel with a kind of fatalism that made many feel as if they were visiting him for the last time. Others began to wonder if at least some part of him *wanted* to die.

Trotsky himself wrote:

> I know I am condemned. I am a soldier and I can see that all the cards are stacked against me. Stalin is enthroned in Moscow with more power and resources at his disposal than any of the tsars. I am alone with a few friends and almost no resources, against a powerful killing-machine which has already eliminated the other opponents, Lenin's associates in the Politburo and the Soviet government. So what can I do?

Faced with this intransigence, Trotsky's supporters turned to trying to improve the little fortress's defenses. A military engineer was brought in to plan the reconstruction. Once money was raised ($2,250 by American Trotskyists and $6,000 from the sale of Trotsky's papers to Harvard University), the work could begin. They built six-meter-high walls around house as well as a bombproof redoubt complete with walls and floors of reinforced concrete and bulletproof turrets that overlooked the garden and all the adjacent streets.

There were new barriers of barbed wire and flexible mesh designed to withstand grenade attacks. The old wooden portico that looked onto the Avenida Viena, on which Robert Sheldon Harte had been surprised and kidnapped by the NKVD assailants, was replaced by electrically controlled steel doors.

Now when visitors approached the house, its double doors would open a crack and a powerful lamp would shine at them until they had been recognized and identified. Once it was established they could be trusted, the guard would signal to the sentry manning a machine gun in the turret, and the sentry would then open the door.

A spiderweb of electric wires ran across the walls. It was impossible to climb the walls without triggering an alarm, which would also set off colored lights on a board in the guardroom that indicated not only that an attempt was being made, but *where*.

The Mexican government trebled the number of police watching the compound and James Cannon traveled to Minneapolis, hoping to bring back bodyguards from the Truckers Union—some of the Minneapolis Teamsters Union's toughest members.

Trotsky himself remained reluctant about all this. He had long opposed searches for concealed weapons and continued to veto the suggestion that nobody should be allowed to talk to him alone in his study. He still believed that mutual suspicion was a more corrosive force than any spy could ever be.

As the building progressed, he stalked around the patio, suggesting changes and improvements. But just as often he could be seen talking to himself. On one occasion he conducted an imaginary conversation with his old Bolshevik comrades Bukharin, Kamenev, and Zinoviev. Trotsky, who remained incapable of admitting his own errors, attacked them for the mistakes they had made.

The past was never far from his mind. When guests came to stay, Trotsky and Natalia talked for the entire evening about the tragedy of Lev's death. Perhaps even this was preferable to contemplating their present in a house Trotsky referred to endlessly as a jail.

It wasn't just that Trotsky objected to the way his freedom was being restricted in the name of protecting his life; he didn't believe that any of the measures being implemented—the walls, the chain mail suit, the extra guards—would ultimately be enough to protect him. One could not be on the alert every single second of the day. One could not devote one's existence to self-preservation, because by doing so, life lost much of its meaning.

Talking with his guard Joseph Hansen, Trotsky "indicated the way in which he could easily be killed." There was no need for such a big apparatus and so many people if "a single agent of the GPU who passes for my friend could murder me in my own house."

---

THERE WAS A paradoxical quality about the life Trotsky led now. On the one hand, he was increasingly isolated and constrained—his existence confined to a dusty suburb on the outskirts of Mexico City. And yet he continued to look outward, avidly absorbing as much information as he could about a world that seemed on the precipice of another huge fracture, and fighting relentlessly against his ideological enemies.

Stalin remained his chief antagonist. By the middle of August, he could tell a correspondent that having almost completed his project of exposing the perpetrators of the May assault, he was ready to return to his "poor, neglected Stalin book."

Trotsky had set himself a deadline for completing the manuscript by the end of the month. He was obsessed by the idea of finishing it before he died.* But it had not been an easy book to write. Some of this was logistical. It was difficult, confined as he was, to obtain the documents and notes he needed to discover more about his rival's obscure origins or the precise nature of the role he had (or hadn't) played in 1917. It was especially difficult to get anything useful from the Soviet Union, and he was forced to rely on months-old issues of *Pravda* (which were full of fabrications) and barely audible radio broadcasts from Moscow.

The other issue was more profound. Trotsky prided himself on his objectivity, and yet he realized this was precisely what he was incapable of when it came to writing about Stalin. As he told Natalia: "It's hard going. It's incredibly hard to write calmly about the swine.

---

* It was a contract he had entered into reluctantly—he would have preferred to write about the friendship and collaboration of Marx and Engels, a book he had dreamed about for a long time—but he accepted that this was what the public was most interested in. And it would not be published until 1946, in a jumbled, unsatisfactory form. Many of the problems already existed. The translator, Charles Malamuth, was incompetent. As early as 1939, based on what he had seen of Malamuth's initial efforts to translate sections of the manuscript, Trotsky complained: "Malamuth seems to have at least three qualities: he does not know Russian; he does not know English; and he is tremendously pretentious."

It's easier to pour a bottle of black ink on the paper. I can only write about this Cain that way."

He'd spent a decade writing thousands and thousands of pages about the Georgian; now he could barely manage a word. And what he did produce had a different quality. Trotsky might argue, "Generally speaking, in matters of historic import, personal hatred is a petty and contemptible feeling. It is not only degrading but blinding." This, however, was not enough to stop him from introducing into the book hysterical speculation (which even he admitted was supposition) that Stalin had poisoned Lenin: "I began to ask myself with growing insistency: What was Stalin's actual role at the time of Lenin's illness? Did not the disciple do something to expedite his master's death?"

He knew that he was writing his worst book, that hatred froze his mind every time he tried to sit down and work on it, but he had to finish it, if only so he could honor contracts and avoid the financially ruinous route of having to repay advances.

Once he had recovered in July from an attack of "his old and mysterious illness" that arrived without warning, leaving him with crippling back pain and a high temperature, he was able to sit up in bed and dictate both the draft of the biography and the letters he still sent to his dwindling band of sympathizers.

For all this, he was clearly a physically diminished figure. Natalia noted his almost constant exhaustion. "He slept poorly," she said, "dozing off and waking up in the self-same thoughts." Each time this happened, she was seized by a "feeling of the greatest alarm."

The man who had led two revolutions and won a civil war was no longer capable of serious work.

AND THEN THERE was Frank Jacson, or Jacques Mornard, or whatever his name *actually* was. Nobody in Trotsky's circle had quite been able to fathom this strange man who had appeared on the periphery of their life months previously and had been working his way closer to the center ever since. He was louche, overfond of luxury, clearly adrift, but he was nice enough and helpful and he didn't try to poke his nose where it wasn't wanted. Moreover, he was sweet and attentive to Sylvia, whom everyone liked. But something about him had changed since he returned, looking thin and sick, from his rather abrupt disappearance to New York.

For one thing, they were seeing more of him.

He rarely stayed long—usually restricting his interactions to a few minutes of conversation in the garden. His longest visit, on 29 July, had lasted just over an hour—but over the course of a couple of weeks, he saw them seven or eight times. Once or twice he entered the house. What was also striking was that he often appeared to be nervous or hurried.

Natalia noted how he was a "rather timid . . . irresolute and strange person" who observed everything in an "indifferent and distracted manner." For her, the conversations they had lacked a "definitive character." It was always as if one were meeting him again for the first time.

When she asked him where he had been recently and why he was looking so gray—"awful" as she put it more frankly—he told her that after his return from New York, he'd had to travel to several Mexican cities for business. He added that he'd had a hepatic crisis.

And yet despite his sickness, he appeared keener than ever to make himself amenable—particularly to Natalia, who could often seem somewhat lonely in her busy home. On 1 August Ramón took Natalia on a shopping trip to the center of Mexico City. He carefully helped bring in her purchases, putting them down where she directed. Then he left quite suddenly, claiming he had urgent business.

On 8 August he arrived with no obvious reason to be there. He was carrying with him a bouquet of flowers and an expensive box of chocolates for Natalia; he handed the chocolates over, saying, "Here's a little gift from the minority"—a reference to an ideological split within the American Workers Party, a significant part of the Fourth International. While the majority led by James Cannon still supported Trotsky, the minority, led by Max Shachtman and James Burnham—men Trotsky had believed were loyal friends—had moved away from both Trotskyism and Marxism. Sylvia, otherwise unwavering in her loyalty to Trotsky, had sided with the minority; the chocolates were from her, Ramón said. He gave Trotsky a book called *Hitler and Stalin*. When Natalia mentioned in passing a walk she had taken in the mountainous countryside outside the city after Trotsky had developed a passion for collecting cactus plants, she was surprised by the force of Ramón's interest. In quick succession, he asked how they had got there and why they hadn't taken up his offer to drive them. He would, he said, suddenly seeming very excited, love to escort Trotsky whenever he next decided to make an excursion to the mountains. Did they know that he was an experienced alpinist? Trotsky remained polite but noncommittal.

The next day, Ramón was back again, saying that Ageloff had secured a vacation permit and had arrived in Mexico. He asked if they could come together to the Avenida Viena on Saturday morning.

That Ramón, so diffident up to now, was suddenly being so assertive seized Natalia's attention. She agreed with him, saying, "Well, on Saturday it is," but even as the words left her mouth, she knew that she did not want this visit to go ahead. It seemed too strange. Nevertheless, Natalia must have decided to ignore her doubts, for on 10 August, Sylvia and Ramón came, at Natalia's suggestion, to take tea at the house on the Avenida Viena. It was the first time the couple had received a formal invitation and to start with the conversation focused on them and their future. Natalia was convinced they would marry, and as they sat in the courtyard, "she talked with tact and humor about family life and its diversions."

This coziness soon gave way to an argument about the defense of the USSR, the source of the dispute within the movement. Sylvia argued the minority of the Socialist Workers Party's case heatedly.* Ramón, who appeared to have developed a passionate interest in the dispute ever since his return from New York, simply echoed Trotsky's words. At times he laughed and mocked Sylvia.

Before they left, he offered to write an article that he said might help show the problem in a different light. This was the first surprise. The second surprise was that Trotsky agreed to read it, as long as it had a solid basis.

THE ARGUMENT OVER the factional split was evidence of another strange development: Ramón suddenly seemed passionately interested in politics. When the Trotskyists had first met him, they had found him incapable of carrying on a sustained political conversation. Somehow, he always wandered onto a different subject. For normal people this was unremarkable, but for ardent communists this lack of interest in ideology was perplexing. And yet now he had discovered a devotion to the Fourth International. Ramón had started saying of Trotsky over and over again, always with an eye on his audience, "He has the greatest intellect in the world."

On their journeys back from Coyoacán, he would tell Sylvia that he admired Trotsky because he considered him a great man and that Trotsky's arguments were always brilliant.

His transformation was not entirely convincing. When on 29 July he'd come back to pick up the Buick, he let slip that he hadn't visited any members of the Socialist Workers Party while he was in New York.

This astonished those listening. Undaunted, he explained—rather glibly—that by day he was "slaving in an office on Wall Street" and in

* Natalia did not consider Ageloff's sympathy for the minority of the Socialist Workers Party as proof that Ageloff was against Trotsky or disloyal to him, because, she said, the Trotskyists' party was a living political body in which disagreements were a normal thing.

the evenings he'd spent so much time with Sylvia and her sisters arguing about the issue that was currently splitting the movement that he did not have time to visit the party's headquarters.

The bad impression this created lingered. So much so that the guards challenged Trotsky about it. Trotsky seemed far less troubled than his followers. "It is true, of course," he said, "that he is rather light minded and will probably not become a strong member of the Fourth International. Nevertheless, he can be won closer. In order to build the party we must have confidence that people can be changed."

He added that Ramón was carrying on some studies in French statistics that could prove useful to them.

Joseph Hansen believed that "Trotsky, who saw the possibility for anyone to develop into a revolutionary, wished to utilize Jacson as an example in point. The very distance which the guards kept between themselves and the apparently difficult job of turning this rather unpromising clay into a revolutionary, spurred Trotsky into making a stronger demonstration. He suggested to me specifically that I should go out of my way to become friendly with Jacson in order to help bring him closer to the Fourth International."

Trotsky had, after all, once joined a revolutionary movement that sought to emulate Lenin's practice of persuading individual disciples. He had long boasted that even if the Soviets managed to get a spy into his entourage, he was confident he could change their allegiance. And, anyway, he argued, it was difficult to establish whether or not somebody could be trusted until they'd arrived.

In spring 1938, when looking for a new Russian typist, Trotsky's entourage wrote to several countries for help. The Czech Trotskyists replied, saying that they knew of a young woman who spoke Russian perfectly and was ready to come to Mexico, but that she was suspected of being a Stalinist.

Jean van Heijenoort entered Trotsky's study and explained the situation. The Old Man made a sweeping gesture with his left arm: "Let her come! We shall win her over!"

On 14 May Trotsky wrote to Jan Frankel in New York:

> She is a quite young girl of eighteen. I do not believe that she can be a terrible agent of the G.P.U. Even if she comes with some sympathies for the Stalinists and with some wicked intentions against us (which I consider impossible, for nobody would entrust diabolical schemes to a little girl without experience), even in that case we feel strong enough to watch her, to control her, and to re-educate her.

A month later, he wrote again to Frankel:

> If the Czech girl is a *good typist*, I would be ready to accept her immediately. The political apprehensions are in this case not very serious. A girl of eighteen years cannot make conspiracies in our home: we are stronger. In two or three months she would be totally assimilated.

Perhaps he saw this enigmatic young man as another mind that could be swayed. It's also possible that his faith in his own charisma and powers of argument was not misplaced, that the exaggerated veneration Ramón had suddenly begun to show for him was becoming something more authentic. Months later, after Ramón's arrest, he was presented with a set of written questions. One asked: "Were you right or wrong to kill Trotsky?" When Ramón tried to answer this, he became incredibly nervous and appeared racked by indecision. The space allocated for his response was spattered with ink blots. Then, finally, he wrote: "Yes, since if I had waited and allowed myself to be convinced by him . . ."

His newfound political ardor was accompanied by a disturbing shift in his personality that had become especially pronounced since his return from New York. Ramón was normally gregarious, a man who liked to talk and was good at telling stories. Now this "somewhat vulgar *bon vivant*, who had been content to lead an easy and leisurely life, was suddenly in a terrible state of nerves."

He appeared suddenly older, his skin darker as if some poison had seeped into his body. His features twitched. He talked quickly, and yet, tripped up by his own thoughts, he sometimes appeared to struggle to find the word he wanted.

Ramón's peculiar, morose behavior was punctuated by "sudden outbursts of euphoria and loquacity." He spooked people by saying strange things. One day, while driving some American friends of Trotsky's back from Toluca, he was gripped by a "sudden fit of depression" and threatened to drive his car over a precipice. "Then," he said to one of the stunned passengers, "it would all be over!"

At other times, he boasted about his strength, which was sufficient, he said, to split a huge ice block with a single blow from an ice ax. He talked at length about his morbid fascination with surgery, saying that he used to ask to be allowed to watch doctors as they operated. As an example of the surgical skills he claimed to have picked up, he carved a chicken with great expertise. In one of those odd connections a stray phrase can sometimes set off, this reminded one of the Trotskyists that Jacson had once said he had known the sorely missed Rudolf Klement, one of Trotsky's old secretaries whose killers had dismembered his body with "surgical skill."

Ramón also made offers of unconventional help. He abandoned the discretion that had characterized his business affairs, boasting about the shady speculations he made for his "boss" and asking first the guards and then Trotsky himself if they'd like him to make on their behalf some investments that would "allow substantial profits to help the Fourth International."

Trotsky tried not to engage, confining himself to making "vague remarks about commercial ability and similar things." Both he and Natalia were irritated by these clumsy attempts to involve them in what felt to them like a disreputable moneymaking scheme. "Who is this fabulously rich boss?" the irritated Trotsky asked. "We should find out. After all, he might be some profiteer with Fascist tendencies and it might be best to stop seeing Sylvia's husband altogether."

And yet they did not stop him from coming. He was seen as a "friend of the house." Being Sylvia's "husband" (there was doubt about the precise nature of their relationship, but unconventional romantic arrangements were not viewed by the Trotskyists as being either significant or interesting) helped him avoid suspicion. He also had found a way of making himself useful. He contributed to the costs of building new fortifications after the May assault and helped with the shipping of some of Trotsky's documents to New York.

Ramón also benefitted from a lack of interest, especially on the part of Trotsky himself, about the life he had led before the comrades became aware of his existence. When Cornell was asked later whether he'd ever had any suspicions about Ramón, he said, "Never. Once I heard Trotsky say that Jacson was one of his supporters and that in Paris he had given a lot of money to the party."

There were many irregularities and inconsistencies about who Ramón was, whom he worked for (he told one person that he was importing diamond cutters; another that he dealt in sugar and oil on behalf of the Allies; another that he was a highway engineer sheltering in the city from summer rains), what nationality he held, what he was paid. In this small, incestuous colony of Trotskyists in Mexico, it would have been easy to compare notes or ask questions. But nobody ever checked.

THE PERSON MOST alarmed by the change in Ramón was the woman who was closest to him: Sylvia.

In France, he had been peaceful and friendly. Now, in Mexico City, he became irascible and hot-tempered. Whatever passion she had had for him had begun to decline; and yet here she was.

He told her that he was the victim of malaise. And his green complexion, the tremor in his hands, and his slow, tired walk all appeared to indicate a man whose health was broken. The elegant dresser now spent half the day in pajamas or went out with an old raincoat over his arm. Some days he climbed between the sheets and refused to leave his bed. He'd stare fixedly at the ceiling, lighting one cigarette after another. At intervals, Sylvia tried to begin a conversation, but all she got in return were incoherent, almost inaudible fragments. It was as if, she thought, she were talking to a wall. He seemed aware of this, noting: "For a whole week, I felt like I didn't exist any more: I had an obsession, I was obsessed to the point that I didn't even greet Sylvia. I was sick."

At night he was plagued by strange dreams that caused him to wake "very tired, like someone who had been beaten."* Most frightening of all, he appeared to be getting worse. "As for Jac, I'm glad I came, because he really feels bad and needs attention," Sylvia wrote to her sister Hilda. "Jac has diarrhea or something else terrible. This leaves him totally exhausted."

Ramón himself explained his behavior by referring both to his long-running health problems ("Since the age of six I have suffered in my liver") and to his rage at Trotsky, who he claimed had tried to suborn him into a conspiracy aimed against the USSR.

But he was also carrying a crushing psychological burden. He had

* Ramón would later recall a dream from this time in which "There was a funnel in the shape of a cone. Formidable, enormous, like Popocatépetl; very brilliant as though it were made of chrome steel. It had great resonance, it amplified sound. I was standing on top of the cone, the wide base of which pointed upward and below there was my friend, the pharmacist. I was circling around, on top. My friend said to me: 'Throw yourself down, I have chloroform.' And then waves of color appeared. Behind me there was an old man, could it be a doctor? The old man said: 'No, there is no chloroform.' I was worried because I thought my eardrums would burst. It was like that all night."

so many people to deceive, and there was so much resting on his shoulders. He knew that if he failed, the lives of people he cared about—his mother, Eitingon—would be at risk. He would also have been thinking about what he had been charged with doing. There was the need to choreograph his attack, to find the time and the place that would give him the best chance of completing his task and escaping safely. And he would inevitably have dwelled on what could go wrong: on what a mistake on his part, or simply a piece of bad luck, could mean for him personally. Trotsky's guards might have lacked polish, yet they remained ferociously devoted to their master.

Most of all, though, there was the thought of the act itself. Ramón needed to sink his ice ax deeply into the skull of an old man who sat defenseless and unaware before him. It is one thing to fire at a faraway enemy whose face you may never see, but quite another to contemplate killing a man whose body you can smell; whose coffee you have drunk; whose shoulders you can see rising and falling.

Ramón had once said, "It is ridiculous for a man to spend his days thinking about what he is going to do. I do not do this. I like to act and solve my difficulties while I am acting." Now, though, it appeared that he was becoming tangled in his own complex thoughts. And he was suffering.

During one of the last visits Ramón made to Coyoacán that August, he almost gave himself away. He arrived in the courtyard to find Trotsky discussing with Joseph Hansen and Charles Cornell the improvements being made to security on the Avenida Viena. Trotsky turned to him to ask him what he thought of the fort they were building. "Next time," Ramón said, "the GPU will use other methods."

A surprised Hansen asked, "What methods?"

Ramón simply shrugged.

On 17 August 1940, the day Eduardo Téllez Vargas also saw Trotsky, Ramón announced his arrival—recorded in the register at four thirty-five p.m.—by crashing his Buick into a Dodge that was parked outside the door.

Plainly nervous, he explained himself to one of the guards: "You know, I don't feel well at all. Besides, I have been ill since my early youth."

Trotsky had been busy dictating an article on pacificism, but broke off to receive their visitor. As Trotsky fed his animals, Ramón told him that he was about to leave Mexico City for good in order to return to New York. He had already sold his car and was doing what was needed to liquidate his employer's business.

He then removed a sheet of paper from his blazer—it was the article he had promised a few days earlier. Trotsky agreed to look at it and they walked to the studio, where he read the essay and offered some observations on what needed to be improved. Once their conversation was over, Ramón appeared in a rush to leave. His visit had lasted just eleven minutes.

Talking later that day to Natalia, Trotsky tried to explain the strange feeling that the encounter had left him with. "He showed me a paper devoid of any interest. It's confused and full of banal phrases. He says he can produce some interesting French statistics." It was not just that the article was off. "He did not behave like a Frenchman at all. He sat down on my desk right away and didn't take his hat off."

"That's funny," Natalia replied, "He never wears a hat."

"Well, this time he had one!"

At this he looked uneasy, as if he had registered something about the interloper without being able to identify exactly what it was. "I don't like him," he told his wife. "What sort of fellow is he? We ought to make a few inquiries."

Two days later Ramón woke early. Although both his physical and mental health seemed to be disintegrating, he told Sylvia that he had a meeting with the builders who were working on his firm's office.

Their work had to be completed before the couple returned to New York.

He did not, however, go to his office. Instead, he went to a carpenter's shop on the Avenida Chapultepec, where he asked for the long handle of his ice ax to be cut down, explaining that it was too long to use to easily break ice. When Sylvia had seen the ice ax in their room, he told her he'd used it to climb the Pico de Orizaba and Popocatépetl. He waited patiently, if somewhat anxiously, for the work to be completed; then he headed to the nearby Chapultepec Forest to meet Leonid Eitingon.

Ramón returned to the Hotel Montejo after noon. Without saying a word to Sylvia, he climbed into bed, where he stared at the wall and waited, unsleeping, for dawn.

# 29

# I Feel Really Good

Leon Trotsky spent the morning of the last day of his life feeding rabbits. The night before, he had slept soundly. He woke up feeling full of energy. "Do you know, I feel very well this morning, better than I have felt for a long time. I took a double dose of sleeping-powder last night. I've noticed that it does me good," he told Natalia.

"Yes," she replied, "I remember we noticed this before, in Norway; you were much weaker then than now. But it's not the sleeping pill that makes you feel good: it's sleep, which gives you total rest."

"It's true."

Trotsky looked across to the steel shutters that had been put on their bedroom window, and said: "The Siqueiros won't get to us so easily next time."

Every morning over the last few weeks, almost the first thing he had said to Natalia was: "There you are. We've slept through a whole night and nobody has killed us. And you're still not satisfied." She thought he was looking to reassure himself as much as he was trying to comfort her. A few days before, he had added in a thoughtful voice: "Yes, Natasha; we've been given a short reprieve."

As Trotsky did every day, he had a massage, washed himself vigorously, dressed quickly, then headed off with "a firm step" to the garden, where between seven fifteen and nine he saw to the plants, chickens, and rabbits while it was still fresh and cool. From time to time, he stopped to dictate an order or idea. The courtyard was brilliant with roses and geraniums flowering in the midst of hardy cacti. It was a little paradise inside the grim fortress their home had become.

At nine a.m., he had breakfast. His spirits were lifted further when, on sitting down, he opened a letter from his lawyer, Albert Goldman, informing him that the material from his archives that he had sold to Harvard University had arrived at its destination in perfect condition.

After breakfast he told Natalia once again that he felt "quite well" and that he wanted to sit down to start dictating ideas for an article he planned to write about military mobilization in the United States and the idea of revolutionary defeatism; the article was to be called "Bonapartism, Fascism and War."

What Trotsky produced was wandering and tentative—a record of a man trying to make sense of the way in which old ideas had crashed into new realities. It was only recently that he had stopped arguing for the policy of "revolutionary defeatism," which Lenin had adopted during the Great War. Workers weren't responsible for defending an imperialist fatherland; their duty was to repeat the triumph of 1917: to turn a conflict into a revolution.

The terrifying success of the Third Reich had changed this. Trotsky talked of the "treacherous senile Bonapartism" that now governed the humiliated France, but also of the American workers' desire to fight. Pacifism was futile, he thought, and anyway, war often led to revolution. These new thoughts sat alongside tired arguments about Mensheviks and Bolsheviks, digs at the Trotskyist faction in New York, and long-rehearsed complaints about the ways in which the proletariat had disappointed him.

Trotsky also turned to his correspondence. There were two letters to American comrades who had just been released from prison after having participated in a strike. And a cheerful note to Hank Schultz, one of his American correspondents:

> I received an excellent gift from Grace—a dictionary of slang. There is only one difficulty—that at mealtimes I must permanently keep this book in my hands in order to be able to understand the conversation. However, I shall try to study it between meals in order to better check the "academic" part of the household. In the part I have already studied, which is devoted to college slang, I had hoped to find some abbreviations for the various sciences, philosophical theories, etc., but instead I found merely about 25 expressions for an attractive girl. Nothing at all about dialectics or materialism.

It was clear that he was in high spirits. He did not know that it was the last letter that would ever leave his desk.

At one o'clock, Antonio Rigault, the lawyer who was helping Trotsky deal with the fallout from the May attack, came to see him. After emerging from the meeting looking frustrated, Trotsky told Natalia that he had to delay his work on the article while he drafted a response to *El Popular*'s newest collection of calumnies against him. Then there was a flash of anger. "I'm going to take the offensive and call them cynical slanderers," he said, his voice vibrating with defiance.

"It's a pity you can't write that article on mobilization," said Natalia.

"What can I do? I have to give it up for two or three days. I asked that all the materials be put on my desk. . . . After lunch, I will take a look at them."

At this Trotsky brightened. He said, "I feel really good," as if surprised anew at the change that had come over him.

He took his customary short nap and then sat down at his desk. Natalia felt a surge of pleasure when, having half opened the door so as not to disturb her husband, she glanced at him in his study, bent over papers, pen in hand. She was glad that he was looking so well; in the last few days, he had suffered from a number of distressing fainting attacks and had complained of more general fatigue. When he was in this state, Trotsky thought "of them" more than his wife believed was good for him. And yet it seemed as if he were on the threshold of a new period of better health. This moment of happiness was followed by a sadder observation. The greatest living revolutionary of his era was living like a cloistered monk.

In that glorious year when Trotsky and Lenin had changed the world, there had been so much energy and excitement. He had given speeches from a position in which he was so closely pressed against others that "I seemed to be speaking out of a warm cavern of human bodies." In these ecstatic moments, he had felt the crowd's collective will force its way into his own mind, dictating to him what he should say next.

He had thundered to thousands of men and women, "Let this be your oath—to defend with all your might, at whatever cost, this Soviet which has shouldered the glorious task of leading the Revolution to victory and to give the people land, bread and peace." Then he had watched as those men and women lifted their hands and repeated his words in rhythmic unison.

And in the last months before the Bolshevik seizure of power, he had worked from a large, square, sparsely furnished room in the Smolny Institute. At the heart of the filthy staircases strewn with sunflower seeds; the exhausted men sleeping with rifles cradled in their arms beneath chandeliers in pillared white halls; and the constantly shrilling telephones was the fastidious, precise Trotsky talking endlessly into clouds of tobacco smoke.

Most nights he dropped fully clothed onto his sofa, gripped by nervous exhaustion, sleeping for a few hours at a time. Natalia remembered those days as "a sort of lucid delirium"; it was impossible to arrange properly the jumbled sequence of events. "But," she added, "there was a sense of contained happiness, and we felt there was not a moment to spare for anything but the task at hand."

This all seemed impossibly distant. Now he was impotent, hunted, a prisoner of his own past who had been defeated utterly by the man he had dismissed as an "oafish provincial."

---

Ramón started the morning in a hurry. By the time he had breakfasted (alone, away from the other guests in the hotel), the sun had already come up, shining fiercely even though it was the rainy season. But in the distance, dark clouds collected above the twin volcanic peaks of Popocatépetl and Izaccihuatl.

He had been feeling sick all week and rarely left room 113. When he came out to take his meals in the hotel's garden, he appeared withdrawn and did not speak with any of the other guests. The manager, Miss Noriega, thought that he and his partner just wanted to be left alone.

Despite the mounting heat, Ramón strode out of the hotel with his English khaki raincoat under his arm after announcing to Sylvia that he was going to the US embassy—they needed, he said, to urgently check his visa ahead of his departure the following day for New York. He would be back for lunch.

When interrogated later, he told the police that he had instead gone to the Chapultepec Forest. Perhaps he walked around the park, trying to summon the strength he knew he needed for the task that lay ahead of him. It is possible that he used the time to go over the details of his plan in his head once more or to finesse one or two outstanding points. He might also have met with his coconspirators—this might have been the moment when Eitingon handed him the typewritten explanation for his actions that formed the basis for his cover story.

At noon, Ramón returned in an angry mood, and he headed out for lunch with Sylvia, who was dressed in a "white piqué sports ensemble" over which she wore a worn beige coat trimmed with faded fur.

As they passed the gleaming white marble of the Palacio de Bellas Artes, they were spotted by Otto Schüssler and his partner, Gertrude Schrotter, who were heading toward an art gallery near the Alameda Central. Ramón and Sylvia did not see them. Schüssler approached the other couple and touched Sylvia's right arm gently to draw her attention.

Sylvia smiled and was cheerful, telling Schüssler: "Oh it is so good to see you, we are leaving for the USA tomorrow morning but first we wanted to say our goodbyes to you and Mr. Trotsky this afternoon."

Schüssler replied that he would not be at the house on the Avenida Viena that afternoon; it was his afternoon off. At this, Ramón, who appeared pale and almost unable to speak from nerves, opened his mouth for the first time.

"You will not be in the house this afternoon?"

Schüssler confirmed that he would not be there and suggested that they should go the following morning instead.

Sylvia pointed out that it would be better for Ramón and her to go that afternoon. Time would be tight in the morning; they needed to arrange the dispatch of their luggage and then catch their flight.

Schüssler then told them that Trotsky would not be free until after four p.m. This appeared to end Ramón's interest in the conversation and he sank back into himself.

Sylvia told Otto that she was worried about her partner. Although he was an athlete, he was in delicate health. "The altitude, the food of the country do not seem to suit him. Better we get out of here." Otto thought that she was sincerely concerned.

She also suggested that since they would not be able to bid Schüssler farewell at Trotsky's compound, perhaps they could meet for dinner once Ramón and she had returned from Coyoacán.

Ramón proposed that they all meet at seven o'clock on the corner of San Juan de Letrán Street and Madero Street. As soon as everybody had agreed, Ramón brought the exchange to a conclusion, saying: "Excuse me, Otto, but we have an appointment at two o'clock." Schüssler noted the difference between his habitual courtesy and the bluntness with which he was now speaking.

After parting ways with the Schüsslers, Ramón and Sylvia ate their lunch in the Don Quixote Salon of the St. Regis Hotel. Ramón still seemed agitated throughout the meal, so much so that they left the restaurant before they had finished their food. He told his lover that he was in a hurry because he had urgent business—he had to work at a bank and then attend a phone conference with his employers in New York regarding the commercial assets of a man named Alfredo Viñas, who lived in the Las Lomas neighborhood. He also asked her to pay the bill. She did this and then they both took a cab back to their hotel.

If anything, Ramón seemed even more uneasy by the time they arrived. He tried to explain himself, saying that he was just anxious because he was late for work. Then he promised her that he would return to the Montejo at around four, after which they could travel to Coyoacán together to say their goodbyes and to show Trotsky the corrected version of his article "The Third Camp and the Popular Front."

Sylvia asked him if he was going to wear his gabardine raincoat. Yes, he said, and she watched him walk to their closet and take it. She did not know that sewn into its lining was a six-inch knife with a blue metal cuff and silver inlays he had bought at La Lagunilla, the big Mexico City secondhand market. The knife was encased in a bay-colored leather sheath embroidered with silver thread. In one of the coat's pockets was a Spanish-made .45-caliber Star automatic pistol with eight bullets in the magazine and one in the firing chamber. It was a powerful weapon, capable of knocking a man off his feet. There were also his piolet, or ice ax, which was attached to his pocket by a cord, and $890 in cash. Finally, Ramón had a typewritten confession in French explaining why he was doing what he was about to do; the confession had that day's date and the signature of "Jac" added in pencil.

At somewhere between two and two thirty, he left the hotel. After this, Ramón wandered aimlessly around the city for three hours. He turned up to collect his mail from the Wells Fargo office, and then between four and five p.m., he drove to a deserted lot close to a railway crossing near where the city ended and Coyoacán began. Here he burned the fake passport he used to enter the country and various other papers. In doing so, he was destroying any documents that might suggest his true identity or the role he was about to play.

This done, he slid back into his Buick and took the road for the Avenida Viena.

# 30

# Him Again

At five p.m., the bell at the fortress in Coyoacán rang out.

Twenty minutes later, Ramón pulled up in his Buick. He was ready for what he called "my great historic act."

Charles Cornell, Melquíades Benítez, and Joseph Hansen were on the roof connecting a siren with the alarm system; it had been sent to them by an enthusiastic supporter from Los Angeles—another precaution in case of a mass attack.* They were nearing the end of the process of strengthening the house's defenses, but progress was slowing and they were still waiting for barbed wire and sandbags.

The guards were surprised to see Ramón. They were unaware of any appointment Trotsky had made with him or Sylvia, but then this in itself was not unusual. Trotsky was often guilty of such oversights. Hansen also noticed that while Ramón usually parked his car so that its grille faced the compound, today he had turned around in the Avenida Viena and parked the Buick parallel to the wall, with its nose pointed toward Coyoacán.

Hansen did not attach much significance to either of these things,

* Trotsky: "The siren provoked even more admiration. It is wonderful enough just in appearance. We have not yet tried it out . . . for we are told that this siren can be heard from here to Los Angeles. I, personally, consider this an exaggeration."

and he watched as Ramón got out of his car, waved, and asked the guards, "Has Sylvia arrived yet?"

He needed to establish if she had arrived early. Sylvia, with the exception of the investigation she tried to instigate about his phantom office, had rarely been anything other than obedient. When he asked her to do something, she did it. It was not in her nature to act too independently. But if she had decided to break their arrangement and come straight to the house, it would throw his plans into disarray.

"No," Hansen told him, "wait a moment." At this, Cornell operated the electrical controls on the double doors, and they swung open to let Ramón into the patio, where he found the thin, wiry Harold Robins. Robins had his pistol in his hand, yet like all of the others, he trusted Ramón and neglected to search him. Nor did he record his arrival in the ledger—this was something the guards had been told they needed to do only for strangers.

Robins noticed nothing unusual about their guest's behavior. He registered the raincoat slung over Ramón's arm, but did not think much of it. It was the rainy season, and although the sun was high in the sky, he could also see ominous-looking clouds massing over the mountains to the southwest.

Hansen, Melquíades, and Cornell returned to their work, spending the next ten minutes or so sitting in the main tower writing out the names of all the guards on white labels that were to be attached to the switches connecting their rooms with the alarm system.

As they walked farther into the compound, Harold asked Ramón about the scratch he'd left on the house's Dodge. Ramón explained that he was responsible and that he'd already agreed with the Old Man that he'd cover the cost of the repair.

The secretaries called down to them, saying something Ramón couldn't make out, and he resumed his conversation with Robins, talking about how keen Sylvia was to say her goodbyes. "She may come later," he told Harold as they arrived at the rabbit hutch, where Trotsky was feeding the animals. Trotsky greeted his visitor politely, but continued to carefully load the feed troughs with dried alfalfa. He appeared reluctant to leave the rabbits alone—partly because of his obsessive attachment to his own rituals; partly because he felt as if he had already discussed Ramón's unsatisfactory article with him; and partly because he was still baffled by the strange encounter with Ramón a few days before.

As Ramón waited patiently, Trotsky explained, in French, that it was dangerous to give the rabbits damp weeds, because their bellies would swell up. At some point, Ramón's patience gave way to distraction and he stopped taking in anything his interlocuter was saying: "He explained why but I don't remember. I know nothing about rabbits."

NATALIA WAS ENJOYING a day that she felt was "one of the smoothest we have ever known." Trotsky had been productive, and she had been able to show him how much she cared for him. At noon she had seen him striding around the garden bareheaded, defenseless against the blazing sun. She ran out with a white cap to protect him.

There had been a "perfect balance" in the hours that followed. She enjoyed the perfume of flowers in full bloom and the brilliant green of the lawn. Everything felt so ordinary, so safe; she and her husband had discussed summoning a barber to cut Trotsky's hair before deciding that there wasn't time. Then they had taken tea at five, as always, and thirty minutes later, she went out to the balcony. She could see her husband standing on the patio by the open hutch, and beside him was somebody that she recognized only when he took off a gray hat with a black band and walked toward the house.

*Him again*, she thought. *Why does he come here so often?*

Something about Ramón's demeanor had changed since he had been chatting amiably with Robins. Natalia instantly noticed and was troubled by his ashy green countenance and his nervous air, which shaded into irritability.

Ramón approached her, and they spoke in French. "I am terribly thirsty," he said. "Could I have a glass of water?"

"Wouldn't you like a cup of tea?"

"No, I had a late lunch," he said. "I'm full up to here. It's choking me." At this, he pointed to his throat.

It was only now Natalia noticed that despite the heat he wore a dark suit and carried a raincoat. This was also strange; he had once told her that he never wore a coat, even in the cold.

"Why are you wearing your hat and raincoat in such fine weather?"

"Because it might rain."

Natalia realized this was absurd but remained more mystified than alarmed.

"And how is Sylvia?"

For a moment Ramón didn't reply. The mention of his raincoat had clearly disturbed him. He seemed absorbed, as if he had suddenly awakened from a deep sleep. With some effort, he recovered. "Sylvia? Sylvia? She is always well."

Once he had drunk the water, he turned back to the hutch. Natalia went with him and asked, "Is your article ready?"

"Yes," he said, "it is completed."

Natalia asked him whether he had typed the text up. He made a clumsy gesture with the hand that held the raincoat. He kept the arm close to his body and showed her some typed sheets.

They reached Trotsky, who spoke to his wife in Russian. "You know, he's waiting for Sylvia. They leave tomorrow." He suggested that perhaps they could invite Ramón, if not to dinner, then at least to tea, and he urged her to think about what they might drink.

Natalia turned to Ramón. "I didn't know you were expecting Sylvia and leaving tomorrow."

"Oh yes!" he replied. "I forgot to tell you."

"Too bad we didn't know!" Natalia said, "I could have given you a commission for New York."

"Oh, I can come back tomorrow morning." There was a flash of the obliging young man whom they had got to know over the last few months, but just as quickly Natalia appeared to regret the opening she had offered him.

"No, no, thank you. It would bother us."

Speaking again in Russian, she told Trotsky that she had already offered their guest tea and that he had refused.

Trotsky examined the younger man, looking into his eyes, which were barely blinking. "You don't look well. That's not good." For a few tense seconds, there was silence; then Ramón, his hand trembling now, produced a sheaf of typed sheets of paper.

Without even a "glimpse of enthusiasm," Trotsky said, "Oh well, are you going to show me your article?"

Ramón simply nodded.

At that moment Natalia sensed that something had shifted in her husband's feelings about this young man, but that he was still trying to work out exactly what. She watched as he tried to shrug off this uncertainty as he carefully closed the hutch's doors and peeled off his gardening gloves; always meticulous, Trotsky was especially careful of his hands, because they were easily injured and even the slightest scratch could interfere with his writing. Then he shook off his blue French peasant blouse, which he wore to protect his clothes.

The two men crossed the courtyard without speaking. "Then," Ramón later recalled, "he invited me to step into his office. Of course I was counting on that."

Natalia watched as the door, with its stained-glass windowpanes, closed behind them. There was time for Trotsky to have a final thought as Ramón followed him in: *This man could kill me.*

Trotsky's whitewashed study, which abutted his simply furnished bedroom, was bright, high ceilinged, and unadorned, though its floor was painted a striking deep red. In its stern elegance, the study was in many ways a reflection of its owner.

Light streamed through a balcony window on which Trotsky usually turned his back while working. He spent so much of his time here that there was even a couch for his daily siestas. There were no ornaments, no photos, no paintings, no figurines. The chairs were simple and cane bottomed.

What decoration there was came from a map of Mexico that hung on one wall and from the books—the works of Lenin bound in red and blue cloth and titles by Herzen, Tolstoy, Taine, Nietzsche, Ibsen, Schnitzler, Dos Passos, Langston Hughes, London, Malraux, Freud, Maurras, Henri Béraud, Serge, Barbusse, and Souchy—that filled almost every other space in the room. Most of these books' margins were covered in notes and comments. In one of them, Boris Souvarine's recent biography of Stalin, a string of angry exclamation marks perforated the paper.

Trotsky sat down in his usual armchair. Ramón felt a rush of confidence. Everything was going as well as he could possibly have hoped. The desk behind which Trotsky sat was a broad, rough-hewn table piled with magazines and books. His pen tray contained an ivory paper knife, a pair of spectacles, and some cartridge cases that had been collected in the aftermath of the attack in May. There were pens and pencils in a jar, along with an old-fashioned blotter, a gooseneck lamp, and his bulky Dictaphone. Centimeters away from his hand was a .25-caliber automatic pistol. Elsewhere in the study was a Colt .38. Both were loaded with six bullets.

Ramón stood on Trotsky's left, inserting himself between the Russian and the recently installed alarm switch. The reconnaissance he had made the week before meant that he knew exactly where it was located. He casually tossed his overcoat onto the table to ensure that Trotsky could not reach for the switch; then he sat on the desk's edge and watched as Trotsky bent over the manuscript of his article.

Ramón's position gave him a view of Trotsky's bare head, with its crown of thinning white hair. He could see that alongside his own shoddy article was one that Trotsky was drafting about Siqueiros's assault. One second, maybe two passed.

Then Ramón acted. Later he said that he was anxious "not to lose the brilliant opportunity which was offered me." At the "exact moment" that Trotsky started to read—he had skimmed the first page and was about to start on the second—Ramón took the piolet from the pocket of his raincoat. At the end of a heavy, foot-long wooden stock was a steel head that ran seven inches tip to tip. One end was sharpened to a vicious point; the other was a forked hammer claw. It was this broad end—which climbers used to detach and split blocks of ice—that crashed into Trotsky's skull, leaving a gory three-inch deep wound.

But it did not kill him instantly. Trotsky, who had been totally absorbed in the article, shook his head just as the weapon descended. This changed the direction of the blow and weakened the impact.

Trotsky screamed in such a way that Ramón instantly knew that he would never forget the sound as long as he lived. "His scream was a long, endlessly long 'aaaa' and it still seems to me as if that scream were piercing my brain."

Ramón's excitement in this moment had reached such a pitch that he did not reach for the knife. The impact of the scream paralyzed him. Blood spattered onto Trotsky's papers, which included his biography of Stalin and a file he had been keeping on the NKVD.

Trotsky clawed at whatever was at hand—books, the inkpot, the Dictaphone—and hurled them at Ramón before stealing the pick from his grip. He then leaped up "like a madman" and threw himself at his assassin, biting his hand with such force that toothmarks were still visible during Ramón's interrogation a few days later.

Ramón pushed Trotsky to the floor, and running and stumbling, he escaped from the room. Trotsky staggered out of the study in the other direction. Natalia had heard "a terrible, soul-shaking cry," although she didn't immediately realize it had come from her husband.

She rushed toward the sound and was confronted by the sight of him leaning against the door that led from the study to the balcony, arms hanging limply by his side. His face was covered in blood, but what really struck Natalia was the way that his blue eyes, unshielded by glasses, glittered.

"What is happening? What is happening?" she cried, and flung her arms around him in utter confusion. Trotsky became briefly unresponsive as Natalia frantically tried to work out what had gone on. Had something fallen from the ceiling?

At that moment he said one word, calmly, without any "distortion, bitterness or despair": "Jacson." It was as if, Natalia later thought, he were conveying a last message: *Now it is done.*

As SOON AS he heard Trotsky's scream, Joseph Hansen felt an unidentifiable dread surge through his body. He sprinted from the guardhouse to the roof, where he switched on the alarm.

His first thought that one of the builders had had an accident. But then he heard the unmistakable sounds of a life-or-death confrontation coming from the study. He glimpsed Melquíades pointing his rifle at the window below and caught a flash of Trotsky's blue work jacket in a "body to body" struggle with another.

"Don't shoot!" he shouted at Melquíades. "You might hit the Old Man!"

He slid down a ladder to the study, and just as he entered the door that connected it to the dining room, he encountered a bloodied Trotsky. By this point, Trotsky had sunk to the ground. Hansen asked him what had happened.

"Jacson shot me with a revolver," Trotsky told him. "I am seriously wounded. . . . I feel that this time it is the end."

"It's only a surface wound. You will recover."

"We talked about French statistics."

"Did he hit you from behind?"

Trotsky made no answer.

"No, he did not shoot you. We didn't hear any shot. He struck you with something."

Trotsky looked skeptical and pressed Hansen's hand. He had been speaking to Natalia in Russian at the same time he had been answering his secretary's questions. At intervals he brought her hand to his lips.

"Natasha, I love you. Oh . . . Oh . . ."

"No one, no one, must be allowed to see you without being searched."

Natalia placed a pillow beneath his "broken head," held a piece of ice to his rapidly swelling wound, and wiped blood from his face with a cotton ball.

Speaking with mounting effort, his voice getting fainter and coming close to breaking, Trotsky ordered that Seva be taken away to safety. But it was obvious that he did not realize that he was having difficulty speaking.

"You know, in *there*," he said, indicating the study with his eyes, "I sensed . . . I understood what *he wanted to do*. . . . He wanted to strike me . . . once more. . . . But I didn't let him."

There was a deep note of satisfaction in his words.

HANSEN CLAMBERED BACK up to the roof, where he shouted across the wall to the police: "Get an ambulance!" Then he found Cornell and Melquíades and told them, "It's an assault—Jacson." His voice was staccato with stress and fear. He looked down at his wristwatch and saw that it read ten minutes to six.

He then returned to Trotsky's side, this time followed by Cornell. They hurriedly discussed how they could get the Old Man help. It would be too long to wait for an ambulance, so it was decided that Cornell should go to summon Dr. Dutren, whose home was close and who had treated the family before. The comrade's car was locked away behind double doors in the garage, so Cornell indicated he'd take Ramón's car, which they thought was still on the street.

Trotsky then looked at Hansen and spoke to him in English. Although Natalia and Joseph were kneeling on either side of Trotsky, neither could make out what he was saying.

Their attempt was interrupted when Charles Cornell, his face "chalk-white" and a revolver in his hand, rushed in. His appearance suddenly reminded Natalia of the existence of her husband's attacker.

"What about *that one*?" she asked Trotsky. "They will kill him."

"No," he said, his speech coming painfully slowly now, ". . . impermissible to kill, he must be *forced to talk*."

Trotsky's whispered orders were suddenly obscured by a cry of pain and renewed sounds of a struggle. Natalia looked at her husband questioningly. He winked, almost imperceptibly, in the direction of his office and said "indifferently," "It's him. . . . Hasn't the doctor arrived?"

HANSEN LEFT TROTSKY with Natalia and entered the dining room. He found a panic-stricken Ramón desperately trying to escape from Robins. An automatic pistol lay on the table. On the floor was "a blood-spattered instrument which looked to me like a prospector's pick."

Robins and Cornell stood over the injured Ramón, who was covered in both his own and Trotsky's blood. Hansen passed on Trotsky's order.

Robins looked back at Hansen: "I'm not going to kill him. But I'm going to crush his bones and make his body a sieve if he doesn't tell us right away who he worked for."

Robins started methodically hitting Ramón's ribs. Blow followed blow. Robins's shouts of "Admit it, it's the G.P.U. who sent you!" alternated with the dull thump of bone crashing into bone and Ramón's denials: "No! Not the G.P.U." Ramón slipped into unconsciousness twice, resurfacing to offer up more conflicting, ambiguous sentences that seemed like well-rehearsed lines.

One of the guards remembered thinking: "That was the first I realized how hard this person really was. He would sooner die than talk."

The second time Ramón came to, he moaned: "They have imprisoned my mother. . . . Sylvia Ageloff had nothing to do with this. . . . No, it was NOT the GPU; I have NOTHING to do with the GPU."

As if following the stage directions in an unseen script, he put particular emphasis on the words that he thought put distance between himself and the men who had sent him into this room. And then a movement from Robins that slung Ramón back down onto the floor evidently convinced him that his last moment had arrived. He writhed in terror; words he was unable to control spilled out of his lips

"It's them! Them!"

"Who, them?" Robins yelled. "Come on, speak!"

"A man. I don't know him, but he made me do this."

"How did he make you do it?"

"They've got me!" There was a pause, as if Ramón was assessing the wisdom of what he was about to say. Then: "They're holding my mother hostage!"

Robins, convinced he was still being lied to, continued to push for more information. He repeated his questions over and again, each time with more malice in his voice.

Ramón expanded his story. He'd been ordered to kill Trotsky by a man named Paris, who was also known as Bartolo or Bartolo Perez. Ramón had known this Paris or Bartolo or Bartolo Perez in Paris and then encountered him again three weeks earlier in Mexico at the Kit-Kat Club, at the corner of the Avenida Independencia and Calle Dolorès.

At this, Hansen joined in, hitting Ramón on the mouth and on the jaw below his ear so hard that he broke his own hand. Ramón started pleading: "Kill me! Kill me at once! I don't deserve to live! Kill me! I received no orders from the G.P.U. But kill me anyway!"

They were interrupted by Cornell, who exploded into the study. "The keys aren't in his car." Cornell fumbled with Ramón's clothing, trying to find them. Nothing.* As Cornell searched, Hansen ran out and opened the garage doors. Then Cornell sped off in the Avenida Viena's car, and Hansen returned to Trotsky. Like Natalia, he knelt on the floor, holding the Old Man's hands.

"He hit you with a pick," Hansen told Trotsky again. "He did not shoot you. I am sure it is only a surface wound."

"No, I feel here"—Trotsky gestured to his heart—"that this time they have succeeded."

"No, it's only a surface wound; you'll get better."

Trotsky's eyes betrayed gentle amusement at Hansen's clumsy attempt to reassure him. "Take care of Natalia. She has been with me many, many years." With this request, he began gazing at his wife.

"He seemed to be drinking in what her features were like," remembered Hansen later, "as if he were leaving her forever—in these fleeting seconds compressing all the past into a last glance."

Hansen promised, "We will."

All three knew that Trotsky was nearing the end. He pressed Natalia's and Hansen's hands "convulsively"; his eyes suddenly filled with tears. Natalia simply wept, bent over her husband, and kissed his hand.

---

* What the guards did find: a steel Longines watch with a worn-out brown leather strap; two empty glasses cases; seventy-six pesos and four $20 bills; and a handful of cartridges for Ramón's pistol.

# 31

# AFTERMATH

Sylvia and Ramón were supposed to be meeting Schüssler and Schrotter for dinner at seven p.m. that evening. They had agreed to meet them on the corner of Madero Street and San Juan de Letrán Street.

An anxious-looking Ageloff arrived fifteen minutes late, without Ramón. She explained that he had gone to work but had still not returned. "I don't know what's wrong with Jacson," she told Schüssler. "He is acting strange. When he is late, he usually calls me and tells me the reason, but today he only told me to meet him in the hotel at four p.m. so we could go together to Trotsky's house. But he has not called."

Sylvia had been sure that there had been a miscommunication and that she would find Ramón here. She appeared distressed to find that she had been wrong. The three friends decided to walk until they found a telephone. Having done so, Ageloff called the Hotel Montejo several times, but the staff had not seen him.

Schüssler then suggested calling Ramón's business contact, Alfredo Viñas. Sylvia had a scrap of paper with Viñas's address. They looked without success for his number in the phone book, so they returned to the Hotel Montejo to wait for Ramón.

Sylvia's anxiety mounted as the evening dragged on. She proposed visiting the address she had for Viñas. The trio took a cab to Las Lomas, looking for Paseo de la Reforma 1329 or 1331. There was no building with that number and none of the neighbors they asked knew anything about a man called Viñas.

Next, they took another taxi to Café Swastica. Again, Sylvia called the hotel, this time asking for Jacques Mornard, and again the staff reported no sign of him. They tried to find Alfredo Viñas at the Banco Ejidal, where they believed he worked. The night watchman informed them that nobody of that name worked in the building.

It was now eight ten p.m. Schüssler attempted to persuade Sylvia to call Trotsky. She was reluctant, saying: "It is impossible that Jacson is at Trotsky's house because he never goes there without me."

Schüssler stepped into a shop to buy cigarettes. Once inside, he called the Avenida Viena. The telephone was answered by a man called Mr. Milton. When Schüssler asked if Ramón was there, Milton replied: "Yes, come immediately. Jacson attacked Mr. Trotsky."

Schüssler hung up the phone and with the others leaped into a cab to Coyoacán. As they sped through Mexico City's dark streets, he told his companions what he had just learned.

Sylvia began to cry, saying, "If something happened it must be very serious," and Schüssler tried to reassure her by telling her that the person he had spoken to was excited and that it had been difficult to hear him above the confused street noise. Perhaps there was information about a new assassination attempt and Ramón could not leave the house.

This explanation did not soothe the Sylvia, who said over and over again: "Why did Jacson go to the house alone? Why didn't he go with me? Why didn't he phone me?"

They finally arrived and were met by one of the guards, who confirmed that what Sylvia had feared most had taken place. She started weeping again and asked to be taken to a police station.

Trotsky hung on for another day. He was lucid right up to the end, even though it clearly hurt him to speak. As he was sped through the city in an ambulance, he lay on a stretcher, his left hand paralyzed against his body. The right one was in constant movement, describing circles in the air and occasionally alighting on Natalia's fingers.

When Natalia asked how he was, he told her, "Better now." There was a pause; then he repeated himself. For a moment, a "dull hope" rose within his wife, and it persisted as they arrived at the hospital. Once a bed had been found for him, the doctors bent over the wound in silence while a nurse cut Trotsky's hair. Suddenly a faint smile emerged on his face. "The hairdresser came, you see."

Then he turned to Joseph Hansen. "Joe, you . . . have . . . notebook?" His voice was thick, the words scarcely distinguishable, and he spoke with great effort. His eyes seemed fixed on a distant point invisible to Hansen as if he had stopped being aware of the external world. But still Hansen felt "his enormous will power holding away the extinguishing darkness, refusing to concede to his foe until he had accomplished one last task." Slowly, pausing frequently, as if he needed to summon energy from deep within himself to continue, he dictated in English, because Hansen spoke no Russian:

> I am close to death from the blow of a political assassin . . . struck me down in my room. I struggled with him . . . we entered . . . talk about French statistics . . . he struck me. Please say to our friends . . . I am sure . . . of the victory . . . of the Fourth International . . . Go forward!

He continued trying to speak but Hansen could no longer make out what he was saying. His voice faded away and he closed his eyes.

The doctors began to remove Trotsky's clothes, cutting through his workers' coat with scissors to avoid hurting him; then they moved to his waistcoat and shirt. Before they started on his underwear, he spoke again to Natalia in a very distinct voice that was full of sorrow.

"I don't want them to undress me; I want it to be you." Natalia did not realize at the time that these would be the last words he ever said to her.

When she was done, she leaned down and pressed her lips to his. He returned the kiss, once, twice, a third time. Not long afterward, he lost consciousness. Hansen thought, almost irrelevantly, that with his head shaved and bandaged, Trotsky bore a startling resemblance to Lenin. An operation that revealed that the ice ax had penetrated seven centimeters, destroying considerable brain tissue, could not revive him.

Natalia—refusing food and watching dry-eyed, hands clenched, knuckles white—stayed by his side through the night, never once breaking her watch over him. She tried to take heart from the fact that his breath, although occasionally labored, was always calm. Then, at noon, he seemed to improve. There was another surge of hope. But by the end of the afternoon, his breath was coming in short, quick gasps.

Early that evening, Natalia, who had fallen asleep from exhaustion in an armchair, suddenly awoke as if from a premonition to see two white-clad doctors standing in front of her. She understood immediately what their presence meant.

At seven twenty-five p.m., the old revolutionary heaved his last breath and slipped away.

# EPILOGUE

## "ONE DOES NOT CHOOSE THE TIME TO LIVE, DIE, OR KILL"

While Ramón had been carrying out his attack, Caridad and Eitingon were waiting in a car parked around the corner from the Avenida Viena, expecting to see him emerge, triumphant. They parted as soon as it became clear that he had not escaped.

Eitingon, traveling on false documents, reached Acapulco, where a Soviet cargo ship was waiting for him.

Caridad stayed in Mexico City for one day more, long enough to organize a lawyer for her son; then she made her way to Tampico and took a boat to Japan, where the Japanese authorities held her for two months in Yokohama before the Soviet government secured her release.

Meanwhile, her son lay on a stinking, filthy cot in the same hospital to which his victim had been taken. Bandages covered much of his head as well as his right arm, the legacy of the bite he had received from Trotsky. His expression was vacant, his skin drained of any color. One witness described him as appearing like a ghost of himself; another described him as a "human rag."

Ramón denied furiously that he had any connection with the NKVD. He claimed that he was merely a disaffected Trotskyist who had been revolted by his idol's refusal to allow him to marry Sylvia and attempt to involve him in a plot to kill Stalin.

A letter found in his jacket stated his reasons for murdering Trotsky; and he repeated its sentiments ad nauseam, almost as if it were a script he had learned by heart. One section read:

> instead of finding myself face to face with a political chief who was directing the struggle for the liberation of the working class, I found myself before a man who desired nothing more than to satisfy his needs and desires of vengeance and of hate and who did not utilize the workers' struggle for anything more than a means of hiding his own paltriness and despicable calculations. . . . It was Trotsky who destroyed my nature, my future and all my affections. He converted me into a man without a name, without country, into an instrument of Trotsky. I was in a blind alley. . . . Trotsky crushed me in his hands as if I had been paper.

SYLVIA WAS LEFT reeling from the shock of Ramón's actions. Every time that Trotsky's name was mentioned, she wept and demanded the execution of the man who had betrayed her. She was even more distressed to find herself accused of murder. The authorities did not believe that she had been ignorant of Ramón's plans, nor did they accept his own pleas that she had had nothing to do with the assassination. (The FBI's own representative suggested: "While this girl is very adept in pulling hysterical fits at the proper time, she, in my opinion, is a tough customer and may never tell all that she knows that might be useful in determining just what was behind Jacson's killing of Trotsky.")

Sylvia would see her erstwhile partner just once more, when he was brought by the head of the Mexican police, Colonel Leandro Sánchez Salazar, to the hospital bed where she had retired, seemingly in the grip of a nervous breakdown.

Sylvia collapsed into "convulsive sobs" while Ramón, who had been told that he was simply having an examination on the eye that had been damaged in the fracas following his attack on Trotsky, tried to pull away, shouting, "Why did you bring me here? What have you done, Colonel? What have you done? Take me!"

Sánchez Salazar replied, "If you love Sylvia as much as you say you do, approach her, talk to her, try to console her." He gestured to the soldiers who were supporting Ramón and made them hold his head so that Sylvia could see his face.

At this, Sylvia jerked her head up, fixed Ramón with a vicious stare, and launched a volley of curses at him: "Take that murderer away! Kill him as he killed Trotsky! Kill him! Kill him!"

Sánchez Salazar remained impassive. He turned to Sylvia and invited her to speak again. "Jacson claims that you are the justification of his whole life and that it was because you were the victim of Trotsky's intrigues that he killed him."

"That's not true!" Sylvia screamed in response. "He's a liar! An assassin!" At one point she attempted to attack Ramón; as her fragile body was restrained by guards who had rushed into the room, she spat and shouted, "You are a blackguard! Blackguard! Blackguard!" Ramón endured the onslaught with the patient air of a man submitting to an unpleasant but necessary medical procedure. Finally, though, he turned his head toward Colonel Sánchez Salazar and, in a barely audible voice, asked, "Please, sir, order this woman to be removed from here immediately. Can't you see how crazy she is?"

Shortly afterward, the murderer was ushered out of her room, pursued by Sylvia's insults.

Her release was eventually secured and she returned to the United States. By the mid-forties, she was living under her mother's maiden name—Maslow—in suburban New York and running a kindergarten from one of her father's apartments. She shared a home with her sister Hilda. They lived quietly, only receiving a few female visitors and spending weekends at Ruth's farm in Connecticut. Whenever she was asked about the events of 1940, and her involvement in them, she continued to insist that she had merely been a dupe.

When the FBI arrived at her door on the evening of 15 April 1942 to ask her more questions about the murder, she was "greatly perturbed" that her address had been discovered. Only immediate family members were supposed to know it. More than anything, she wanted to be forgotten. She died in Brooklyn in 1995.

THE MOST MACABRE sequel to the murder came a few days later, when the examining magistrate, Raúl Carrancá y Trujillo, broke the five seals that had prevented entry to Trotsky's office, and began a reconstruction of the crime.

The room had remained untouched. Two pairs of Trotsky's glasses were on the desk. The tortoiseshell pair he had been wearing when Ramón had struck him lay there, their lenses smashed.

Wearing a gray suit and bowing his head, Ramón was brought in. The killer appeared a pathetic specimen, weak and apparently unable to stand without being supported. His face was still swathed in a helmet of bandages from which a single lock of hair escaped.

Ramón moaned with pain continually, though some present believed he was exaggerating his discomfort. When he saw the Trotskyist guard Joseph Hansen, he trembled visibly, then sank into a chair.

Ramón realized that in doing so he had stepped on some dried blood and convulsed violently, then hid his face in his arms as if he could not bear to contemplate what he had wrought.

The reconstruction began with a Major Galindo sitting in Trotsky's chair. Ramón was placed to his left, near the garden window. He whispered, "When I attacked him, he was reading my article. He had skimmed the first page and was about to start the second when I took a step back; I turned around and pulled the ice ax from the raincoat, which I had put down on the table behind me when I entered. And immediately I hit him on the head. Like this." With that, he grabbed a roll of newspapers and made the gesture of hitting Major Galindo. Then he added in a faint voice, "Someone had arrived: Robins,

I believe. I couldn't see anything; I was unable to take a step. I was beaten up and fell to the ground almost unconscious. That's all. Yes, that was it."

WHILE HE AWAITED trial, Ramón was subjected to one of the most detailed interrogations in history. In his first six months behind bars, he spent nine hundred hours alone with psychiatrists.

At their first meeting, he announced, "You are not going to get anything out of me." But after that, he was generally polite and helpful, patiently answering question after question, all the while smoking an unbroken chain of cigarettes.

The psychiatrists carried out an extraordinary range of tests, such as examining Ramón's nervous system and adrenaline levels and making him record dummy radio broadcasts so that they could analyze his voice and determine whether or not he was a journalist as he claimed.

Ramón was asked to assemble a pistol in the dark and to sing four different versions of "The Marseillaise" (two of which were sung during the Spanish Civil War). Other ploys included sending him messages in Russian, subjecting him to encephalograms and dream analysis, giving him provocative books, and making him repeat meaningless phrases. He was asked to touch and then identify objects with his eyes covered.

His reserve could be broken by the evocation of certain precise details of the crime that seemed to disturb him and would leave him almost prostrate with a kind of mental agony. Nevertheless, he clung tenaciously to his story, even at those moments when it was shown to be provably false. At one moment he boasted that he would not relent "Even if you should cut the skin off me centimeter by centimeter."

At the end of all this, the report "The Organic-Functional and Social Study of the Assassin of Leon Trotsky"—which was divided into two volumes and ran more than 1,332,726 words—was submitted to the judge. It is unclear how much, if at all, it influenced his verdict.

In 1941, Ramón was given a prison sentence of twenty years to be served in the infamous Palacio de Lecumberri prison.

TROTSKY'S DEATH MARKED the end of the NKVD's interest in the Fourth International. On 1 July 1941, a little over a week after the Third Reich's invasion of the Soviet Union, state security officials Agoyants and Klykov drafted a memo that officially closed the agency's file on Trotsky, as well as any Trotskyist literature being published abroad. They noted that "all of this material is no longer of any operational interest."

Oddly enough, most witnesses agreed that even Stalin showed "no particular joy" on learning of his old rival's death. Earlier in the same month that Trotsky died, the Soviet Union had annexed Lithuania, Latvia, and Estonia. More pertinently, Stalin knew that the pact that he had signed with Hitler the previous summer was only a temporary expedient. His country would soon be at war again; a more urgent preoccupation. Suddenly, it was as if Stalin could see Trotsky for what he was or had been: an impotent exile banished to a faraway nation.

Nevertheless, the NKVD did not abandon Ramón. Within a month of the killing, Moscow used its special channels to communicate its gratitude for his accomplishment of the mission. Eitingon was ordered to use his agents to find out the condition of the "patient" and to see if anything could be done to help him. The NKVD sent money to Ramón's prison to help make his life there as comfortable as possible, and they paid for the services of Eduardo Ciniceros Ríos, one of Mexico City's most notable lawyers, who would later become Ramón's friend.

Ramón's cell was spacious, sunny, and well ventilated, and he was able to arrange it in the orderly and systematic fashion that suited his orderly and systematic mind. He wore good clothes and slept in silk pajamas. He ate and drank well and smoked the best cigars. He had all the books he wanted, a radio receiver, and the tools to make model airplanes. He was also able to pay another prisoner to clean his cell. Victor Serge secured an audience with him in the mid-forties and found the prisoner dressed in khaki gabardine slacks with a sharp crease, yellow shoes, a silk sport shirt, and an expensive suede jacket. Everything about his bearing exuded mental and physical well-being.

At no point did Ramón's faith in the cause he had served, or the actions he had taken in this service, waver. He believed history would remember him as a soldier in the world revolution who had fought for the working class by killing the man who wanted to betray it. He loved to sing the revolutionary song "The Young Guard," giving extra emphasis to the last line: "We work for a great cause!"

In 1944, Ramón met and fell in love with Roquelia Mendoza, the daughter of a soldier and a former cabaret dancer who had been paid by the Soviets to bring him food and look out for his welfare. Mexico's humane prison regulations allowed them to marry. Although they were unable to have children themselves, they adopted two children; later they would also take in Roquelia's nephew, whose parents had died in a car accident.

RAMÓN WAS KNOWN by fellow prisoners as *el hombre del piolet* (the man with the ice ax), just as others were known as "the brick" or "the hammer" because of the murder weapon they'd used. But the others seemed to respect and like him, largely because he earned this respect. Early on during his sentence, Ramón took courses on electronics and learned a great deal about the subject. The prison authorities were so impressed by his progress that they placed him in charge of the institution's radio and carpentry workshops. He gave lessons to his fellow inmates and repaired lamps, motors, refrigerators, and radios. It is also estimated that over two decades he taught some four hundred prisoners how to read and write.

He was steadfast in holding on to his assumed identity. It was only in 1950 that cracks began to appear in the carapace he had built. Warders heard him sing a lullaby in Catalan. This set off a chain of events that led investigators to Spain, where Franco's police supplied a "thick dossier" on Ramón Mercader, including photographs and fingerprints.

Ramón remained dismissive of any attempts to persuade him to acknowledge his true identity. Following the revelations, *Life* magazine arrived in Mexico and offered him $50,000 for his memoirs, with the only condition being that he reveal his name and nationality. Ramón pretended to accept the proposal, received the journalists in his cell, and even took the check between his fingers. But when he was handed the contract to sign, he tore it and the check into pieces and threw the scraps into their faces, gleefully informing them, "Journalism is one of the human race's most detestable activities."

Ramón wrote occasional letters to Luis, though he said very little of his own circumstances except "Dear brother, I'm fine." In turn, Luis tried to persuade him to write his own memoir, "maybe just for me." Ramón had clearly been drafting something in his cell—another inmate remembered him constantly writing in a notebook—but his response to his brother was categorical: "I have never been a traitor, I will never betray my parents."

EITINGON WORRIED THAT Caridad, who was in a febrile state of mind, might lurch into an indiscretion of some kind as soon as they were in Russia.

Initially, his fears seemed overstated. Caridad was received in the Kremlin. Mikhail Kalinin, who was, formally at least, the head of the Soviet state, pinned the Order of Lenin on her uniform. She was also awarded a Hero of the Soviet Union medal on Ramón's behalf—Moscow's way of reassuring her it had not forgotten about her son.

Caridad was reunited with Luis and given an apartment in a building largely occupied by secret service agents. Later, after the German invasion, she lived with Luis and Elena Imbert, until Elena's death from tuberculosis in 1943.

The Soviet Union still had tasks for Caridad. She spied on communist émigrés from other countries. Sometimes she was sent on missions to neutral countries such as Turkey and Spain. But over time, her bitterness and frustration grew. She was an uninhibited cosmopolitan woman who had traveled the world and, thanks to largesse of the NKVD, had become accustomed to living comfortably. She felt caged in Moscow, despising everybody who lived around her. She hated the weather, the hardships, and the "leaden and terrifying environment." She had become something strange: a "blind-eyed believer" in Stalin who could not tolerate her existence in the USSR.

Another émigré remembered the time he spent with Caridad "in her little apartment in Kaluzhskaya." Here she lay in bed with a cape over her shoulders, knitting and smoking one cigarette after another, only getting up to make coffee. Stricken by insomnia and the guilt she felt for having embroiled her family in such catastrophes, she lived behind closed windows and locked doors, rarely venturing out into the streets below.

Instead, she spoke longingly of other places—like Cuba, Mexico, and Paris—as if lingering on the past could help obscure the misery of her present existence. Occasionally, her frustration and bitterness overflowed. She would break out into hysterics, saying "unimaginable things" and threatening to kill herself.

One day, Caridad started ranting: "They cheated us. . . . They deceived us with their revolutionary books, their propaganda and their so-called paradise. It is the worst hell that has ever existed. I never can get used to it. I have only one desire, only one thought: to run away, to run away from here. . . . You don't know these people the way I do . . . they don't have a soul or a conscience. They annihilate your will, they force you to kill and then make you die, all at once or slowly, as they are making me die at this moment."

Then she narrated the whole story of Trotsky's assassination. By the end, she was lying on her bed once more, sobbing, her head buried in her hands. "I made Ramón an assassin, my poor Luis a hostage and my two other children wrecks. What reward did I receive in return? Two bastards!" At this, she stood up, went to a chest of drawers, and, with a disgusted look, pulled out the decorations she and Ramón had been awarded.

She wrote unceasingly to Beria and Sudoplatov, alternately threatening them with exposure or pleading for permission to leave the Soviet Union. They responded with Georgian wines (obtained from prerevolutionary cellars), bouquets of flowers, and soothing postcards.

Occasionally, Eitingon would pay Caridad visits to urge patience on her, but the only person who seemed able to calm her was her son Luis. Finally, she threatened to either kill herself or take refuge in the Cuban embassy if she was not allowed to leave the country. Beria acquiesced and allowed her to go to Cuba on the condition that she would not try to visit Mexico; she was considered too unstable, too unpredictable to be allowed to return.

She agreed; then, as soon as she had escaped from the Soviet Union, she headed for Mexico. Here she made an abortive attempt to rescue Ramón; its only material impacts were to delay his release and to engender in him lasting resentment that he would spend much of the rest of his life trying to suppress.

ON 6 MAY 1960 at nine in the morning, Ramón's sentence came to an end. He traveled first to Czechoslovakia. Within days of his arrival in Moscow, he was awarded the rank of a retired KGB colonel with the right to a monthly pension. Twenty years after his "great act," he had finally officially entered the Soviet intelligence service.

His appointment was accompanied by another new identity: Spanish-Soviet citizen Ramón Ivanovich López.

The first question Ramón asked on his arrival in the Soviet Union was: "Where is Leonid?" He was horrified to learn that his friend was in prison. After Mexico, Eitingon had continued to provide valuable services to the Soviet Union, working as Sudoplatov's deputy in the

Fourth Directorate of the NKVD. Together they, among other things, stole atomic secrets from the United States and helped organize partisan movements behind enemy lines. After the war they continued the struggle against anti-communist movements in Eastern Europe, even as his own faith began to wane. As Sudoplatov remembered, "Leonid said that the party was no longer an association of people devoted to socialist ideas and justice but had become the machinery for ruling the country."

His career was brought to a halt by Stalin's paranoia. Eitingon had once commented sardonically, "There is one small guaranteed way not to end up in jail under our system. Don't be a Jew or a general in the state security service." He was both. In 1951 the ailing Stalin launched one last purge, this time directed at what he characterized as a cabal of (largely) Jewish doctors and their comrades who had plotted to murder Soviet leaders. Eitingon, whose sister Sonia was a doctor, became embroiled. Although Stalin had professed himself so pleased with Eitingon's role in the assassination of Trotsky that he personally promised that "not a hair will ever fall from your head," Eitingon, along with others, was imprisoned and pressured to make a false confession. Eitingon denied his involvement, but Sonia was sentenced to ten years behind bars.

It seemed as if Stalin's death in 1953, followed by Beria's arrest and execution, might offer respite. Although Sonia was released, Eitingon's perceived allegiance to Beria led to him being thrown into jail and stripped of his rank and all his medals. He was set free only after Khrushchev's deposition in 1964.

Ramón and Eitingon met as soon as the latter was released, and they would spend hours together talking in French. A year before his death in 1977, Ramón dedicated a photo to Eitingon: "Dear Leonid, thank you for your friendship, I am proud to have been able to work under your orders and thus have learned to behave like a true communist."

Ramón met with Sudoplatov too, though their relationship was never warm. (Sudoplatov was also arrested in 1953, but he feigned madness, which postponed his trial for a few years—this was not enough to help him escape prison.) Inevitably, their conversations would stray to the events of 1940. Ramón once told the spy chief: "If we were to relive the 1940s I would do the same thing, but not in the present day." He then quoted a Russian saying: "One does not choose the time to live and die"; then he said, "I would add to that 'One does not choose the time to live, die, or kill.'"

Ramón lived quietly with his wife and their children, working as a translator for magazines and books. His walls were adorned with paintings by Siqueiros, Rivera, and Kahlo. He was the sort of person who, when invited to dinner at someone else's home, would always think hard about which wines he could take to best please his host. Generally, though, he found that other Spaniards kept their distance from him, wary of his connections with the secret police. He was seen as a solitary, lonely presence. His daughter said he was afflicted by nightmares, and sometimes he talked about the terrible moment he struck Trotsky, covering his eyes with his hands and saying, "I can hear that scream."

There were parts of his past that he struggled to leave behind.

Victor Zaslavsky, who would later become a renowned professor of political sociology at several universities in Russia and the United States, had a strange encounter with Ramón.

Zaslavsky often visited the Moscow Central Public Library, the best place to consult books that had been banned elsewhere in the Soviet Union.

Any researcher had to be properly accredited, and what they read was strictly controlled. One day, a man in his sixties—tall, with a broad back and a pronounced chin, and dressed in "the western manner"—sat down beside Zaslavsky and shared his desk.

Unlike everybody else, who worked in stern silence, this man repeated phrases to himself, smiled, and sometimes even laughed openly.

Intrigued, Zaslavsky waited until his desk mate was briefly absent.

"Nimble as a thief, I rummaged through his stack of books." Victor Serge's *L'affaire Toulaev* fell open, but what really struck Zaslavsky were the other books, most of which were in French or Spanish and either by Trotsky or about him.

This was the sort of reading matter that could get you thrown into prison or executed. Who was this man? Through a friend, Zaslavsky discovered that the man was registered under the name Carrasco, which was evidently a pseudonym. Later, however, they discovered his true identity. "For God's sake, don't tell anyone," Zaslavsky's friend told him. "We'll both end up in jail."

Anxiety drove Zaslavsky away from the library. He sensed that contact—any contact—with Ramón might prove dangerous. And yet he saw that he was not the only one who was uncomfortable. Ramón appeared to have trouble reading. He did not notice the agitated student sitting beside him; rather, "he was conducting an endless personal dialogue with Trotsky or, perhaps, with the authors of books on Trotsky. He polemicized, accused, defended himself . . . sometimes he paced up and down the corridor, advancing, clenching his fists."

It was as if Ramón needed to know more about the man whom, decades earlier, he had assaulted with an ice ax. And, perhaps, he needed to establish whether he had done the right thing.

Ramón's calm existence was occasionally interrupted by the arrival in Moscow of Caridad, who made irregular visits from Paris, where she had made a home for herself.

Luis and Ramón tried to preserve her faith in the system, shielding her from the "defects and difficulties of daily life." In the process they "ruined ourselves," borrowing money and consumer goods to no avail because "there was nothing that suited her."

Ramón avoided arguments with his mother and held back from reproaching her for the ways in which she had bent his life out of shape. It was easier to remain silent, perhaps because he knew how deep the guilt she felt was. As she once admitted to Luis, "It's my fault that everything has turned out this way. I've destroyed the family. It's because of me that my family are scattered all over the world. . . . Yes, I've destroyed my family."

After each visit, Caridad left "broken to pieces, disappointed, her spirit depleted"—and yet her faith would always return. She died in October 1975, aged eighty-three, a month before Franco. To the end, she had an enormous portrait of Stalin on her bed's headboard. Her funeral costs were covered by the Soviet embassy in France.

Natalia remained in the house on the Avenida Viena for several years. She had little money and was haunted by the events of August 1940. A visitor noted that she was "physically reduced to nothing, [with] the body of a worn-out little girl; a tragic face, wrinkled, tense, ravaged, pale, and much aged." She reminded him of an exhausted shadow. Occasionally, she would travel to France to stay with friends. "For months at a time she would wander about in Paris, visiting theaters and museums, trying to recover the happiness she had enjoyed in Paris with her husband."

In order to relieve Natalia's straitened circumstances, the Mexican government bought the property and turned it into a museum. She stayed for a while longer in Mexico City before eventually resettling in Paris. When she died in 1962, her ashes were buried next to those of her husband in Coyoacán.

Luis had tried to persuade his brother to remain in the more westernized Czechoslovakia, which he thought would suit him better. From the late fifties onward, Luis entertained doubts about the system; he saw that the blind faith displayed by his mother and brother was an abyss that they had fallen into.

Ramón ignored these warnings, and for some years relations between the siblings cooled. "I could not speak frankly about anything with him," remembered Luis. "He was completely mesmerized by the idea of communism, and absolutely sure that there was nothing in the world better than the Soviet Union."

Steadily, however, disillusionment set in, though Ramón remained a discreet dissenter. Once, Eusebio Cimorra, an announcer for Radio Moscow's Spanish broadcasts, said in a whispered conversation, "Ramón, they have deceived us."

His friend let out a self-pitying sigh: "Some more than others."

Luis suggested that Ramón move to Cuba, which seemed to promise a freer, more cosmopolitan existence. Ramón wrote to Fidel Castro, who replied immediately, inviting him to settle in Cuba.

The KGB blocked Ramón's plans to relocate, though Roquelia and their children were allowed to travel without him. At around this time, Ramón began suffering from a mysterious illness that resembled cancer in many ways, even if multiple examinations failed to detect cancerous cells.

Eitingon would later speculate that his friend had been poisoned, potentially by a gold watch engraved with "To the hero of the Soviet Union Ramón López, in remembrance of Victory Day"; he was given the watch at a party to celebrate Victory Day. Ramón's health deteriorated further—to some who knew him he resembled a man who was centuries old—and he continued to petition to be allowed to go to the Caribbean.

Eventually, permission was granted. His last years passed fairly comfortably, though each night he suffered from a fever he called "*la moth,*" and his departure from the communist paradise was the occasion for a break with his siblings Jorge and Montserrat, who saw it as an act of betrayal. Ramón was scathing in return, calling his sister and brother "ignorant petty bourgeois."

He was killed in 1978 by lung cancer at the age of sixty-five. Although he died in Havana, his body was brought back to Moscow's Kuntsevo Cemetery, where he was buried as Ramón Ivanovich López, the name he had been given on his arrival in the Soviet Union.

In the years after his release from prison, Leonid Eitingon was employed as an interpreter and editor at the International Book Organization in Moscow. When not working, he made repeated attempts to secure official rehabilitation, which were rewarded in 1992, when the Russian Supreme Court agreed to annul his conviction. But Eitingon was not around to see his name cleared; he died of natural causes in 1981.

Sudoplatov lived long enough to see the collapse of the Soviet Union and his own official rehabilitation. His entertaining, loquacious, and only partially misleading memoir, *Special Tasks*, was published in 1994, two years before his death in 1996.

Mark Zborowski, or Etienne, emigrated to the United States in 1941. Although he was charged with getting "very close" to Jean van Heijenoort, Trotsky's former secretary, who was in charge of the Trotsky archive at Harvard, it's not clear how long his spying continued. He forged a successful career as a medical anthropologist and became known for groundbreaking research on the cultural mitigation of pain and for an ethnohistoric account of life in the shtetls of Eastern Europe. He died of heart failure at San Francisco's Mount Zion Hospital on 30 April 1990, aged eight-two, though not before he was confronted by Elsa Reiss, who had belatedly discovered his true allegiance during this period.

# ACKNOWLEDGMENTS

This book would not exist without the encouragement and skill of my agent, Chris Wellbelove. Or the enthusiasm shown by my publishers in the United States, Dutton, notably Brent Howard, who commissioned it; and Lindsey Rose, whose edit improved my text immeasurably. I'm also grateful to David Howe, Charlotte Peters, and senior production editor LeeAnn Pemberton for everything they have done to make the book better.

In December 2022, I traveled to Mexico City to visit some of the locations mentioned in the book, as well as archives held at the Palacio de Lecumberri, which in a former life was the prison in which Ramón Mercader spent two decades. Mario Arévalo helped me navigate my way through the documents, as well as conducting a great deal of valuable research after I had left. It was a real pleasure to collaborate with him. Also in Mexico City, Leonardo Ruíz Gómez and Alberto De la Barreda were very generous with the help they provided.

Roland Philipps has long been a source of good advice and support, but I'm particularly grateful to him for sending me the manuscript of Zita James's unpublished memoir, which contained a wonderful account of an encounter with Trotsky.

Any book of this kind stands on the shoulders of the many scholars and writers who have written brilliantly and knowledgeably about their areas of expertise for many years. I've relied especially on the work of Isaac Deutscher, Simon Sebag Montefiore, Stephen Kotkin, Isaac Don Levine, Christopher Andrew, Robert Service, and Dmitri Volkogonov, authors whose insights have helped shape my understanding of this era and the men and women who inhabited it.

Most of all I want to thank my wife, Victoria, and daughter, Ivy, who mean everything to me.

# AUTHOR'S NOTE

Soviet Russia's first secret police organization, the Cheka (the All-Russian Extraordinary Commission), was established on 20 December 1917, just weeks after the Bolsheviks had seized power. It was dissolved in 1922 and replaced by a new organization, the GPU, which was replaced in turn by the OGPU, which was itself replaced, in July 1934, by the NKVD (People's Commissariat for Internal Affairs).

To avoid a proliferation of confusing titles, and because most of this book's narrative unfolds during the period when the Soviet Union's clandestine operations were presided over by the NKVD, I have used this term consistently throughout the text.

# Notes

## Prologue

1 **At some point:** Gary Kern, *A Death in Washington: Walter G. Krivitsky and the Stalin Terror* (Enigma Books, 2004), 13–14, 26; Gérard Rosenthal, *Avocat de Trotsky* (Robert Laffont, 1975), 209–11, 214; Elisabeth K. Poretsky, *Our Own People: A Memoir of "Ignace Reiss" and His Friends* (Oxford University Press, 1969), 1–3, 9, 23–24; KV 2 1898; KV 2 2878; KV 2 2879.

4 **The letter contained continued in:** Poretsky, *Our Own People*, 188, 222–28; KV 2 1898.

6 **After Reiss had:** Poretsky, *Our Own People*, 231–35; KV 2 1898.

9 **Renata Steiner, an:** Christopher Andrew and Vasili Mitrokhin, *The Mitrokhin Archive: The KGB in Europe and the West* (Allen Lane, 2005), 103; Rosenthal, *Avocat de Trotsky*, 211–13; Poretsky, *Our Own People*, 239.

10 **Later that afternoon:** Rosenthal, *Avocat de Trotsky*, 211–12, 214; Victor Serge, *Notebooks: 1936–1947* (New York Review Books Classics, 2019), 21–22, 171.

## 1: Death Solves All Problems

15 **Perhaps it was:** Dmitri Volkogonov, *Trotsky: The Eternal Revolutionary*, trans. Harold Shukman (HarperCollins, 1996), 47, 260–61; Leon Trotsky, *Stalin: An Appraisal of the Man and His Influence*, trans. Charles Malamuth (Harper & Brothers, 1946), 90.

15 **Trotsky was tall:** Volkogonov, *Trotsky*, 216; Clare Sheridan, *Russian Portraits* (Jonathan Cape, 1921), 129; Max Eastman, *Leon Trotsky: The Portrait of a Youth* (Faber and Gwyer, 1926), 28–29, 39; Joel Carmichael, *Trotsky: An Appreciation of His Life* (Hodder & Stoughton, 1975), 162; Robert Service, *Trotsky: A Biography* (Belknap Press of Harvard University Press, 2010), 1.

16 **This precocious son:** Volkogonov, *Trotsky*, 3, 41, 84–85; Eastman, *Leon Trotsky*, iv–v.

16 **He studied philosophy:** Volkogonov, *Trotsky*, 10, 16.

17 **One thing led:** Carmichael, *Trotsky*, 233; Yuri Slezkine, *The House of Government: A Saga of the Russian Revolution* (Princeton University Press, 2017), xii; Martin Amis, *Koba the Dread: Laughter and the Twenty Million* (Jonathan Cape, 2002), 14.

18 **Joseph Stalin was:** Trotsky, *Stalin*, 66, 87; Stephen Kotkin, *Stalin, vol. 1: Paradoxes of Power, 1878–1928* (Allen Lane, 2014), 427; Robert C. Tucker, *Stalin as Revolutionary 1879–1929: A Study in History and Personality* (Chatto & Windus, 1974), 432; Dmitri Volkogonov, *Stalin: Triumph and Tragedy*, trans. Harold Shukman (Weidenfeld & Nicolson, 1991), 155; Amis, *Koba the Dread*, 101; Robert Conquest, *The Great Terror: A Reassessment* (Hutchinson, 1990), 54, 64; Simon Sebag Montefiore, *Stalin: The Court of the Red Tsar* (Weidenfeld & Nicolson, 2003), 2–4; Milovan Djilas, *Conversations with Stalin* (Penguin, 1962), 52.

19 **Nobody was better:** Kotkin, *Stalin, vol. 1*, xii, 26; Tucker, *Stalin as Revolutionary*, 212; Volkogonov, *Stalin*, 3, 46.

20 **Their paths crossed:** Trotsky, *Stalin*, 99; Service, *Trotsky*, 1; Montefiore, *Stalin*, 25.

20 **Stalin was not:** Tucker, *Stalin as Revolutionary*, 429–30.

21 **He was intoxicated:** Volkogonov, *Trotsky*, 60, 125; Nicholas Mosley, *The Assassination of Trotsky* (Sphere Books Ltd., 1972), 83; Angelica Balabanova, *Impressions of Lenin* (University of Michigan Press, 1964), 128; Victor Serge and Natalia Sedova Trotsky, *The Life and Death of Leon Trotsky*, trans. Arnold J. Pomerans (Wildwood House, 1975), 2.

22 **The jet-black:** Volkogonov, *Trotsky*, xxix, 152–54, 164–67; Kotkin, *Stalin, vol. 1*, 327; Antony Beevor, *Russia: Revolution and Civil War, 1917–1921* (Weidenfeld & Nicolson, 2022), 233, 258.

22 **There was another:** Slezkine, *The House of Government*, 165; Volkogonov, *Trotsky*, 156; Mosley, *The Assassination of Trotsky*, 68; Service, *Trotsky*, 197; John J. Dziak, *Chekisty: A History of the KGB* (Lexington Books, 1988), 35, 75; Amis, *Koba the Dread*, 252.

23 **In a very:** Volkogonov, *Trotsky*, xxxii.

24 **He used his:** Volkogonov, *Trotsky*, 140–43; Trotsky, *Stalin*, 288, 293–300; Kotkin, *Stalin, vol. 1*, 304, 308–9; Amis, *Koba the Dread*, 57; Montefiore, *Stalin*, 28.

24 **Stalin was convinced:** N. N. Sukhanov, *The Russian Revolution 1917: A Personal Record*, trans. Joel Carmichael (Oxford University Press, 1955), 230; Trotsky, *Stalin*, 48; Serge and Trotsky, *The Life and Death of Leon Trotsky*, 133; Montefiore, *Stalin*, 28.

## 2: LIAR, TRAITOR, SCUM

25 **Trotsky despised a:** Trotsky, *Stalin*, 289; Max Eastman, *Love and Revolution: My Journey Through an Epoch* (Random House, 1964), 561, 563; Service, *Trotsky*, 37, 119, 337; Conquest, *The Great Terror*, 9.

26 **Where Trotsky mocked:** Volkogonov, *Trotsky*, 241–45, 253; Kotkin, *Stalin, Vol. 1*, 419, 425, 469; Tucker, *Stalin as Revolutionary*, 348, 353; Volkogonov, *Stalin*, 88, 134; Serge and Trotsky, *The Life and Death of Leon Trotsky*, 117; Montefiore, *Stalin*, 30, 43–44.

28 **Slowly, relentlessly, Trotsky:** Volkogonov, *Trotsky*, 199–201, 266, 274; Eastman, *Leon Trotsky*, 42–43; Carmichael, *Trotsky*, 338; Mosley, *The Assassination of Trotsky*, 85, 92; Service, *Trotsky*, 325, 344.

28 **As an exasperated-sounding:** Leon Trotsky, *Trotsky's Diary in Exile 1935*, trans. Elena Zarudnaya (Faber and Faber, 1958), 37–38; Volkogonov, *Trotsky*, 270.

29 **There were still:** Volkogonov, *Trotsky*, 295–96, 299; Kotkin, *Stalin, vol. 1*, 615, 646–48; Serge and Trotsky, *The Life and Death of Leon Trotsky*, 150–51.
31 **In the months:** Andrew and Mitrokhin, *The Mitrokhin Archive*, 51; Serge and Trotsky, *The Life and Death of Leon Trotsky*, 149; Montefiore, *Stalin*, 39; Serge, *Notebooks*, 90–91.

## 3: ATTRITION

33 **Trotsky was optimistic:** Robert Payne, *The Life and Death of Trotsky* (W. H. Allen, 1978), 330; Isaac Deutscher, *The Prophet Outcast: Trotsky, 1929–1940* (Oxford University Press, 1963), 9.
33 **Trotsky also struggled:** Christopher Andrew and Oleg Gordievsky, *KGB: The Inside Story of Its Foreign Operations from Lenin to Gorbachev* (Hodder & Stoughton, 1990), 120; Deutscher, *The Prophet Outcast*, 9.
34 **Even this confidence:** Deutscher, *The Prophet Outcast*, 19.
34 **In France, where:** Trotsky, *Trotsky's Diary in Exile 1935*, 101–2, 365; Payne, *The Life and Death of Trotsky*, 353; Andrew and Mitrokhin, *The Mitrokhin Archive*, 51; Serge and Trotsky, *The Life and Death of Leon Trotsky*, 193–95.
35 **The discomfort Trotsky:** Jean van Heijenoort, *With Trotsky in Exile: From Prinkipo to Coyoacán* (Harvard University Press, 1978), 130; Deutscher, *The Prophet Outcast*, 58–61.
36 **One of Stalin's:** Andrew and Mitrokhin, *The Mitrokhin Archive*, 52; Serge and Trotsky, *The Life and Death of Leon Trotsky*, 132.
37 **As Olga Grebner:** Volkogonov, *Trotsky*, 7.
37 **It had never:** Volkogonov, *Trotsky*, 312, 348.
38 **Zina, Trotsky's firstborn:** Volkogonov, *Trotsky*, 349–52; van Heijenoort, *With Trotsky in Exile*, 35; Service, *Trotsky*, 385–86; Deutscher, *The Prophet Outcast*, 145, 149–51, 178–79, 195–97; Serge and Trotsky, *The Life and Death of Leon Trotsky*, 190.

## 4: KREMLIN COMPLEXION

40 **Stalin had last:** Boris Souvarine, *A Critical Survey of Bolshevism* (Alliance Book, 1939), 431; Kotkin, *Stalin, vol. 1*, 469; Tucker, *Stalin as Revolutionary*, 432–33; Volkogonov, *Stalin*, xxi; 146–48, 167, 190, 201; Amis, *Koba the Dread*, 112; Montefiore, *Stalin*, 101, 103.
42 **Stalin was the:** Volkogonov, *Stalin*, 196–98, 259–60; Serge and Trotsky, *The Life and Death of Leon Trotsky*, 171.
43 **Trotsky knew that:** Trotsky, *Trotsky's Diary in Exile 1935*, 66; Trotsky, *Stalin*, 18; Tucker, *Stalin as Revolutionary*, 211.
44 **Stalin never forgot:** Tucker, *Stalin as Revolutionary*, 438, 449; Volkogonov, *Stalin*, 63.
44 **Trotsky had belittled:** Andrew and Gordievsky, *KGB*, 121; Volkogonov, *Stalin*, 259, 261, 318; Conquest, *The Great Terror*, 56; Montefiore, *Stalin*, 4.

## 5: A PERFECT COMMUNIST FAMILY

49 **Ramón Mercader del Río:** Isaac Don Levine, *The Mind of an Assassin* (New American Library, 1960), 157–70; Luis Mercader, *Ramón Mercader, mi hermano: cincuenta años después* (Espasa-Calpe, 1990), 21, 50; Eduard Puigventós López, *Ramon Mercader, l'home del piolet: Biografia de l'assasí de Trotski* (Ara Llibres, 2015).
51 **Eustacia María Caridad:** Levine, *The Mind of an Assassin*, 13–16, 156, 158; José Luis López-Linares and Javier Rioyo, dirs., *Storm the Skies* (Cero en Conducta,

1996); Mercader, *Ramón Mercader, mi hermano*, 17–18, 56; José Ramón Garmabella, *El grito de Trotsky: Ramón Mercader, el asesino de un mito* (Debate, 2007), 12; Puigventós López, *Ramon Mercader, l'home del piolet*, 297, 328.

52 **It was only:** Levine, *The Mind of an Assassin*, 158; López-Linares and Rioyo, *Storm the Skies*; Mercader, *Ramón Mercader, mi hermano*, 17, 80; Garmabella, *El grito de Trotsky*, 13; Puigventós López, *Ramon Mercader, l'home del piolet*, 386.

54 **In 1925, when:** Levine, *The Mind of an Assassin*, 16–19; Mercader, *Ramón Mercader, mi hermano*, 17, 20; Puigventós López, *Ramon Mercader, l'home del piolet*, 402.

55 **Ramón had returned to:** Levine, *The Mind of an Assassin*, 19–20; Mercader, *Ramón Mercader, mi hermano*, 21, 53; Puigventós López, *Ramon Mercader, l'home del piolet*, 297.

57 **In the summer of 1936:** Teresa Pàmies, *"Ramón Mercader: misión cumplida," Triunfo*, 28 October 1978, 22; Garmabella, *El grito de Trotsky*, 21–22, 258; Puigventós López, *Ramon Mercader, l'home del piolet*, 513.

## 6: BLACK WORK

60 **The purge that:** Marc Jansen and Nikita Petrov, *Stalin's Loyal Executioner: People's Commissar Nikolai Ezhov, 1895–1940* (Hoover Institution Press, 2002), 20, 195–99; Garmabella, *El grito de Trotsky*, 102.

62 **But Trotsky was:** J. Arch Getty and Oleg V. Naumov, *The Road to Terror: Stalin and the Self-Destruction of the Bolsheviks, 1932–1939* (Yale University Press, 1999), 20; Kotkin, *Stalin, vol. 1*, 470, 591, 679; Orlando Figes, *The Whisperers: Private Life in Stalin's Russia* (Allen Lane, 2007), 239, 277.

63 **The victims were:** Conquest, *The Great Terror*, 149–51.

64 **As the Terror:** Figes, *The Whisperers*, 232–33; Ilya Ehrenburg, *Men, Years—Life* (MacGibbon & Kee, 1961–1966), 193–94; Conquest, *The Great Terror*, 121–23, 127, 130; Montefiore, *Stalin*, 198, 230.

65 **More than half:** Vladimir Petrov and Evdokia Petrov, *Empire of Fear* (Deutsch, 1956), 71; Montefiore, *Stalin*, 175, 219.

## 7: SUPER-BANDIT

66 **Trotsky was still:** Serge and Trotsky, *The Life and Death of Leon Trotsky*, 206, 210.

66 **In the pages:** Trotsky, *Trotsky's Diary in Exile 1935*, 53.

67 **Trotsky's anxiety at:** Trotsky, *Trotsky's Diary in Exile 1935*, 90; Volkogonov, *Trotsky*, 366; Serge and Trotsky, *The Life and Death of Leon Trotsky*, 206; Montefiore, *Stalin*, 169.

68 **The gentle Sergei:** Trotsky, *Trotsky's Diary in Exile 1935*, 61–66, 69, 79–81, 116, 117; Volkogonov, *Trotsky*, 355–56; Sèrvice, *Trotsky*, 346; Deutscher, *The Prophet Outcast*, 281–83.

70 **At one point:** Alain Dugrand, *Trotsky in Mexico 1937–40* (Carcanet, 1992), 38; van Heijenoort, *With Trotsky in Exile*, 41.

71 **Natalia's life had:** Volkogonov, *Trotsky*, 24; Eastman, *Leon Trotsky*, 165; Service, *Trotsky*, 85, 108, 262, 345, 446–47; Serge and Trotsky, *The Life and Death of Leon Trotsky*, 12.

## 8: THE CRUCIBLE

73 **Once the first:** Levine, *The Mind of an Assassin*, 21; Puigventós López, *Ramon Mercader, l'home del piolet*, 620.

74 **Around the same:** Mercader, *Ramón Mercader, mi hermano*, 22, 53; Puigventós López, *Ramon Mercader, l'home del piolet*, 635.

75 **And yet there:** Amanda Vaill, *Hotel Florida: Truth, Love, and Death in the Spanish Civil War* (Bloomsbury, 2014), 42–46; Giles Tremlett, *The International Brigades: Fascism, Freedom and the Spanish Civil War* (Bloomsbury, 2020), 27; Ehrenburg, *Men, Years—Life*, 110–13; Puigventós López, *Ramon Mercader, l'home del piolet*, 687.

75 **Combative, daring, energetic:** Levine, *The Mind of an Assassin*, 13, 61; Pàmies, *"Ramón Mercader: misión cumplida,"* 22; Garmabella, *El grito de Trotsky*, 28.

76 **A month later:** Mercader, *Ramón Mercader, mi hermano*, 23; Pàmies, *"Ramón Mercader: misión cumplida,"* 22; Garmabella, *El grito de Trotsky*, 22; Puigventós López, *Ramon Mercader, l'home del piolet*, 722.

## 9: The Only Honest Government in the World

82 **And yet, as:** Dugrand, *Trotsky in Mexico 1937–40*, 15; Payne, *The Life and Death of Trotsky*, 391–92; Serge and Trotsky, *The Life and Death of Leon Trotsky*, 210.

83 **Mexico was a:** Susan Weissmann, *Victor Serge: The Course Is Set on Hope* (Verso, 2001), 176; Deutscher, *The Prophet Outcast*, 166; Hayden Herrera, *Frida: A Biography of Frida Kahlo* (Harper & Row, 1983), 204–5.

83 **Within days of:** Volkogonov, *Trotsky*, 365, 387.

83 **The house in:** Evelyn Waugh, *Robbery Under Law: The Mexican Object-Lesson* (Catholic Book Club, 1939), 19–25; Matías Gueilburt, dir., *El asesinato de Trotsky*, Anima Films, 2007; Anita Burdman Feferman, *Politics, Logic, and Love: The Life of Jean van Heijenoort* (Jones and Bartlett, 1993), 143; Jonathan Kandell, *La Capital: The Biography of Mexico City* (Random House, 1988), 10–11, 123, 203, 386–87, 389, 485–86; Service, *Trotsky*, 429; Herrera, *Frida*, 206; Kingsley Martin, "Kingsley Martin: Trotsky in Mexico, 10 April 1937," *The New Statesman*, 10 May 2013, https://www.newstatesman.com/long-reads/2013/05/kingsley-martin-trotsky-mexico; Garmabella, *El grito de Trotsky*, 75; Serge and Trotsky, *The Life and Death of Leon Trotsky*, 211.

86 **These trips, which:** Dugrand, *Trotsky in Mexico 1937–40*, 38; Gueilburt, *El asesinato de Trotsky*; Service, *Trotsky*, 430; Joseph Hansen, "With Trotsky to the End," *Fourth International* 1, no. 5 (1940); Deutscher, *The Prophet Outcast*, 448–49; Herrera, *Frida*, 208; Garmabella, *El grito de Trotsky*, 73.

87 **Once they were:** Volkogonov, *Trotsky*, 386.

88 **In Mexico Trotsky:** Serge and Trotsky, *The Life and Death of Leon Trotsky*, 225, 228.

88 **They were watched:** Alan Wald, "Memories of the John Dewey Commission: Forty Years Later," *Antioch Review* 35, no. 4 (1977); Service, *Trotsky*, 429; Garmabella, *El grito de Trotsky*, 74–75; Serge and Trotsky, *The Life and Death of Leon Trotsky*, 221.

## 10: *Piochitas*

90 **Diego Rivera, one:** Frida Kahlo, *The Letters of Frida Kahlo: Cartas Apasionadas* (Chronicle Books, 1995), 64, 83, 151; Bertram D. Wolfe, *Diego Rivera: His Life and Times* (Robert Hale, 1939), 10–11, 14, 19, 51, 77, 194; Kandell, *La Capital*, 444–45, 453; Herrera, *Frida*, 81.

92 **His commitment to:** Wolfe, *Diego Rivera*, 107, 167, 169, 237, 243; van Heijenoort, *With Trotsky in Exile*, 132; Kandell, *La Capital*, 451–52; Herrera, *Frida*, 102.

94 **Trotsky, who had:** van Heijenoort, *With Trotsky in Exile*, 134; Kandell, *La Capital*, 482–83; Deutscher, *The Prophet Outcast*, 358–59; Herrera, *Frida*, 209; Garmabella, *El grito de Trotsky*, 71.

95 **Frida Kahlo was:** Frida Kahlo, *The Diary of Frida Kahlo: An Intimate Self-Portrait* (Bloomsbury, 1995), 12, 20; Wolfe, *Diego Rivera*, 205; Feferman, *Politics, Logic, and Love*, 143, 169; Herrera, *Frida*, x–xi, 49, 62, 73–74, 181, 197.

96 **Frida started to:** Feferman, *Politics, Logic, and Love*, 144, 170; Service, *Trotsky*, 448–49; Deutscher, *The Prophet Outcast*, 384, 399; Herrera, *Frida*, 209–10, 215.

## 11: Comrade Pablo

99 **As always, what:** López-Linares and Rioyo, *Storm the Skies*; Mercader, *Ramón Mercader, mi hermano*, 23–26.

99 **In October 1936:** Levine, *The Mind of an Assassin*, 12–14.

101 **There was only:** John Costello and Oleg Tsarev, *Deadly Illusions* (Century, 1993), 16, 258–63, 270–71; Paul Preston, *The Spanish Holocaust: Inquisition and Extermination in Twentieth-Century Spain* (HarperPress, 2012), 351; Boris Volodarsky, *Stalin's Agent: The Life and Death of Alexander Orlov* (Oxford University Press, 2015), xxvi, 166–67, 283, 322; Andrew and Mitrokhin, *The Mitrokhin Archive*, 96.

102 **The Soviet intelligence:** Andrew and Gordievsky, *KGB*, 121–22; John Barron, *KGB: The Secret Work of Soviet Secret Agents* (Hodder & Stoughton, 1974), 308; Preston, *Spanish Holocaust*, 407; Volodarsky, *Stalin's Agent*, 18, 239, 245–48, 263; Andrew and Mitrokhin, *The Mitrokhin Archive*, 53–54, 97; Ronald Radosh, Mary R. Habeck, and Grigory Nikolaevich Sevostianov, eds., *Spain Betrayed: The Soviet Union in the Spanish Civil War* (Yale University Press, 2001), 107; Serge and Trotsky, *The Life and Death of Leon Trotsky*, 224, 225.

105 **There was another:** Costello and Tsarev, *Deadly Illusions*, 276.

105 **Leonid Eitingon was:** Andrew and Gordievsky, *KGB*, 131; Pavel Sudoplatov and Anatoli Sudoplatov, with Jerrold L. Schecter and Leona P. Schecter, *Special Tasks: The Memoirs of an Unwanted Witness—A Soviet Spymaster* (Little, Brown, 1994), 31; Mercader, *Ramón Mercader, mi hermano*, 29–30; Mary-Kay Wilmers, *The Eitingons: A Twentieth-Century Story* (Faber & Faber, 2009), 104, 107, 113–16, 266, 285.

107 **Eitingon gave the:** Volodarsky, *Stalin's Agent*, 451; Sudoplatov and Sudoplatov, with J. Schecter and L. Schecter, *Special Tasks*, 33–34; Wilmers, *The Eitingons*, 117, 119, 124, 149.

108 **Eitingon's secret work:** Volodarsky, *Stalin's Agent*, 168; Wilmers, *The Eitingons*, 126.

109 **There is no:** Costello and Tsarev, *Deadly Illusions*, 279–80; Mercader, *Ramón Mercader, mi hermano*, 27–29.

111 **That he agreed:** Ehrenburg, *Men, Years—Life*, 196; Mercader, *Ramón Mercader, mi hermano*, 16; Pàmies, *"Ramón Mercader: misión cumplida,"* 21.

112 **There was one last sighting:** Levine, *The Mind of an Assassin*, 37.

## 12: The Kid

113 **But those who:** Volkogonov, *Trotsky*, 357; Victor Serge, *Memoirs of a Revolutionary* (New York Review Books Classics, 2011), 344; Deutscher, *The Prophet Outcast*, 347; Rosenthal, *Avocat de Trotsky*, 186; Phillip Hall, "My Grandfather the Revolutionary," *The Guardian*, 13 February 2003, https://www.theguardian.com/artanddesign/2003/feb/13/heritage.russia.

115 **Sometimes, though, the:** Serge, *Memoirs of a Revolutionary*, 327–28; Deutscher, *The Prophet Outcast*, 389–90; Rosenthal, *Avocat de Trotsky*, 221, 227; Michael B. Miller, *Shanghai on the Métro: Spies, Intrigue, and the French Between the Wars* (University of California Press, 1994), 218.

115 **The persecution left:** Dugrand, *Trotsky in Mexico 1937–40*, 28; Gueilburt, *El asesinato de Trotsky*; Deutscher, *The Prophet Outcast*, 165, 179–80, 366; Rosenthal, *Avocat de Trotsky*, 222; Poretsky, *Our Own People*, 259–61.

117 **Trotsky placed strenuous:** Dugrand, *Trotsky in Mexico 1937–40*, 28–29; Service, *Trotsky*, 383–84; Deutscher, *The Prophet Outcast*, 144–45, 180–81; Rosenthal, *Avocat de Trotsky*, 179.

118 **All he received:** Deutscher, *The Prophet Outcast*, 144–45, 180.

119 **Lev's anxieties about:** Volodarsky, *Stalin's Agent*, 320; Andrew and Mitrokhin, *The Mitrokhin Archive*, 53–54, 91–92, 98–99; Helen Rappaport, *After the Romanovs: Russian Exiles in Paris Between the Wars* (Scribe, 2022), 209–12; Rosenthal, *Avocat de Trotsky*, 211; Poretsky, *Our Own People*, 238.

### 13: Polecats

121 **At some point:** Andrew and Gordievsky, *KGB*, 121; Volkogonov, *Trotsky*, 336; Service, *Trotsky*, 415; Deutscher, *The Prophet Outcast*, 347–48; Rosenthal, *Avocat de Trotsky*, 261; Poretsky, *Our Own People*, 263, 273; International Committee of the Fourth International, "The Story of Mark Zborowski: Stalin's Spy in the Fourth International," World Socialist Web Site, 17 November 2011, https://www.wsws.org/en/articles/2011/11/zbor-n17.html.

123 **And almost everything about:** Volkogonov, *Trotsky*, 335; "Testimony of Mark Zborowski, Accompanied by Herman A. Greenberg, Esq., His Attorney," *Scope of Soviet Activity in the United States, Hearing Before the Subcommittee to Investigate the Administration of the Internal Security Act and Other Internal Security Laws of the Committee on the Judiciary, United States Senate, Eighty-Fourth Congress, Second Session, February 29, 1956*, pt. 4, Washington, Government Printing Office, 1956; Volodarsky, *Stalin's Agent*, 409–10; David J. Dallin, *Soviet Espionage* (Yale University Press, 1955), 29; Rosenthal, *Avocat de Trotsky*, 264–65; Poretsky, *Our Own People*, 262; International Committee of the Fourth International, "The Story of Mark Zborowski: Stalin's Spy in the Fourth International."

124 **The keen student:** Costello and Tsarev, *Deadly Illusions*, 50, 59; Dallin, *Soviet Espionage*, 9–10, 54.

125 **Moscow was delighted:** Volkogonov, *Trotsky*, 335–36, 372, 448; "Testimony of Mark Zborowski," *Scope of Soviet Activity in the United States*; van Heijenoort, *With Trotsky in Exile*, 99–100; Service, *Trotsky*, 416; Rosenthal, *Avocat de Trotsky*, 262.

127 **His work was:** Levine, *The Mind of an Assassin*, 29.

127 **Etienne was not:** "Testimony of Mark Zborowski," *Scope of Soviet Activity in the United States*; Service, *Trotsky*, 416; Poretsky, *Our Own People*, 263.

129 **One incident that:** Andrew and Mitrokhin, *The Mitrokhin Archive*, 92–93.

131 **After Reiss's friend:** Rosenthal, *Advocat de Trotsky*, 218–220; Poretsky, *Our Own People*, 250–52.

### 14: Walking in a Graveyard

133 **When he replaced:** Costello and Tsarev, *Deadly Illusions*, 294; Conquest, *The Great Terror*, 408; Montefiore, *Stalin*, 217–18.

135 **As time passed:** Andrew and Mitrokhin, *The Mitrokhin Archive*, 101–3.
136 **The same tragedies:** Weissmann, *Victor Serge*, 215; Kern, *A Death in Washington*, 46; Rosenthal, *Avocat de Trotsky*, 230; Arthur Koestler, *Bricks to Babel: Selected Writings with Author's Comments* (Hutchinson, 1980), 62–63, 70–72; Poretsky, *Our Own People*, 30.

## 15: Our Little Lyova

139 **As 1937 wore:** Serge, *Memoirs of a Revolutionary*, 344; Service, *Trotsky*, 433.
141 **Trotsky's primary concern:** Volkogonov, *Trotsky*, 358–59; Service, *Trotsky*, 431–32; Deutscher, *The Prophet Outcast*, 392–93.
143 **Yet there was defiance:** Dugrand, *Trotsky in Mexico 1937–40*, 29; "Testimony of Mark Zborowski," *Scope of Soviet Activity in the United States*; Service, *Trotsky*, 434; Deutscher, *The Prophet Outcast*, 362, 395; Rosenthal, *Avocat de Trotsky*, 230–34; Poretsky, *Our Own People*, 273.
145 **The Trotskyists immediately:** van Heijenoort, *With Trotsky in Exile*, 119–20; Payne, *The Life and Death of Trotsky*, 401–2; Deutscher, *The Prophet Outcast*, 144–45, 398, 401; Serge and Trotsky, *The Life and Death of Leon Trotsky*, 228; Alfred Rosmer, *Trotsky and the Origins of Trotskyism* (Francis Boutle, 2002), 19.
147 **The question as:** Sudoplatov and Sudoplatov, with J. Schecter and L. Schecter, *Special Tasks*, 82–83; Service, *Trotsky*, 435; Andrew and Mitrokhin, *The Mitrokhin Archive*, 99–100; Kern, *A Death in Washington*, 104.
148 **Elsa Reiss saw:** Costello and Tsarev, *Deadly Illusions*, 294–98; Deutscher, *The Prophet Outcast*, 144–45, 405–7; Rosenthal, *Avocat de Trotsky*, 271; Poretsky, *Our Own People*, 265.
149 **Once Trotsky had:** Volkogonov, *Trotsky*, xxxiii.
150 **Trotsky knew nothing:** Volkogonov, *Trotsky*, 361; Serge and Trotsky, *The Life and Death of Leon Trotsky*, 251.

## 16: The Citadel

151 **It was inevitable:** van Heijenoort, *With Trotsky in Exile*, 134, 137–38; Payne, *The Life and Death of Trotsky*, 409; Feferman, *Politics, Logic, and Love*, 173; Herrera, *Frida*, 247.
152 **His appeal fell:** Kahlo, *Letters*, 99, Herrera, *Frida*, 248–49.
153 **It was Jean:** Dugrand, *Trotsky in Mexico 1937–40*, 27; van Heijenoort, *With Trotsky in Exile*, 138–39; Deutscher, *The Prophet Outcast*, 447; Garmabella, *El grito de Trotsky*, 137; Serge and Trotsky, *The Life and Death of Leon Trotsky*, 251.
153 **"I am not":** General Leandro A. Sánchez Salazar with Julian Gorkin, *Murder in Mexico: The Assassination of Leon Trotsky* (Secker & Warburg, 1950), 80.
153 **A watchtower was:** Volkogonov, *Trotsky*, 396.
154 **Keys were left:** Sánchez Salazar with Gorkin, *Murder in Mexico*, 13.
154 **The file on:** Andrew and Gordievsky, *KGB*, 131.
154 **It was easy:** Cass Canfield, *Up & Down & Around: A Publisher Recollects the Time of His Life* (Collins, 1972), 146–47; Deutscher, *The Prophet Outcast*, 447.
154 **But there were:** Volkogonov, *Trotsky*, 396; Gueilburt, *El asesinato de Trotsky*; Payne, *The Life and Death of Trotsky*, 413–14.
158 **Looking after Trotsky:** Gueilburt, *El asesinato de Trotsky*; van Heijenoort, *With Trotsky in Exile*, 20; Payne, *The Life and Death of Trotsky*, 428; Feferman, *Politics, Logic, and Love*, 57–59, 80, 117, 127, 134; Mosley, *The Assassination of Trotsky*, 17, 73; Wald, "Memories of the John Dewey Commission: Forty Years Later";

Hansen, "With Trotsky to the End"; Deutscher, *The Prophet Outcast*, 144–45, 435, 448, 486; Zita James, unpublished journal, September 1930, private collection.

160 **Trotsky remained almost absurdly**: Clare Sheridan, *To the Four Winds* (Andre Deutsch, 1957), 131; van Heijenoort, *With Trotsky in Exile*, 28; Wald, "Memories of the John Dewey Commission: Forty Years Later"; Eastman, *Love and Revolution*, 332; Service, *Trotsky*, 163, 336, 345; Serge and Trotsky, *The Life and Death of Leon Trotsky*, 52, 119.

161 **Days were "run"**: Dugrand, *Trotsky in Mexico 1937–40*, 39; van Heijenoort, *With Trotsky in Exile*, 16–18, 61, 72; Feferman, *Politics, Logic, and Love*, 119; Mosley, *The Assassination of Trotsky*, 30, 73, 144; Rosenthal, *Avocat de Trotsky*, 72.

163 **More than anything:** Volkogonov, *Trotsky*, 384; Serge and Trotsky, *The Life and Death of Leon Trotsky*, 4, 255; Serge, *Notebooks*, 100–101.

## 17: I LIKE TO ACT

167 **Ageloff was frail:** Sánchez Salazar with Gorkin, *Murder in Mexico*, 107; Levine, *The Mind of an Assassin*, 56, 130; Mosley, *The Assassination of Trotsky*, 163; Eric M. Gurevitch, "Thinking with Sylvia Ageloff," Hypocrite Reader, August 2015, https://hypocritereader.com/55/thinking-with-sylvia; Eric London, "Sylvia Ageloff and the Assassination of Leon Trotsky," World Socialist Website, 5 February 2021, https://www.wsws.org/en/articles/2021/02/06/sylv-f06.html.

169 **Sylvia's life was quiet:** Levine, *The Mind of an Assassin*, 47–48; van Heijenoort, *With Trotsky in Exile*, 146; Gurevitch, "Thinking with Sylvia Ageloff"; Committee on Un-American Activities, *American Aspects of Assassination of Leon Trotsky: Hearings Before the Committee on Un-American Activities, House of Representatives, Eighty-First Congress, Second Session; July 26, August 30, October 18 and 19, and December 4, 1950* (Forgotten Books, 2018), vii–viii, 3401–2, 3405; NY 100-775, https://vault.fbi.gov/leon-trotsky/leon-trotsky-part-1-of-5/view; Louis Francis Budenz, *Men Without Faces: The Communist Conspiracy in the U.S.A.* (Harper & Brothers, 1950), 1, 127–28.

173 **One man who:** Sánchez Salazar with Gorkin, *Murder in Mexico*, 127; Levine, *The Mind of an Assassin*, 56, 165, 170; Mercader, *Ramón Mercader, mi hermano*, xii.

173 **Ramón Mercader and:** Levine, *The Mind of an Assassin*, 48–50; López-Linares and Rioyo, *Storm the Skies*; Committee on Un-American Activities, *American Aspects of Assassination of Leon Trotsky*, 3403, 3409; NY 100-775; TSJDF/siglo XX/Archivo histórico/caja 3265/folio.602993; Garmabella, *El grito de Trotsky*, 122–23.

176 **He never drank:** Sánchez Salazar with Gorkin, *Murder in Mexico*, 127; Levine, *The Mind of an Assassin*, 164; López-Linares and Rioyo, *Storm the Skies*; NY 100-775; TSJDF/siglo XX/Archivo histórico/caja 3265/folio.602993; Garmabella, *El grito de Trotsky*, 129.

176 **Still, as a:** Levine, *The Mind of an Assassin*, 165.

177 **Still stranger was:** Levine, *The Mind of an Assassin*, 44–47; TSJDF/siglo XX/Archivo histórico/caja 3265/folio.602993.

177 **Each night she:** Levine, *The Mind of an Assassin*, 155.

178 **Sometimes a new:** Dugrand, *Trotsky in Mexico 1937–40*, 47; López-Linares and Rioyo, *Storm the Skies*; Maria Crapeau, *"J'ai connu l'assassin de Trotsky," France-Observateur*, 19 May 1960, 11.

179 **Ramón did not:** Sánchez Salazar with Gorkin, *Murder in Mexico*, 127; Levine, *The Mind of an Assassin*, 171, 174; López-Linares and Rioyo, *Storm the Skies*;

Mercader, *Ramón Mercader, mi hermano*, 63; Crapeau, *"J'ai connu l'assassin de Trotsky,"* 11; Puigventós López, *Ramon Mercader, l'home del piolet*, 2418.

## 18: He Couldn't Be Forgiven

181 **Stalin never stopped:** Levine, *The Mind of an Assassin*, 67; Andrew and Gordievsky, *KGB*, 120; Andrew and Mitrokhin, *The Mitrokhin Archive*, 93; Montefiore, *Stalin*, 59–60, 101; Djilas, *Conversations with Stalin*, 52.

181 **Individual articles were:** Volkogonov, *Trotsky*, 342, 373, 397, 442, 445.

183 **No Soviet official:** Costello and Tsarev, *Deadly Illusions*, 295, 299; Jansen and Petrov, *Stalin's Loyal Executioner*, 68; Conquest, *The Great Terror*, 409.

184 **Shpiegelglass was next:** Volkogonov, *Trotsky*, 443.

184 **Pavel Sudoplatov was:** Barron, *KGB*, 309; Sudoplatov and Sudoplatov, with J. Schecter and L. Schecter, *Special Tasks*, xiii, 7–10, 12–13, 22–24.

186 **At eleven fifty a.m.:** Hugo Dewar, *Assassins at Large: Being a Fully Documented and Hitherto Unpublished Account of the Executions Outside Russia Ordered by the GPU* (Wingate, 1951), 59; Sudoplatov and Sudoplatov, with J. Schecter and L. Schecter, *Special Tasks*, 27–28, 30, 31, 38–39; Serhii Plokhy, *The Man with the Poison Gun* (Oneworld, 2016), 14–15.

187 **And yet his:** Volodarsky, *Stalin's Agent*, 18; Sudoplatov and Sudoplatov, with J. Schecter and L. Schecter, *Special Tasks*, 41, 47; Andrew and Mitrokhin, *The Mitrokhin Archive*, 112.

189 **Beria's appointment was:** Figes, *The Whisperers*, 280; Volkogonov, *Stalin*, 333; Garmabella, *El grito de Trotsky*, 104; Montefiore, *Stalin*, 67, 244, 252.

189 **On the eve:** Volkogonov, *Trotsky*, 443; Sudoplatov and Sudoplatov, with J. Schecter and L. Schecter, *Special Tasks*, 41, 47, 56–58, 60–62.

## 19: Childish Games

193 **By March 1939:** Sudoplatov and Sudoplatov, with J. Schecter and L. Schecter, *Special Tasks*, 4, 64–68; Montefiore, *Stalin*, 102, 261.

197 **Things continued to:** Volodarsky, *Stalin's Agent*, 359; Wilmers, *The Eitingons*, 284–85.

197 **To execute his:** Volkogonov, *Trotsky*, 449; Sudoplatov and Sudoplatov, with J. Schecter and L. Schecter, *Special Tasks*, 68–72; E. B. Held, *A Spy's Guide to Santa Fe and Albuquerque* (University of New Mexico Press, 2011), 7.

## 20: So Funny

200 **Early in 1939:** Garmabella, *El grito de Trotsky*, 147.

201 **The conference itself:** Levine, *The Mind of an Assassin*, 52; Andrew and Gordievsky, *KGB*, 129; Service, *Trotsky*, 443–44; Deutscher, *The Prophet Outcast*, 419–20; Rosenthal, *Avocat de Trotsky*, 263, 276–77; Serge and Trotsky, *The Life and Death of Leon Trotsky*, 245.

202 **In February 1939:** Sudoplatov and Sudoplatov, with J. Schecter and L. Schecter, *Special Tasks*, 72; Andrew and Mitrokhin, *The Mitrokhin Archive*, 113.

203 **The most significant:** Levine, *The Mind of an Assassin*, 69; Wolfe, *Diego Rivera*, 170–71; Leonard Folgarait, *So Far from Heaven: David Alfaro Siqueiros'* The March of Humanity *and Mexican Revolutionary Politics* (Cambridge University Press, 1987), 33–34; Matthew Affron et al., *Paint the Revolution: Mexican Modernism, 1910–1950* (Philadelphia Museum of Art, 2016), 7, 183; Kandell, *La Capital*, 451–52; Andrew and Mitrokhin, *The Mitrokhin Archive*, 113–14; NY 100-775.

204 **There was also:** Volodarsky, *Stalin's Agent*; Andrei Znamenski, "Joseph Grigulevich: A Tale of Identity, Soviet Espionage, and Storytelling," *The Soviet and Post-Soviet Review* 44, no. 3 (2017): 328; Held, *A Spy's Guide to Santa Fe and Albuquerque*, 7–9.
205 **Alongside all this:** Herrera, *Frida*, 249–50; Crapeau, *"J'ai connu l'assassin de Trotsky,"* 11.
207 **They had established:** Costello and Tsarev, *Deadly Illusions*, 59, 93; Volodarsky, *Stalin's Agent*, 113; Kern, *A Death in Washington*, 67–68.
208 **Ramón had carried:** López-Linares and Rioyo, *Storm the Skies*; NY 100-775; Wilmers, *The Eitingons*, 287; Crapeau, *"J'ai connu l'assassin de Trotsky,"* 11.
209 **Eitingon had no:** Sudoplatov and Sudoplatov, with J. Schecter and L. Schecter, *Special Tasks*, 72–73.

## 21: PICTURES AND EVERYTHING

210 **Frank Jacson passed:** NY 100-775.
211 **Once Ramón had:** Levine, *The Mind of an Assassin*, 62; Committee on Un-American Activities, *American Aspects of Assassination of Leon Trotsky*, 3405, 3408; NY 100-775.
211 **As she had:** Committee on Un-American Activities, *American Aspects of Assassination of Leon Trotsky*, 3406, 3408; TSJDF/siglo XX/Archivo histórico/caja 3265/folio.602993; Crapeau, *"J'ai connu l'assassin de Trotsky,"* 11; Puigventós López, *Ramon Mercader, l'home del piolet*, 3272.
213 **Sylvia and her:** Andrew and Gordievsky, *KGB*, 131; Andrew and Mitrokhin, *The Mitrokhin Archive*, 140.
213 **There was also:** Sudoplatov and Sudoplatov, with J. Schecter and L. Schecter, *Special Tasks*, 73–74; Mercader, *Ramón Mercader, mi hermano*, xxxvi, 36; Puigventós López, *Ramon Mercader, l'home del piolet*, 3290.
214 **He told her:** Sánchez Salazar with Gorkin, *Murder in Mexico*, 145; Committee on Un-American Activities, *American Aspects of Assassination of Leon Trotsky*, 3403; NY 100–775;. TSJDF/siglo XX/Archivo histórico/caja 3265/folio.602993; Puigventós López, *Ramon Mercader, l'home del piolet*, 3292.

## 22: *SÍ, NO, GRACIAS*

217 **One day in:** López-Linares and Rioyo, *Storm the Skies*; Garmabella, *El grito de Trotsky*, 153.
218 **Caridad was the:** Levine, *The Mind of an Assassin*, 169–70; Puigventós López, *Ramon Mercader, l'home del piolet*.
218 **In the meantime:** David Wingeate Pike, *In the Service of Stalin: The Spanish Communists in Exile, 1939–1945* (Clarendon Press, 1993), 51; Volodarsky, *Stalin's Agent*, 360–61.
219 **In order to:** van Heijenoort, *With Trotsky in Exile*, 147; TSJDF/siglo XX/Archivo histórico/caja 3265/folio.602993.
220 **Ramón also began:** Levine, *The Mind of an Assassin*, 71–72; van Heijenoort, *With Trotsky in Exile*, 146; TSJDF/siglo XX/Archivo histórico/caja 3265/folio.602993; Puigventós López, *Ramon Mercader, l'home del piolet*, 3496.

## 23: *MUERTE A TROTSKY*

221 **Most evenings after:** Volkogonov, *Trotsky*, 409; Andrew and Mitrokhin, *The Mitrokhin Archive*, 100.

222 **His only real:** Dugrand, *Trotsky in Mexico 1937–40*, 38; Mosley, *The Assassination of Trotsky*, 72–73; Deutscher, *The Prophet Outcast*, 449.
222 **The arrival of:** Dugrand, *Trotsky in Mexico 1937–40*, 46–47; Deutscher, *The Prophet Outcast*, 449; Garmabella, *El grito de Trotsky*, 142–43; Serge, *Notebooks*, 529.
223 **Trotsky was grappling:** Trotsky, *Trotsky's Diary in Exile 1935*, 68; Deutscher, *The Prophet Outcast*, 466–68.
224 **It was in:** Trotsky, *Trotsky's Diary in Exile 1935*, 139–40; Service, *Trotsky*, 484; Hansen, "With Trotsky to the End."
225 **Ramón continued to:** Committee on Un-American Activities, *American Aspects of Assassination of Leon Trotsky*, 3403; NY 100-775.
227 **At some point:** Levine, *The Mind of an Assassin*, 78; Deutscher, *The Prophet Outcast*, 483; Garmabella, *El grito de Trotsky*, 158.
228 **the great metallic:** Sánchez Salazar with Gorkin, *Murder in Mexico*, 5.
228 **To begin with:** Alan Woods, "The House in Coyoacan: Reflections on Trotsky's Last Years," In Defense of Marxism, 16 June 2009, https://marxist.comhouse-in-coyacan-reflections-trotsky.htm; Mercader, *Ramón Mercader, mi hermano*, xxxvii.
228 **Ramón also began:** Volkogonov, *Trotsky*, 458.
230 **And yet, for:** Sánchez Salazar with Gorkin, *Murder in Mexico*, 146; NY 100-775; TSJDF/siglo XX/Archivo histórico/caja 3265/folio.602993.
231 **Sylvia had little:** Sánchez Salazar with Gorkin, *Murder in Mexico*, 146; Levine, *The Mind of an Assassin*, 80; TSJDF/siglo XX/Archivo histórico/caja 3265/folio.602993.
232 **On 11 April:** Levine, *The Mind of an Assassin*, 91–92; NY 100-775; Puigventós López, *Ramon Mercader, l'home del piolet*, 3525.
234 **Calls for Trotsky's:** Volkogonov, *Trotsky*, 447; Deutscher, *The Prophet Outcast*, 482.

## 24: Two Hundred Bullets

236 **In April 1940:** Levine, *The Mind of an Assassin*, 99; Payne, *The Life and Death of Trotsky*, 431; Serge and Trotsky, *The Life and Death of Leon Trotsky*, 257.
236 **Some members of:** Gueilburt, *El asesinato de Trotsky*; Serge, *Notebooks*, 547.
238 **His band of:** Sánchez Salazar with Gorkin, *Murder in Mexico*, 45; Mosley, *The Assassination of Trotsky*, 36–37; Wilmers, *The Eitingons*, 302.
238 **His right-hand man, Pujol:** Levine, *The Mind of an Assassin*, 82.
238 **It was a:** Julian Gorkin, *L'assassinat de Trotski* (Livre de Poche, 1973), 370; Puigventós López, *Ramon Mercader, l'home del piolet*, 4193.
239 **The raiders flowed:** Mosley, *The Assassination of Trotsky*, 38–39; Woods, "The House in Coyoacan: Reflections on Trotsky's Last Years"; Gorkin, *L'assassinat de Trotski*, e-book 792.
241 **As soon as:** Payne, *The Life and Death of Trotsky*, 428; Mosley, *The Assassination of Trotsky*, 39–41; Znamenski, "Joseph Grigulevich: A Tale of Identity, Soviet Espionage, and Storytelling," 329; Mercader, *Ramón Mercader, mi hermano*, 39; Gorkin, *L'assassinat de Trotski*, 448; Serge and Trotsky, *The Life and Death of Leon Trotsky*, 257.
243 **Natalia and Trotsky:** Andrew and Mitrokhin, *The Mitrokhin Archive*, 114; Pike, *In the Service of Stalin*, 52; Mercader, *Ramón Mercader, mi hermano*, xlii; Serge and Trotsky, *The Life and Death of Leon Trotsky*, 256–57.

244 **By the time:** Sánchez Salazar with Gorkin, *Murder in Mexico*, 5, 99; Mosley, *The Assassination of Trotsky*, 40–41; Gorkin, *L'assassinat de Trotski*, 237, 509.

## 25: THINGS ARE BETTER AS THEY ARE

246 **It was only:** Gorkin, *L'assassinat de Trotski*, 1512–17.
247 **By the end:** Folgarait, *So Far from Heaven*, 34.
247 **It was covered:** Sánchez Salazar with Gorkin, *Murder in Mexico*, 75.
247 **It was discovered:** Volodarsky, *Stalin's Agent*, 363–64; Mosley, *The Assassination of Trotsky*, 44; Sudoplatov and Sudoplatov, with J. Schecter and L. Schecter, *Special Tasks*, 74; Andrew and Mitrokhin, *The Mitrokhin Archive*, 115; Deutscher, *The Prophet Outcast*, 492; John Earl Haynes, Harvey Klehr, and Alexander Vassiliev, *Spies: The Rise and Fall of the KGB in America* (Yale University Press, 2009), 476; Gorkin, *L'assassinat de Trotski*, 838; Puigventós López, *Ramon Mercader, l'home del piolet*, 3883.
250 **One of the:** Garmabella, *El grito de Trotsky*, 185.
250 **On 27 May:** Levine, *The Mind of an Assassin*, 93–94; Dugrand, *Trotsky in Mexico 1937–40*, 48–49; Hansen, "With Trotsky to the End"; TSJDF/siglo XX/Archivo histórico/caja 3265/folio.602993; Serge and Trotsky, *The Life and Death of Leon Trotsky*, 264.
251 **She was unwilling:** TSJDF/siglo XX/Archivo histórico/caja 3265/folio.602993.

## 26: SHIPPING DOCUMENTS

254 **The return to:** Andrew and Gordievsky, *KGB*, 132; NY 100-775; TSJDF/siglo XX/Archivo histórico/caja 3265/folio.602993; Crapeau, *"J'ai connu l'assassin de Trotsky,"* 12.
255 **Then, almost as:** NY 100-775.
256 **Alone in New:** Levine, *The Mind of an Assassin*, 104; NY 100-775.
257 **She thought Sylvia:** Levine, *The Mind of an Assassin*, 116.
257 **Sightings of him:** TSJDF/siglo XX/Archivo histórico/caja 3265/folio.602993.

## 27: FEAR

261 **After the attack:** Sudoplatov and Sudoplatov, with J. Schecter and L. Schecter, *Special Tasks*, 75–81; Wilmers, *The Eitingons*, 305.
263 **At some point:** Wilmers, *The Eitingons*, 151.
264 **As soon as:** Volkogonov, *Trotsky*, 459; Garmabella, *El grito de Trotsky*, 188, 190, 194; Serge and Trotsky, *The Life and Death of Leon Trotsky*, 257; Wilmers, *The Eitingons*, 307.
266 **Perhaps too Ramón:** López-Linares and Rioyo, *Storm the Skies*.
266 **The year before:** Andrew and Gordievsky, *KGB*, 133.

## 28: OTHER METHODS

268 **In the weeks:** David North, "Trotsky's Last Year," World Socialist Web Site, 19 August 2020, https://www.wsws.org/en/articles/2020/08/20/anni-a20.html.
268 **many of Trotsky's:** Volkogonov, *Trotsky*, 454; Deutscher, *The Prophet Outcast*, 494.
269 **I know I:** Dugrand, *Trotsky in Mexico 1937–40*, 49.
269 **Faced with this:** Sánchez Salazar with Gorkin, *Murder in Mexico*, 13; Dugrand, *Trotsky in Mexico 1937–40*, 49–50; Hansen, "With Trotsky to the End"; Levine, *The Mind of an Assassin*, 108–10.

271 **By the middle:** Volkogonov, *Trotsky*, 454, 463; Trotsky, *Stalin*, 372; Hansen, "With Trotsky to the End"; Garmabella, *El grito de Trotsky*, 144.
272 **Once he had:** Mosley, *The Assassination of Trotsky*, 52; Service, *Trotsky*, 487.
273 **On 8 August:** Levine, *The Mind of an Assassin*, 113; Volkogonov, *Trotsky*, 464; Hansen, "With Trotsky to the End"; TSJDF/siglo XX/Archivo histórico/caja 3265/folio.602993; Serge and Trotsky, *The Life and Death of Leon Trotsky*, 265.
275 **His transformation was:** Levine, *The Mind of an Assassin*, 104–5; Hansen, "With Trotsky to the End"; TSJDF/siglo XX/Archivo histórico/caja 3265/folio.602993.
276 **In spring 1938:** van Heijenoort, *With Trotsky in Exile*, 101; Service, *Trotsky* 415.
277 **Months later, after:** Levine, *The Mind of an Assassin*, 105.
277 **His newfound political:** Levine, *The Mind of an Assassin*, 53; Hansen, "With Trotsky to the End"; TSJDF/siglo XX/Archivo histórico/caja 3265/folio.602993; Serge and Trotsky, *The Life and Death of Leon Trotsky*, 264–65.
278 **Ramón also made:** Serge, *Notebooks*, 101.
281 **Trotsky turned to:** Levine, *The Mind of an Assassin*, 110; Crapeau, *"J'ai connu l'assassin de Trotsky,"* 12.
281 **On 17 August:** Serge and Trotsky, *The Life and Death of Leon Trotsky*, 265.
282 **Two days later:** TSJDF/siglo XX/Archivo histórico/caja 3265/folio.602993.

## 29: I Feel Really Good

284 **Leon Trotsky spent:** Sánchez Salazar with Gorkin, *Murder in Mexico*, 113; Mosley, *The Assassination of Trotsky*, 155; Service, *Trotsky*, 487, 489; Serge and Trotsky, *The Life and Death of Leon Trotsky*, 264, 266–67.
285 **The courtyard was:** Sánchez Salazar with Gorkin, *Murder in Mexico*, 5, 115; Serge and Trotsky, *The Life and Death of Leon Trotsky*, 264, 266.
285 **At nine a.m., he:** Deutscher, *The Prophet Outcast*, 501–2.
287 **In that glorious:** Slezkine, *The House of Government*, 129; Trotsky, *Stalin*, 194; Serge and Trotsky, *The Life and Death of Leon Trotsky*, 52, 55, 59, 70.
288 **Ramón started the:** Levine, *The Mind of an Assassin*, 115–16; Hansen, "With Trotsky to the End"; Puigventós López, *Ramon Mercader, l'home del piolet*, 4832.
288 **"white piqué sports":** Sánchez Salazar with Gorkin, *Murder in Mexico*, 107; TSJDF/siglo XX/Archivo histórico/caja 3265/folio.602993; Gorkin, *L'assassinat de Trotski*, 1633; Puigventós López, *Ramon Mercader, l'home del piolet*, 4849.
288 **As they passed:** Levine, *The Mind of an Assassin*, 117; TSJDF/siglo XX/Archivo histórico/caja 3265/folio.602993.
290 **Ramón still seemed:** Sánchez Salazar with Gorkin, *Murder in Mexico*, 148; TSJDF/siglo XX/Archivo histórico/caja 3265/folio.602993.
290 **She did not:** Sánchez Salazar with Gorkin, *Murder in Mexico*, 105; Levine, *The Mind of an Assassin*, 118; Hansen, "With Trotsky to the End"; TSJDF/siglo XX/Archivo histórico/caja 3265/folio.602993.

## 30: Him Again

292 **At five p.m., the:** Sánchez Salazar with Gorkin, *Murder in Mexico*, 135–36, 140; Levine, *The Mind of an Assassin*, 120–23; Payne, *The Life and Death of Trotsky*, 452–53; Mosley, *The Assassination of Trotsky*, 139; Hansen, "With Trotsky to the End"; TSJDF/siglo XX/Archivo histórico/caja 3265/folio.602993; Garmabella, *El grito de Trotsky*, 213.

294 **Natalia was enjoying:** Sánchez Salazar with Gorkin, *Murder in Mexico*, 116–20; Levine, *The Mind of an Assassin*, 124; Mosley, *The Assassination of Trotsky*, 158; Hansen, "With Trotsky to the End"; TSJDF/siglo XX/Archivo histórico/caja 3265/folio.602993; Serge and Trotsky, *The Life and Death of Leon Trotsky*, 266–67.

296 **Trotsky's whitewashed study:** Dugrand, *Trotsky in Mexico 1937–40*, 44; Payne, *The Life and Death of Trotsky*, 454; Mosley, *The Assassination of Trotsky*, 139, 144; TSJDF/siglo XX/Archivo histórico/caja 3265/folio.602993.

297 **Trotsky sat down:** Sánchez Salazar with Gorkin, *Murder in Mexico*, 135–36; Levine, *The Mind of an Assassin*, ix–x, 124–25; Dugrand, *Trotsky in Mexico 1937–40*, 50; Payne, *The Life and Death of Trotsky*, 455; TSJDF/siglo XX/Archivo histórico/caja 3265/folio.602993; Wilmers, *The Eitingons*, 7.

298 **Ramón pushed Trotsky:** Sánchez Salazar with Gorkin, *Murder in Mexico*, 120–25; Levine, *The Mind of an Assassin*, ix–x, 125; Hansen, "With Trotsky to the End"; TSJDF/siglo XX/Archivo histórico/caja 3265/folio.602993; Serge and Trotsky, *The Life and Death of Leon Trotsky*, 267.

301 **Hansen left Trotsky:** Sánchez Salazar with Gorkin, *Murder in Mexico*, 141; Levine, *The Mind of an Assassin*, 125; Hansen, "With Trotsky to the End"; TSJDF/siglo XX/Archivo histórico/caja 3265/folio.602993; Serge and Trotsky, *The Life and Death of Leon Trotsky*, 267–68.

## 31: AFTERMATH

304 **Sylvia Ageloff had:** Mosley, *The Assassination of Trotsky*, 163; TSJDF/siglo XX/Archivo histórico/caja 3265/folio.602993.

305 **Trotsky hung on:** Hansen, "With Trotsky to the End"; TSJDF/siglo XX/Archivo histórico/caja 3265/folio.602993; Serge and Trotsky, *The Life and Death of Leon Trotsky*, 268–69.

## EPILOGUE: "ONE DOES NOT CHOOSE THE TIME TO LIVE, DIE, OR KILL"

308 **Caridad and Eitingon:** López-Linares and Rioyo, *Storm the Skies*; Garmabella, *El grito de Trotsky*, 236; Wilmers, *The Eitingons*, 8; Puigventós López, *Ramon Mercader, l'home del piolet*, 5245.

309 **Sylvia would see:** Sánchez Salazar with Gorkin, *Murder in Mexico*, 152; Garmabella, *El grito de Trotsky*, 237.

310 **Her release was:** NY 100-775; Crapeau, *"J'ai connu l'assassin de Trotsky,"* 12.

312 **While he awaited:** Levine, *The Mind of an Assassin*, 147; Payne, *The Life and Death of Trotsky*, 470; Mosley, *The Assassination of Trotsky*, 147, 168.

313 **Trotsky's death marked:** Volkogonov, *Trotsky*, 487.

313 **Oddly enough, most:** Volkogonov, *Stalin*, 378.

313 **Nevertheless, the NKVD:** Mercader, *Ramón Mercader, mi hermano*, 45.

314 **At no point:** Andrew and Gordievsky, *KGB*, 133.

314 **Ramón was known:** López-Linares and Rioyo, *Storm the Skies*; Garmabella, *El grito de Trotsky*, 297; Serge, *Notebooks*, 102, 588.

314 **He was steadfast:** Pike, *In the Service of Stalin*, 53; Mercader, *Ramón Mercader, mi hermano*, 41, 55; Garmabella, *El grito de Trotsky*, 259, 293.

315 **Eitingon worried that:** Volkogonov, *Trotsky*, 468; Mercader, *Ramón Mercader, mi hermano*, xlviii, xlix, l.

317 **On 6 May:** Sudoplatov and Sudoplatov, with J. Schecter and L. Schecter, *Special Tasks*, 35–36; Donald Rayfield, *Stalin and His Hangmen: An Authoritative Portrait*

*of a Tyrant and Those Who Served Him* (Viking, 2004), 373; Mercader, *Ramón Mercader, mi hermano*, 32; Garmabella, *El grito de Trotsky*, 334.

319 **Ramón lived quietly:** López-Linares and Rioyo, *Storm the Skies*; Garmabella, *El grito de Trotsky*, 343.

320 **Ramón's calm existence:** López-Linares and Rioyo, *Storm the Skies*; Mercader, *Ramón Mercader, mi hermano*, 49, 56, 58, 63.

321 **Occasionally, she would:** Dugrand, *Trotsky in Mexico 1937–40*, 30; Serge, *Notebooks*, 89.

321 **Luis had tried to:** Mercader, *Ramón Mercader, mi hermano*, lii, 60, 62, 66–72, 76–77.

323 **Mark Zborowski, or:** Volodarsky, *Stalin's Agent*, 409.

# BIBLIOGRAPHY


Affron, Matthew, et al. *Paint the Revolution: Mexican Modernism, 1910–1950.* Philadelphia Museum of Art, 2016.

Amis, Martin. *Koba the Dread: Laughter and the Twenty Million.* Jonathan Cape, 2002.

Andrew, Christopher, and Oleg Gordievsky. *KGB: The Inside Story of Its Foreign Operations from Lenin to Gorbachev.* Hodder & Stoughton, 1990.

Andrew, Christopher, and Vasili Mitrokhin. *The Mitrokhin Archive: The KGB in Europe and the West.* Allen Lane, 2005.

Baĭkalov, Anatoliĭ V. *I Knew Stalin.* Burns, Oates, 1940.

Balabanova, Angelica. *Impressions of Lenin.* University of Michigan Press, 1964.

Barmine, Alexandre. *One Who Survived: The Life Story of a Russian Under the Soviets.* G. P. Putnam's Sons, 1945.

Barron, John. *KGB: The Secret Work of Soviet Secret Agents.* Hodder & Stoughton, 1974.

Beevor, Antony. *The Battle for Spain: The Spanish Civil War 1936–1939.* Weidenfeld & Nicolson, 2006.

Beevor, Antony. *Russia: Revolution and Civil War, 1917–1921.* Weidenfeld & Nicolson, 2022.

Budenz, Louis Francis. *Men Without Faces: The Communist Conspiracy in the U.S.A.* Harper & Brothers, 1950.

Canfield, Cass. *Up & Down & Around: A Publisher Recollects the Time of His Life.* Collins, 1972.

Carmichael, Joel. *Trotsky: An Appreciation of His Life.* Hodder & Stoughton, 1975.

Chambers, Roland. *The Last Englishman: The Double Life of Arthur Ransome.* Faber and Faber, 2009.

Churchill, Winston. *Great Contemporaries.* Macmillan, 1942.

Committee on Un-American Activities. *American Aspects of Assassination of Leon Trotsky: Hearings Before the Committee on Un-American Activities, House of Representatives, Eighty-First Congress, Second Session; July 26, August 30, October 18 and 19, and December 4, 1950.* Forgotten Books, 2018.

Conquest, Robert. *The Great Terror: A Reassessment.* Hutchinson, 1990.

Costello, John, and Oleg Tsarev. *Deadly Illusions.* Century, 1993.

Cotterill, D. J., ed. *The Serge-Trotsky Papers.* Pluto Press, 1994.

Crook, David. *Hamstead Heath to Tian An Men: The Autobiography of David Crook.* Published by the author, 1990. Accessed 16 October 2023, www.davidcrook.net.

Dallin, David J. *Soviet Espionage.* Yale University Press, 1955.

Deutscher, Isaac. *The Prophet Armed: Trotsky, 1879–1921.* Oxford University Press, 1954.

Deutscher, Isaac. *The Prophet Outcast: Trotsky, 1929–1940.* Oxford University Press, 1963.

Deutscher, Isaac. *The Prophet Unarmed: Trotsky, 1921–1928.* Oxford University Press, 1959.

Dewar, Hugo. *Assassins at Large: Being a Fully Documented and Hitherto Unpublished Account of the Executions Outside Russia Ordered by the GPU.* Wingate, 1951.

Djilas, Milovan. *Conversations with Stalin.* Penguin, 1962.

Dugrand, Alain. *Trotsky in Mexico 1937–40.* Carcanet, 1992.

Dziak, John J. *Chekisty: A History of the KGB.* Lexington Books, 1988.

Eastman, Max. *Leon Trotsky: The Portrait of a Youth.* Faber and Gwyer, 1926.

Eastman, Max. *Love and Revolution: My Journey Through an Epoch.* Random House, 1964.

Ehrenburg, Ilya. *Men, Years—Life.* MacGibbon & Kee, 1961–1966.

Feferman, Anita Burdman. *Politics, Logic, and Love: The Life of Jean van Heijenoort.* Jones and Bartlett, 1993.

Feuchtwanger, Lion. *Moscow 1937: My Visit Described for My Friends.* Victor Gollancz, 1937.

Figes, Orlando. *A People's Tragedy: The Russian Revolution 1891–1924.* Pimlico, 1997.

Figes, Orlando. *The Whisperers: Private Life in Stalin's Russia.* Allen Lane, 2007.

Fischer, Louis. *Men and Politics: An Autobiography.* Jonathan Cape, 1941.

Folgarait, Leonard. *So Far from Heaven: David Alfaro Siqueiros'* The March of Humanity *and Mexican Revolutionary Politics.* Cambridge University Press, 1987.

Garmabella, José Ramón. *El grito de Trotsky: Ramón Mercader, el asesino de un mito.* Debate, 2007.

Garros, Véronique, Natalia Korenevskaya, and Thomas Lahusen. *Intimacy and Terror: Soviet Diaries of the 1930s.* New Press, 1995.

Getty, J. Arch, and Oleg V. Naumov. *The Road to Terror: Stalin and the Self-Destruction of the Bolsheviks, 1932–1939.* Yale University Press, 1999.

Gitlow, Benjamin. *The Whole of Their Lives: Communism in America.* Western Islands, 1965.

Goldman, Albert. *The Assassination of Leon Trotsky: The Proofs of Stalin's Guilt.* Pioneer Publishers, 1940.

González, Valentín R. *Listen Comrades: Life and Death in the Soviet Union.* Heinemann, 1952.

Gorkin, Julian. *L'assassinat de Trotski.* Livre de Poche, 1973.

Hansen, J. *Leon Trotsky: The Man and His Work.* Merit, 1969.

Haynes, John Earl, Harvey Klehr, and Alexander Vassiliev. *Spies: The Rise and Fall of the KGB in America.* Yale University Press, 2009.

Held, E. B. *A Spy's Guide to Santa Fe and Albuquerque.* University of New Mexico Press, 2011.

Herrera, Hayden. *Frida: A Biography of Frida Kahlo.* Harper & Row, 1983.

Høidal, Oddvar K. *Trotsky in Norway: Exile, 1935–37.* Northern Illinois University Press, 2013.

Hughes, Robert. *Barcelona*. Harvill, 1992.
James, Zita. Unpublished journal, September 1930. Private collection.
Jansen, Marc, and Nikita Petrov. *Stalin's Loyal Executioner: People's Commissar Nikolai Ezhov, 1895–1940*. Hoover Institution Press, 2002.
Johnston, Robert H. *New Mecca, New Babylon: Paris and the Russian Exiles, 1920–1945*. McGill–Queen's University Press, 1988.
Kahlo, Frida. *The Diary of Frida Kahlo: An Intimate Self-Portrait*. Bloomsbury, 1995.
Kahlo, Frida. *The Letters of Frida Kahlo: Cartas Apasionadas*. Chronicle Books, 1995.
Kandell, Jonathan. *La Capital: The Biography of Mexico City*. Random House, 1988.
Kern, Gary. *A Death in Washington: Walter G. Krivitsky and the Stalin Terror*. Enigma Books, 2004.
Klehr, Harvey, John Earl Haynes, and Fridrikh Igorevich Firsov. *The Secret World of American Communism*. Yale University Press, 1995.
Koestler, Arthur. *Bricks to Babel: Selected Writings with Author's Comments*. Hutchinson, 1980.
Kotkin, Stephen. *Stalin*. Vol. 1, *Paradoxes of Power, 1878–1928*. Allen Lane, 2014.
Kotkin, Stephen. *Stalin*. Vol. 2, *Waiting for Hitler, 1928–1941*. Allen Lane, 2017.
Levine, Isaac Don. *Eyewitness to History: Memoirs and Reflections of a Foreign Correspondent for Half a Century*. Hawthorn Books, 1973.
Levine, Isaac Don. *The Mind of an Assassin*. New American Library, 1960.
Lokhova, Svetlana. *The Spy Who Changed History: The Untold Story of How the Soviet Union Won the Race for America's Top Secrets*. William Collins, 2018.
Mandelstam, Nadezhda. *Hope Against Hope: A Memoir*. Translated by Max Hayward. Collins & Harvill Press, 1971.
Marnham, Patrick. *Dreaming with His Eyes Open: A Life of Diego Rivera*. Bloomsbury, 1998.
Mercader, Luis. *Ramón Mercader, mi hermano: cincuenta años después*. Espasa-Calpe, 1990.
Miller, Michael B. *Shanghai on the Métro: Spies, Intrigue, and the French Between the Wars*. University of California Press, 1994.
Mitrokhin, Vasily. *"Chekisms"—Tales of the Cheka: A KGB Anthology*. Yurasov Press, 2008.
Mitrokhin, Vasily, ed. *KGB Lexicon: The Soviet Intelligence Officer's Handbook*. Routledge, 2002.
Montefiore, Simon Sebag. *Stalin: The Court of the Red Tsar*. Weidenfeld & Nicolson, 2003.
Montefiore, Simon Sebag. *Young Stalin*. Weidenfeld & Nicolson, 2007.
Mosley, Nicholas. *The Assassination of Trotsky*. Sphere Books, 1972.
Orlov, Aleksandr. *The March of Time: Reminiscences*. St. Ermin's Press, 2004.
Orlov, Aleksandr. *The Secret History of Stalin's Crimes*. Jarrolds, 1954.
Patenaude, Bertrand M. *Stalin's Nemesis: The Exile and Murder of Leon Trotsky*. Faber and Faber, 2009.
Payne, Robert. *The Life and Death of Trotsky*. W. H. Allen, 1978.
Petrov, Vladimir, and Evdokia Petrov. *Empire of Fear*. Deutsch, 1956.
Pike, David Wingeate. *In the Service of Stalin: The Spanish Communists in Exile, 1939–1945*. Clarendon Press, 1993.
Plokhy, Serhii. *The Man with the Poison Gun*. Oneworld, 2016.
Poretsky, Elisabeth K. *Our Own People: A Memoir of "Ignace Reiss" and His Friends*. Oxford University Press, 1969.

Preston, Paul. *The Spanish Holocaust: Inquisition and Extermination in Twentieth-Century Spain.* HarperPress, 2012.

Puigventós López, Eduard. *Ramon Mercader, l'home del piolet: Biografia de l'assasí de Trotski.* Ara Llibres, 2015.

Radosh, Ronald, Mary R. Habeck, and Grigory Sevostianov, eds. *Spain Betrayed: The Soviet Union in the Spanish Civil War.* Yale University Press, 2001.

Ransome, Arthur. *Six Weeks in Russia in 1919.* George Allen & Unwin, 1919.

Rappaport, Helen. *After the Romanovs: Russian Exiles in Paris Between the Wars.* Scribe, 2022.

Rayfield, Donald. *Stalin and His Hangmen: An Authoritative Portrait of a Tyrant and Those Who Served Him.* Viking, 2004.

Richardson, R. Dan. *Comintern Army: The International Brigades and the Spanish Civil War.* University Press of Kentucky, 1982.

Rosenthal, Gérard. *Avocat de Trotsky.* Robert Laffont, 1975.

Rosmer, Alfred. *Trotsky and the Origins of Trotskyism.* Francis Boutle, 2002.

Sánchez Salazar, General Leandro A., with Julian Gorkin. *Murder in Mexico: The Assassination of Leon Trotsky.* Secker & Warburg, 1950.

Serge, Victor. *Memoirs of a Revolutionary.* New York Review Books Classics, 2011.

Serge, Victor. *Notebooks: 1936–1947.* New York Review Books Classics, 2019.

Serge, Victor, and Natalia Sedova Trotsky. *The Life and Death of Leon Trotsky.* Translated by Arnold J. Pomerans. Wildwood House, 1975.

Service, Robert. *Stalin: A Biography.* Macmillan, 2004.

Service, Robert. *Trotsky: A Biography.* Belknap Press of Harvard University Press, 2009.

Sheridan, Clare. *Russian Portraits.* Jonathan Cape, 1921.

Sheridan, Clare. *To the Four Winds.* Andre Deutsch, 1957.

Slezkine, Yuri. *The House of Government: A Saga of the Russian Revolution.* Princeton University Press, 2017.

Souvarine, Boris. *A Critical Survey of Bolshevism.* Alliance Book, 1939.

Sudoplatov, Pavel, and Anatoli Sudoplatov, with Jerrold L. Schecter and Leona P. Schecter. *Special Tasks: The Memoirs of an Unwanted Witness—A Soviet Spymaster.* Little, Brown, 1994.

Sukhanov, N. N. *The Russian Revolution 1917: A Personal Record.* Translated by Joel Carmichael. Oxford University Press, 1955.

Teffi. *Memories: From Moscow to the Black Sea.* Translated by Robert Chandler, Elizabeth Chandler, Anne Marie Jackson, and Irina Steinberg. Pushkin Press, 2016.

Teffi. *Rasputin and Other Ironies.* Translated by Robert Chandler. Pushkin Press, 2016.

Thomas, Hugh. *The Spanish Civil War.* Hamish Hamilton, 1977.

Tremlett, Giles. *The International Brigades: Fascism, Freedom and the Spanish Civil War.* Bloomsbury, 2020.

Trotsky, Leon. *My Life: An Attempt at an Autobiography.* Pathfinder Press, 1970.

Trotsky, Leon. *Portraits: Political and Personal.* Pathfinder Press, 1977.

Trotsky, Leon. *Stalin: An Appraisal of the Man and His Influence.* Translated by Charles Malamuth. Harper & Brothers, 1946.

Trotsky, Leon. *Trotsky's Diary in Exile 1935.* Translated by Elena Zarudnaya. Faber and Faber, 1958.

Tucker, Robert C. *Stalin as Revolutionary, 1879–1929: A Study in History and Personality.* Chatto & Windus, 1974.

Ulam, Adam B. *The Bolsheviks: The Intellectual and Political History of the Triumph of Communism in Russia.* Collier-Macmillan, 1965.

Vaill, Amanda. *Hotel Florida: Truth, Love, and Death in the Spanish Civil War*. Bloomsbury, 2014.
Valtin, Jan. *Out of the Night*. Alliance Book Corporation, 1941.
van Heijenoort, Jean. *With Trotsky in Exile: From Prinkipo to Coyoacán*. Harvard University Press, 1978.
Volkogonov, Dmitri. *Stalin: Triumph and Tragedy*. Translated by Harold Shukman. Weidenfeld & Nicolson, 1991.
Volkogonov, Dmitri. *Trotsky: The Eternal Revolutionary*. Translated by Harold Shukman. HarperCollins, 1996.
Volodarsky, Boris. *Stalin's Agent: The Life and Death of Alexander Orlov*. Oxford University Press, 2015.
Waugh, Evelyn. *Robbery Under Law: The Mexican Object-Lesson*. Catholic Book Club, 1939.
Weissmann, Susan. *Victor Serge: The Course Is Set on Hope*. Verso, 2001.
Wilmers, Mary-Kay. *The Eitingons: A Twentieth-Century Story*. Faber & Faber, 2009.
Wolfe, Bertram D. *Diego Rivera: His Life and Times*. Robert Hale, 1939.
Wolfe, Bertram D. *The Fabulous Life of Diego Rivera*. Barrie and Rockliff, 1968.
Wolfe, Bertram D. *Three Who Made a Revolution: A Biographical History*. Beacon Press, 1955.
Wyndham, Francis, and David King, *Trotsky: A Documentary*. Allen Lane, 1972.

## ARTICLES

Crapeau, Maria. *"J'ai connu l'assassin de Trotsky." France-Observateur*, 19 May 1960.
Gurevitch, Eric M. "Thinking with Sylvia Ageloff." Hypocrite Reader, August 2015. https://hypocritereader.com/55/thinking-with-sylvia.
Hall, Phillip, "My Grandfather the Revolutionary." *The Guardian*, 13 February 2003. https://www.theguardian.com/artanddesign/2003/feb/13/heritage.russia.
Hansen, Joseph. "With Trotsky to the End." *Fourth International* 1, no. 5 (1940): 115–23.
International Committee of the Fourth International. "The Story of Mark Zborowski: Stalin's Spy in the Fourth International." World Socialist Web Site, 17 November 2011. https://www.wsws.org/en/articles/2011/11/zbor-n17.html.
London, Eric. "Sylvia Ageloff and the Assassination of Leon Trotsky." World Socialist Web Site, 5 February 2021. https://www.wsws.org/en/articles/2021/02/06/sylv-f06.html.
Martin, Kingsley. "Kingsley Martin: Trotsky in Mexico, 10 April 1937." *The New Statesman*, 10 May 2013. https://www.newstatesman.com/long-reads/2013/05/kingsley-martin-trotsky-mexico.
North, David. "Trotsky's Last Year." World Socialist Web Site, 19 August 2020. https://www.wsws.org/en/articles/2020/08/20/anni-a20.html.
Pàmies, Teresa. *"Ramón Mercader: misión cumplida." Triunfo*, 28 October 1978.
Wald, Alan. "Memories of the John Dewey Commission: Forty Years Later." *The Antioch Review* 35, no. 4 (1977): 438–51.
Woods, Alan. "The House in Coyoacan: Reflections on Trotsky's Last Years." In Defense of Marxism, 16 June 2009. https://marxist.comhouse-in-coyacan-reflections-trotsky.htm.
Znamenski, Andrei. "Joseph Grigulevich: A Tale of Identity, Soviet Espionage, and Storytelling." *The Soviet and Post-Soviet Review* 44, no. 3 (2017): 314–41.

## DOCUMENTARIES

López-Linares, José Luis, and Javier Rioyo, dirs. *Storm the Skies.* Cero en Conducta, 1996.

Matías Gueliburt, dir. *El asesinato de Trotsky.* Anima Films, 2007.

## ARCHIVES

### FBI

NY 100-775, https://vault.fbi.gov/leon-trotsky/leon-trotsky-part-1-of-5/view.

### Archivo General de la Nación (Mexico)

TSJDF/siglo XX/Archivo histórico/caja 3265/folio.602993.

### National Archives (United Kingdom)

KV 2 1898.
KV 2 2878.
KV 2 2879.

"Testimony of Mark Zborowski, Accompanied by Herman A. Greenberg, Esq., His Attorney," *Scope of Soviet Activity in the United States, Hearing Before the Subcommittee to Investigate the Administration of the Internal Security Act and Other Internal Security Laws of the Committee on the Judiciary, United States Senate, Eighty-Fourth Congress, Second Session, February 29, 1956, pt. 4.* Government Printing Office, 1956.

# INDEX

Note: Italicized page numbers indicate material in photographs or illustrations.

# About the Author

**Josh Ireland** is the author of *Churchill & Son* and *The Traitors: A True Story of Blood, Betrayal and Deceit*, an account of four Britons who betrayed their country during World War II. He has written for *The Daily Telegraph*, *Prospect*, *The Spectator*, and *The Times Literary Supplement*.